TAKE YOUR LIFE BACK

DAY BY DAY

*Inspiration to Live Free
One Day at a Time*

STEPHEN ARTERBURN, M.Ed.
DAVID STOOP, Ph.D.

TYNDALE®
MOMENTUM

*An Imprint of
Tyndale House Publishers, Inc.*

Visit Tyndale online at www.tyndale.com.

Visit Tyndale Momentum online at www.tyndalemomentum.com.

Tyndale Momentum and the Tyndale Momentum logo are registered trademarks of Tyndale House Publishers, Inc. Tyndale Momentum is an imprint of Tyndale House Publishers, Inc., Carol Stream, Illinois 60188.

Take Your Life Back Day by Day: Inspiration to Live Free One Day at a Time

Designed by Ron Kaufmann

The authors are represented by the literary agency of WordServe Literary Group, www.wordserveliterary.com.

Printed in the United States of America

22	21	20	19	18	17	16
7	6	5	4	3	2	1

INTRODUCTION

By opening this devotional, you have revealed some positive things about yourself. First, you realize that your life could be better and you know that something needs to change in order for that to happen. You also understand that taking your life back is a day-by-day process, and it helps to get some encouragement and reinforcement along the way. We're happy to join you on this journey and offer some hope and some practical ideas along the way. Thank you for allowing us an opportunity to help you.

God created you for freedom, joy, and peace. For meaningful relationships and productive work. But somewhere in your past you got off track. Because of your own sin, or sins committed against you—abuse, neglect, bad choices, misunderstandings—you lost the sense of freedom and peace that God intends for you. You may have developed unhealthy habits and coping mechanisms that cause more problems than they solve. Instead of responding appropriately to what life sends your way, you may react blindly. You worry about what others think. You carry a heavy weight of guilt, shame, or anger.

You know all too well what the apostle Paul meant when he said, "I don't really understand myself, for I want to do what is right, but I don't do it. Instead, I do what I hate. . . . I want to do what is good, but I don't. I don't want to do what is wrong, but I do it anyway."* Sometimes it feels as if your life isn't your own anymore.

But that can change. With God's help, you can take your life back. You can experience healing for your pain and recovery from an unhealthy reactive

---

* Romans 7:15, 19

lifestyle. But it won't happen all at once. It's a daily journey, not a one-time experience. We created this devotional to be a companion on the road to recovery. It combines nuggets of encouragement with wisdom from God's Word, some questions to stimulate thought, and a suggested prayer to pull you closer to the Source of all true healing.

If you haven't already, we suggest that you also read our book *Take Your Life Back*, which explains many of the concepts and strategies we refer to in this devotional. We have also created a *Take Your Life Back Workbook*, which will guide you through a five-week study and can be used for personal reflection or as the basis for a group discussion. The purpose for the *Take Your Life Back* series is to help you find healing, purpose, and meaning in life, and to inspire you to do precisely what the title suggests.

This 365-day devotional is designed to give you daily encouragement, wisdom, and insight as you progress toward wholeness. Our hope is that you will come to realize that real and lasting change is not only worth *pursuing*, but it is also *achievable*. We all must learn how to stop *reacting* to life and begin to *respond* appropriately instead. If you're ready to take your life back, this devotional will be your daily companion and encourager along the way.

May God greatly bless you, and may you experience his presence as you read the daily devotions and begin to experience the life you were born to live.

Looking Ahead

Go in peace . . . for the LORD is watching over your journey.

JUDGES 18:6

As you embark on this day-by-day journey toward taking your life back, it might help to take a quick look at your desired destination. Though you will never achieve perfection in this world, you can reach a place where you are happier, healthier, and more attuned to God than you ever thought possible.

What will your life look like when you have taken it back? You will feel relatively safe and confident, not tossed to and fro by the whims of other people or by the extremes of your own emotions. Instead of blindly reacting to every little thing that might threaten your comfort or safety, you'll respond appropriately and effectively.

As you discover your real self and begin to live comfortably without pretense or façades, you will develop standards that you intend to keep and expect others to honor. You'll have a good sense of where you end and others begin, and you'll be capable of healthy attachments. You'll give other people grace for their imperfections, but not allow those imperfections to hurt or dominate you. You'll be free to be yourself, free to choose, free to heal, and free to be a healthy, loving adult.

ASK YOURSELF

> » What are your feelings as you read through this description of the destination? Does it seem possible? Desirable? Why or why not?

> » How far along are you on this journey? What choice can you make today to take you further?

ASK GOD

Heavenly Father, thank you for your gifts of wholeness and healing. I ask for your guidance, your protection, your provision, and most of all your presence as I travel toward becoming the person you created me to be.

A Tool for the Journey

So we can say with confidence, "The LORD is my helper, so I will have no fear. What can mere people do to me?" Remember your leaders who taught you the word of God. Think of all the good that has come from their lives, and follow the example of their faith.

HEBREWS 13:6-7

When we're wounded—as we all inevitably are—we tend to *react* to what happens to us instead of responding in a healthy way.

Our reactiveness can take a variety of forms. Some people *act out* in rebellion and anger. Others *act in* by becoming envious, judgmental, or depressed. Either way, when we're living reactively, our lives become contingent on what others do and say. But God longs to set us free from our bondage to such dependency. He wants us to take our lives back—to recover from these unhealthy patterns.

The writer of Hebrews offers a valuable tool for our recovery in the form of a question: "What can mere people do to me?" In other words: "What others say and do can no longer affect me in any significant way. In fact, I'm fearless now because instead of reacting to other people, I trust in God to shape my responses."

When you feel yourself pulled into old patterns, try speaking this verse aloud. It can help you turn reactive living on its head.

ASK YOURSELF

» What (if any) reactive patterns do you recognize in yourself?

» How does turning to God as your Helper change that?

ASK GOD

Lord, with confidence I say that because you are my Helper, I do not fear. Thank you for the ways you are helping me break free from old patterns and find new life in you.

Would You Like to Get Well?

One of the men lying there had been sick for thirty-eight years. When Jesus saw him
and knew he had been ill for a long time, he asked him, "Would you like to get well?"

JOHN 5:5-6

It sounded like a no-brainer. Of course the sick man wanted to get well.

Or did he?

Jesus knew that being healed would change the man's life forever. Begging at the pool was all he knew. All his friends were there. If he was healed, he'd have to leave them and find a new way to support himself. He'd have to learn to care for himself instead of relying on others. In light of all these potential changes, no wonder Jesus asked the man if he really wanted to be healed.

Jesus asks us a similar question: *Do we really want to take our lives back?* Our relationships will shift, and some people in our lives will resist us. We'll have to develop new habits and find a better balance between caring for others and caring for ourselves. A lot will change, and change is almost always difficult, even when the outcome is good.

It's not an idle question: *Do you want to get well?* Be careful how you answer.

ASK YOURSELF

» Are you willing to do the work that will be required of you as you take your life back? What part do you think will be the hardest?

» Who in your life do you think will be the most resistant to your changing? How will you handle that person?

ASK GOD

Jesus, I do want to get well, but I know that changing isn't easy. Please give me the strength to meet resistance with grace and to persevere. Thank you.

Grow with Confidence

This is my command—be strong and courageous! Do not be afraid or discouraged. For the LORD your God is with you wherever you go.

JOSHUA 1:9

After the death of Moses, Joshua was in charge. His task was huge. The Hebrew people he was leading were about to enter the Promised Land, and they would have to take the land from the current inhabitants. To lead them, Joshua needed all the courage—and encouragement—God could give him. But God told him clearly what to do. He was to obey all the instructions Moses had given him and not deviate from them. Only if he did that, God said, would he "prosper and succeed" (Joshua 1:8). In other words, God said to do the next right thing—and then to keep on doing the next right thing until he achieved success.

The same is true for those of us who are in the process of taking our lives back. We know what to do—heal our inner wounds, repair or replace our broken attachments, and confront our trauma. To do this, we need to be strong and courageous. But God's promise to us is the same as his promise to Joshua. He will be with us wherever we go in our quest for wholeness.

ASK YOURSELF

> » Where in your recovery process does your fear tend to rise up and threaten to stop you?

> » How can you live more fully in the promise that God will be with you wherever you go?

ASK GOD

Father God, I need to be strong and courageous, but I get stymied by my fear. Help me to face my fear and overcome the barriers to my recovery.

Surefooted Faith

Give your burdens to the LORD, and he will take care of you.
He will not permit the godly to slip and fall.

PSALM 55:22

Most of the psalms written by David were expressions of his troubles and affirmations of his faith. And David had enough troubles (and enough faith) to last many lifetimes.

Life was turbulent for David as a young man. He spent more than twenty years running for his life from King Saul and other enemies. He lived in caves and never knew whom he could trust. Later, as king, he endured multiple disappointments, including the rebellion and death of a beloved son. When David advises us to give our burdens to the Lord, he knows what he's talking about.

But David also got into some serious sin during his lifetime. He even had an adulterous affair and arranged for his lover's husband to be killed. How could he say that God doesn't let the godly slip and fall?

David slipped when he *stopped* giving his burdens to the Lord and tried to manage life on his own. But when he confessed his sin and returned to relying on God—to being "godly"—he found his footing again.

ASK YOURSELF

» Are you anxious about situations you can't control? How can you give that burden to the Lord?

» Have you ever slipped and fallen and felt that getting up was impossible? How did you finally find your footing?

ASK GOD

Dear God, I want to be strong and surefooted as I walk through this life. Remind me that this will never happen unless I give you my burdens and trust in your care. Help my understanding of you to grow each day so that I can experience you fully.

The Grown-Up Alternative

When I was a child, I spoke and thought and reasoned as a child.
But when I grew up, I put away childish things.

1 CORINTHIANS 13:11

Counselors often ask their clients how old they feel on the inside, especially when in the presence of a parent, a boss, or some other authority figure. Most people answer that they feel somewhere between four and sixteen years old. And that can be a problem.

If I feel like I'm only eight or ten when I'm in the presence of a parent, part of me is still living as a wounded child, probably because I experienced some kind of emotional injury that left me stuck. So even though I am chronologically an adult, I am still speaking, thinking, and reasoning childishly. To take my life back, I need to address those childhood wounds and grow up mentally and emotionally.

One childish thing many of us do is to try to get another person to validate us and make us feel worthwhile. We give away part of ourselves every time we do that. The grown-up alternative is to remember that we are loved and validated by the Creator, the one who made us in the first place.

ASK YOURSELF

» What is it you are seeking when you react as a child? What childhood wounds in you need healing?

» What does it mean to you to be loved by the Creator of the universe— the one who made you?

ASK GOD

Loving Father, help me as I go through this day to feel that you love all of me, especially those parts of me that are still childish. Give me patience as I learn more about myself and work to "grow up" the child within me.

I'm Experiencing a New Life

Anyone who belongs to Christ has become a new person.
The old life is gone; a new life has begun!

2 CORINTHIANS 5:17

When we acknowledge Jesus as our higher power, we start a new life—one characterized by being loved and accepted instead of being shamed or condemned. But the fullness of this life doesn't come to us automatically.

Notice that Paul says, "A new life has *begun.*" It's as if God has erased the slate, giving us a fresh start. But now we must learn new behaviors and attitudes that allow us to take back the life God intended us to experience.

Part of the new life we've begun is learning to care about ourselves as well as others. For too long we have believed that we can care for others only at our own expense. But that makes us feel like we are trying to fill someone else's glass with an empty pitcher. We need God's help to learn how to balance our caring. That's an important way to take our lives back.

ASK YOURSELF

> » Think of a situation in which you cared for someone else at the cost of your physical, mental, or emotional health. What was your motivation in doing so?

> » What makes it hard for you to practice self-care, to make certain you have something to give?

ASK GOD
Heavenly Father, you gave so much for me by sending Jesus to die on my behalf. Help me to see how much you value me as a person. Help me to see that you love me no matter what.

God Strengthens Me

He gives power to the weak and strength to the powerless.

ISAIAH 40:29

One of the key principles in taking your life back is to recognize how powerless you are—on your own—to change. But that's just the first step. The next is to recognize where the power you need will come from. Isaiah says it comes from God himself. And Zechariah echoes this idea: "It is not by force nor by strength, but by my Spirit, says the LORD" (4:6).

What a relief! Change is based not on our ability but on God's power. And as Isaiah reminds us, we are talking about

> the everlasting God,
> > the Creator of all the earth.
> He never grows weak or weary.
> > No one can measure the depths of his understanding.

ISAIAH 40:28

That's who is waiting to give us power and strength. So as we work at understanding our past and its effect on our present, we must do so in complete dependence on God.

By ourselves, we can't do it. But we never have to do it by ourselves.

ASK YOURSELF

» What are some specific situations in which you feel weak and powerless to change?

» What can you do to remind yourself to depend on God's power and strength, not your own?

ASK GOD

God, it's so easy—and so futile—for me to try to change on my own. Help me to remember that you are my power and my strength. Give me the courage to trust in you.

God Is Not Judging Me

There is no judgment against anyone who believes in him.

JOHN 3:18

Why do we tend to give away too much of ourselves to others and neglect to care for ourselves? Often we're driven by a fear of being judged. We are haunted by a sense that we haven't done enough or we haven't done what was expected. And at the root of those fears is the sense that the one who is most critical of us is God himself.

But that's just not true. John tells us plainly that when we believe in Jesus, God does *not* judge us. Paul makes this even clearer when he asserts, "So now there is no condemnation for those who belong to Christ Jesus" (Romans 8:1). No ifs, no ands, no buts—absolutely no condemnation, simply because we belong to Jesus. And that freedom from judgment is not based on how we feel about it. It's reality—based on a transaction we made with God when we affirmed our belief and he adopted us into his family.

So that critical voice we so often hear in our heads is not God speaking; it's us. God speaks only in the language of love.

ASK YOURSELF

» How loud is the critical, judgmental voice in your head? Who first told you the things that your critical voice now repeats?

» Since the critical voice is not telling the truth, how can you argue against it?

ASK GOD

Loving heavenly Father, thank you for not judging me. Help me not to listen to that critical voice within me, for I know it is not you. Help me to know that I am loved by you and accepted for who I am.

What Do You Expect?

Always be humble and gentle. Be patient with each other, making
allowance for each other's faults because of your love.

EPHESIANS 4:2

It is so easy to place our values and expectations upon others, measuring them by our standards and grading them on how well they fit into our plans. And sadly, we are most prone to do this with those closest to us. They sometimes become our emotional punching bags because we know they are the least likely to abandon us when we show our demanding side.

Expectations create unnecessary disappointments. Try to approach each day, each relationship, and each situation with the conscious thought that God wants you to be humble and gentle with others.

Think about how patient God is with you. He meets you right where you are, loves you unconditionally, and focuses on your possibilities, not your faults or failures. This is how he wants you to be with the people in your life as well. If you will allow those who are closest to you the opportunity to be human, you will be surprised at how quickly they grow.

ASK YOURSELF

» Do you tend to judge others too harshly at times? Which of your expectations for others might be too high?

» How are your expectations for yourself tied up with your expectations for others? Can being patient with yourself help you be patient with others?

ASK GOD

Dear Lord, please help me to be as patient with others as you have been with me, and keep me ever conscious of the fact that you work with each of us on an individual basis. Help me to focus on what is expected of me today and not busy myself with the faults of others.

My Hope Is in the Lord

"Everything I had hoped for from the LORD is lost!" The thought
of my suffering and homelessness is bitter beyond words. I will
never forget this awful time. . . . Yet I still dare to hope.

LAMENTATIONS 3:18-21

The prophet Jeremiah was devastated as he looked over the ruins of Jerusalem. He had tried to warn his people of what was coming, but they wouldn't listen. So how could Jeremiah still hold on to hope? Read on:

> The faithful love of the LORD never ends!
> His mercies never cease.
> Great is his faithfulness;
> his mercies begin afresh each morning.
> I say to myself, "The LORD is my inheritance;
> therefore, I will hope in him!"

LAMENTATIONS 3:22-24

Jeremiah held on to hope by refocusing his thinking. Instead of continuing to mourn the loss of all of his dreams for himself and for his people, he chose to focus on God's faithfulness. All of his circumstances shouted "hopeless," but he chose instead to hope in God.

ASK YOURSELF

» Sometimes it takes a faithful friend to help us focus on hope during dark times. Who in your life can help you refocus on God's faithfulness?

» What would it take for you to live today in the reality Jeremiah experienced—the belief that God is faithful?

ASK GOD

Lord Jesus, help me to remember that my hope is based on what I focus on—and that I need to focus on you and your faithfulness. Help me remember that when I'm tempted to focus on the wrong things.

Do Something Different

If you try to hang on to your life, you will lose it. But if you
give up your life for my sake, you will save it.

MATTHEW 16:25

In this Matthew passage, Jesus expresses a profound truth as a paradox—a seemingly self-contradictory statement that proves true upon further examination. Jesus is saying that if we hold too tightly to something, we will lose it.

We are all too familiar with the paradox that sometimes the harder we try to change our lives, the more stubbornly they refuse to change. In such situations, instead of just trying harder, we must be willing to try something *different*.

This doesn't mean giving up. It just means trying a new tactic—maybe even doing the opposite of what we've been doing.

Try that the next time you encounter a familiar but uncomfortable situation. Instead of reacting the usual way—lashing out, clamming up, or pretending to be all right with something when you're not—try to take a mental step back. Take a deep breath. Say a little prayer. Then deliberately do something different. Walk away. Speak up. Say no.

Try it just this once. For a change.

ASK YOURSELF

» Is there a stubborn issue in your life that seems to resist every effort at changing? Brainstorm some different tactics for responding to this issue.

» What internal arguments hold you back from trying something new in response to a painful stimulus?

ASK GOD

Lord, I need you so much in this process of breaking free from reactive patterns in my life. Help me loosen my grip on old habits and trust you enough to try something completely different. Help me better understand why I do what I do, and deliver me from my reactive lifestyle.

God Will Guide Us

The LORD directs the steps of the godly. He delights in every detail of their lives.
Though they stumble, they will never fall, for the LORD holds them by the hand.

PSALM 37:23-24

We've all watched a mom walking with her toddler, holding his hand. Suddenly something catches the little guy's attention, and he pulls his hand away. More often than not, he quickly gets into something he shouldn't. He might even stumble and land flat on his face—something that would never happen if his mom had his hand.

What a great picture of the way we are with God. He seeks to hold our hand and guide us, but we are stubbornly determined to go off on our own. Instead of letting our loving Father direct our steps, we toddle off and get ourselves into trouble.

The other part of this passage that is special is the fact that God delights "in every detail" of our lives. It's like the loving grandfather who listens to his little grandchild prattle on about something that happened to her. He may know all about it, but he still enjoys listening. Why? Because she's his and he loves her dearly.

ASK YOURSELF

» Describe some times when you pull your hand away from God. What typically diverts your attention?

» As a child, did you know anyone who delighted in every detail of your life? How does this affect your ability to experience God's love?

ASK GOD

Lord, it's hard for me to believe you are interested in the details of my life, let alone that you delight in them. Help me to understand that and to spend more time talking with you about everything. And remind me always that my life goes better when I keep my hand in yours.

Worth Protecting

The LORD himself watches over you! The LORD stands
beside you as your protective shade.
PSALM 121:5

When we learn of vulnerable children or helpless animals being mistreated, most of us feel enraged. We understand, at a very deep level, that what they've endured is wrong. But if we were exposed to abuse or neglect when we were young, if no one effectively stood up for us or protected us, we might have internalized the message that we are not *worth* protecting.

As we take our lives back, however, we can begin resisting that faulty assumption. We learn to value ourselves, our lives, and the progress we've made. We gather with others for strength and protect ourselves with truth. We also develop strategies for avoiding places and people that could reverse the gains we've made. We become so grounded in reality that we're no longer confused about where we've been or where we're going. We even have a plan in place for what to do if we stumble and fall.

We learn to protect ourselves because we finally believe, in our bones, that we are *worth* protecting.

ASK YOURSELF

> » Was there someone committed to protecting you when you were young? If not, what has been the fallout in your life?

> » What measures have you put in place to protect yourself today?

ASK GOD

Lord, you are my Protector. Your love has convinced me, at last, that I am worth protecting. Strengthen me to be wise as I live as a new person, holy and beloved.

They Did What Their Friend Couldn't Do

Four men arrived carrying a paralyzed man on a mat. They couldn't bring him to Jesus because of the crowd, so they dug a hole through the roof above [Jesus'] head.

MARK 2:3-4

Imagine the scene: Jesus is teaching in a home, and people are so eager to hear him that they pack tightly into the house and outside as well. Four men have agreed to bring their paralyzed friend to Jesus, but they realize there is no way they can get their friend in front of the Master. Then one of the men suggests they climb to the roof and cut a hole through it so they can lower the man's pallet down in front of Jesus. When they accomplish this task, Jesus is so moved by their faith that he heals the paralyzed man.

How are the actions of these four men different from ours when we are overly involved in others' lives and need to take our own lives back? Quite simply, they did for the paralyzed man what he couldn't do for himself. If they had carried a friend to Jesus who was perfectly capable of walking there on his own, they would have been caring for him inappropriately—and not really helping him or themselves.

ASK YOURSELF

» Make a list of things you tend to do for others that they can—and should—do for themselves. Why do you think you do these things?

» By contrast, what are some things you do—or could do—for others that they cannot do for themselves?

ASK GOD

Father, help me to examine my motives as I seek to care for others. Help me to still be caring, but give me the wisdom to know when I'm helping inappropriately.

The Money Trap

If a bird sees a trap being set, it knows to stay away. . . . Such is the
fate of all who are greedy for money; it robs them of life.

PROVERBS 1:17, 19

Do you ever feel overwhelmed when dealing with your finances? Does it feel like you are running on that hamster wheel of life, just trying to keep up? If you aren't careful, your finances can become a trap that dictates your mood and takes control of your life. In this fast-paced world, it is easy to become addicted to accomplishments without having a real purpose. If you are chasing money for money's sake, you will find that you never have enough.

Whether you are in a comfortable financial position or find yourself with a shortfall, remember that money, although a necessary part of life, is not something to be held in such high esteem that it causes you to neglect the things that are eternal. It can be either a blessing or a curse, depending on the place you choose give it in your life.

ASK YOURSELF

» Have your finances become an unhealthy part of your daily life, wielding more power over you than they should?

» What can you do to keep your finances in the right perspective?

ASK GOD

Dear Lord, there are times when I let my financial situation take control of my life. I never want to give money more value than it should have. Help me to find that healthy balance so that my life is never controlled by need or by greed.

I Am God's Masterpiece

What are mere mortals that you should think about them, human
beings that you should care for them? Yet you made them only a little
lower than God and crowned them with glory and honor.

PSALM 8:4-5

All of us long to feel like we matter, like we have value. But so many of us struggle with feelings of being unworthy. That's one reason we spend so much time trying to make people like and respect us. We think that helping others or winning success will fill in the holes in our sense of self. But life doesn't work that way. We'll never get an accurate picture of our own worth through another person's eyes. For that, we need to see ourselves through *God's* eyes.

David addresses this issue in today's reading: He basically asks God, "Why are we important to you?" And he finds his answer in the way we humans were created. God made us only a little lower than himself and crowned us with glory and honor.

That's where true self-worth comes from. It's an internal realization that God, whose "majestic name fills the earth" (Psalm 8:1), gives each of us glory and honor just for being who we are—his beloved creation.

ASK YOURSELF

» Where do you tend to find your sense of your own value? Do you tend to rely on outside sources (such as other people) or on internal attitudes?

» All through today, personalize and ponder the words of David: "God has crowned *me* with glory and honor!"

ASK GOD

Creator God who made me, forgive me for disrespecting your creation. Help me adjust my attitude and my behaviors to reflect how much you value me.

The One Who Understands

This High Priest of ours understands our weaknesses, for he faced all
of the same testings we do, yet he did not sin. So let us come boldly
to the throne of our gracious God. There we will receive his mercy,
and we will find grace to help us when we need it most.

HEBREWS 4:15-16

The Scriptures assure us that Jesus, our faithful High Priest, knows what our lives are like. He understands our weaknesses because he faced the same kinds of testing that we do, though he didn't sin.

The kinds of temptations Jesus understands include some of the "biggies," like the sins we find in the Ten Commandments and elsewhere throughout the Bible. But have you considered that Jesus probably also faced the same temptation to live reactively that we do?

Like us, Jesus was in relationship with some people who were healthy and others who weren't. So he surely understands our temptation to avoid pain in unhealthy ways—such as denying or minimizing it, complying with unreasonable demands, adhering to bad relationships, placating those who mistreat us, covering up our wounds, enabling dysfunctional behavior in others, becoming controlling, attacking others, or isolating ourselves.

He understands, and he gives us grace as we try to change these behaviors.

ASK YOURSELF

» In what ways are you tempted to deny, minimize, comply, adhere, deceive, placate, cover, enable, control, attack, or isolate?

» What does it mean to you to realize that Jesus probably faced the same "reactive" temptations you do?

ASK GOD

Jesus, my great High Priest, I thank you that you understand the temptations I face. Grant me the courage to turn to you when I'm tempted to live reactively. I trust in your mercy and grace.

Wisdom for Troubled Times

When troubles of any kind come your way, consider it an opportunity for great
joy.... If you need wisdom, ask our generous God, and he will give it to you.
JAMES 1:2, 5

When it comes to how we understand trouble in life, there is wisdom—and
then there's *wisdom*.

Common wisdom counsels that troubles are evidence that God doesn't
care, so we might as well give up. That's what Job's wife advised him to do—to
just "curse God and die" (Job 2:9). Then there's religious "wisdom" that insists
on placing blame. Job's friends took this approach when they said, "God is
doubtless punishing you far less than you deserve" (Job 11:6).

Godly wisdom is completely different. It's based on how big and good our
God is. So it looks at trouble in life as an opportunity to enlarge our understanding of him.

That's why James could say that troubles are "an opportunity for great joy."
They are a sign that we're going to learn something new about God and our
relationship with him. Troubles can also help us rely on God more and ask him
for his wisdom.

It's freely available to us from a God who is bigger than any of our difficulties.
All we have to do is ask.

ASK YOURSELF

» Which type of wisdom do you tend to rely on when troubles come your
way?

» What would it take for you to believe James and actually be joyful
when troubles come?

ASK GOD

Dear God, you know how difficult it is to be joyful when problems come. Please
help me in those times not to listen to common wisdom or even to faulty religious wisdom, to but ask you for godly wisdom.

I Can See Clearly Now

I have come as a light to shine in this dark world, so that all who
put their trust in me will no longer remain in the dark.

JOHN 12:46

You're walking through an unfamiliar building when the lights suddenly go out. You blink, but you can't see a thing. You don't dare walk farther for fear of stumbling or knocking something over. So you stand frozen, unsure of what to do.

Now imagine that the lights come on again. Suddenly you can see clearly. What a relief!

Jesus said, "I am the light of the world. If you follow me, you won't have to walk in darkness, because you will have the light that leads to life" (John 8:12).

Part of Jesus' purpose in coming into this world was to help us see God clearly. He is the light that banishes the darkness. So to follow him is to live in the light.

One of the indicators that we are still living to some degree in the darkness is that we can't find our way. We can't see the issues clearly. But when we surrender our will to seek God's will, it's like someone turned on the lights. We may not see the end of the path, but we can at least see what path to take.

ASK YOURSELF

» Where in your life does it feel like you're still in the dark?

» What do you need to surrender to Jesus in order to bring light to that situation?

ASK GOD

Dear Jesus, please shine your light on any dark places within me. Search me and help me know myself better. Give me the courage to take my entire life back—every part of it.

God Sings Songs over Me!

For the LORD your God is living among you. . . . He will take
delight in you with gladness. With his love, he will calm all
your fears. He will rejoice over you with joyful songs.

ZEPHANIAH 3:17

Some people think of God as a kind of celestial traffic cop, lying in wait for us to mess up. Others envision him as a critical teacher who loves to hand out bad grades. But in this passage, the prophet Zephaniah gives us a completely different picture of God.

Zephaniah begins by reminding us that God is living among and in us—not somewhere far away in the sky. Then he asserts three powerful positive images of how God sees us.

First, God takes delight in us. He enjoys us the way a loving grandfather delights in his grandchildren.

Second, God calms our fears. The apostle John says that love is the opposite of fear and that God loves us perfectly (1 John 4:18).

But Zephaniah's best description is the last one: God rejoices over us "with joyful songs."

What an incredible image! Picture it whenever you feel God is critical or distant. How can you help but feel cherished by a God who sings for you?

ASK YOURSELF

> » Do you struggle at times with seeing God as the "cop in the sky" or the critical teacher? What are some other ways you envision him?

> » Is it hard for you to imagine God delighting in you or singing songs over you? What makes this difficult?

ASK GOD

Father, forgive me for the negative images I have of you—and my fear that I don't bring joy to you. Help me today to realize you are with me, delighting in me and singing over me.

Clean on the Inside

You Pharisees are so careful to clean the outside of the cup and the dish, but inside you are filthy—full of greed and wickedness!

LUKE 11:39

Jesus often didn't follow Jewish customs. He went deeper on issues. Once when he was invited to the home of one of the Pharisees, he skipped the ceremonial hand-washing and simply sat down. This gave him the opportunity to make an important point, that the insides of our lives—our true motivations—need just as much attention as the outsides.

The Pharisees cared deeply about their religious commitments, but much of what they did religiously was for show—to be seen. They did everything right on the outside but neglected to clean up their own selfish and unworthy attitudes.

As we work to take our lives back, we must heed Jesus' message. We gave up control of our lives in the first place by hiding or denying our true motivations. For instance, we may truly care about others, but our acts of kindness may also be motivated by how we want people to perceive us. As we take time to reflect on such mixed motives and focus on fixing what's wrong inside, we'll also become less and less reactive.

ASK YOURSELF

» Think back to a recent time when you did something for someone else. Identify the mix of motives inside of you at that time.

» Is it better to do something good from mixed motives or to hold back from doing good because you know your motives are mixed? What is an even better alternative?

ASK GOD

Father, I know my motives for doing good are mixed. Help me clean my "cup" by shining your light inside me. Help me respond to others with your love rather than out of the "filth" inside me.

Choose a Happy Heart

For the despondent, every day brings trouble; for the
happy heart, life is a continual feast.
PROVERBS 15:15

This proverb seems to say that we can choose how we feel about life. We can choose to be despondent, or we can choose to live with a happy heart.

How can that be a choice? Paul gives us a clue: "Fix your *thoughts* on what is true, and honorable, and right, and pure, and lovely, and admirable. Think about things that are excellent and worthy of praise. . . . Then the God of peace will be with you" (Philippians 4:8-9, emphasis added).

It's been proven that what we think has a huge effect on what we feel. God made us and knows we work that way, so he inspired Paul to remind us to pay attention to what we are telling ourselves. One of God's gifts to you is the ability to choose the focus of your thoughts. And choosing rather than just reacting is key to taking back your life.

Today, when you get a despondent thought, reject it. Argue against it. Remind yourself that you are choosing a happy heart. That may feel phony at first, but it's really not. It's choosing to focus on the truth—which is that God is bigger and more wonderful than any of our day-to-day feelings.

ASK YOURSELF

> » Why do you think so many people, perhaps including yourself, choose to focus on negative thoughts that leave them despondent?

> » Are there times when it's appropriate to feel sad or down? How can you respond to your feelings honestly while still focusing on positive truth?

ASK GOD

Lord, I want to live with a happy heart. Help me to focus my mind on what is beautiful and good—especially you.

Are You Eating?

*Like newborn babies, you must crave pure spiritual milk so that you will
grow into a full experience of salvation. Cry out for this nourishment.*

1 PETER 2:2

Have you ever seen photos of people who don't have enough to eat? The signs
of malnutrition are impossible to ignore. Exposed rib cages, distended bellies,
lost teeth and hair—it is a sobering sight. If these people had the opportunity
to eat a nutritious and balanced diet, they probably would. It is just common
sense to eat what your body requires for proper function. Why, then, is it so
common for people to starve themselves spiritually?

God's Word provides the necessary nutrition for spiritual growth. Are you
spending time in the Word every day so that you can get the spiritual sustenance you need? If not, your walk with God will be negatively impacted. Make
sure that you are not undernourished spiritually. Feast on the Word of God.

ASK YOURSELF

» Do you make a habit of reading the Word of God on a daily basis? What
tends to get in the way of "eating" regularly?

» When you aren't spending enough time in the Word, what are usually
the first signs of spiritual malnutrition?

ASK GOD

Dear Lord Jesus, give me a hunger for your Word. Remind me to ingest your
living Word every day so that I can continue to grow in my knowledge of you.
Make it obvious to me when I am not getting the spiritual nourishment I need
to be the person you want me to be.

Powerless but Not Helpless

*The Scriptures declare that we are all prisoners of sin, so we receive
God's promise of freedom only by believing in Jesus Christ.*

GALATIANS 3:22

Taking our lives back begins with accepting the reality that we *can't* take our lives back. Not on our own. In other words, we must accept the reality that we don't have what it takes to undo the mess our lives have become. As Paul puts it, we are prisoners of sin—our own and the sin of others. We have no ability on our own to break free.

Think of all the times you've tried to change—and failed. All the times you've made some progress, only to find yourself back at square one. We are truly powerless to make any real change in our lives. Powerless, but not helpless—because we *do* have help. In fact, we have a Savior.

Jesus Christ died on the cross to set us free from the destructive consequences of sin that hold us captive. But that freedom is dependent on our believing in Jesus and accepting what he has done for us. Before we can take our lives back, we must give them over to the one who came to set us free.

ASK YOURSELF

» In what areas of your life are you still a prisoner to old behaviors?

» What would it take for you to surrender those parts of your life to the Savior?

ASK GOD

Jesus, thank you for setting me free by your work on the cross. Keep me amazed at the reality that you, the Creator of the universe, would be willing to die for me. Help me to continue to surrender to you those broken areas of my life.

A Rich and Satisfying Life

The thief's purpose is to steal and kill and destroy.
My purpose is to give them a rich and satisfying life.

JOHN 10:10

If a dog or a cat has a wounded foot, it will begin to limp in such a way that the foot no longer bears weight. The animal compensates by changing its behavior so as not to feel or exacerbate the pain.

Those of us who experienced emotional pain as children, without the resources we needed to deal with it, may have grown up on a mission to nullify—or "dullify"—our feelings. We numbed ourselves with denial, rationalization, minimization, and bad habits. We used people and things to survive the pain. When we did that, the thief who comes to steal and kill and destroy was winning.

But Jesus announced that he came to offer something different—"a rich and satisfying life." As we courageously begin to take our lives back and wake up to our feelings, we begin to taste that authentic life he came to bring.

ASK YOURSELF

» Think back on your early experiences. Can you name a time when emotional pain caused you to "limp" or close down your emotions?

» How do you tend to numb your feelings today? What is your "dullifier" of choice?

ASK GOD

God, thank you that you are my Protector and Provider. Though it was once unsafe to feel, I believe I am safe with you. Because I long for the life Jesus came to bring, one that is rich and satisfying, I am willing to trust you on this journey.

God Overcomes Our Guilt

Even if we feel guilty, God is greater than our feelings, and he knows everything.
. . . If we don't feel guilty, we can come to God with bold confidence.

1 JOHN 3:20-21

Guilt is an interesting concept. By definition, it is a legal term. A person is guilty when he or she has actually committed some offense or crime. The definition can also include the *feeling* of having done something wrong. But it is not meant to describe an ongoing emotional state that is generalized into a perpetual sense of shame. That's why John reminds us that God, who knows everything about us, is greater than our guilt feelings.

If we have a chronic or underlying sense of guilt or shame, we need to get to the root of it. One way to do this is to take what people in twelve-step programs call "a fearless moral inventory" of our lives. Do we blame ourselves for what happened to us as kids? Are we holding on to some past failure? Whatever is at the root of those feelings must be brought to God and confessed to someone we trust with the realization that God already knows all about it and has taken away our guilt.

ASK YOURSELF

» What do you think you gain by holding on to feelings of guilt?

» Why is it important to confess those feelings to God and to a trusted person?

ASK GOD

Dear God, help me to see that while feelings of guilt can be an important signal that something is wrong, they can also be a habit. You know everything, so help me as I get to the source of any chronic guilt in my life.

Nothing Will Defeat Me

This makes it clear that our great power is from God, not from ourselves.

2 CORINTHIANS 4:7

The apostle Paul led a hard life. He survived a shipwreck, persecution, and repeated imprisonment, not to mention the rigors of constant travel, the need to make a living while preaching the gospel, and the continual challenge of a chronic personal issue he described only as a "thorn in my flesh" (2 Corinthians 12:7). And yet he wrote, "We are pressed on every side by troubles, but we are not crushed. We are perplexed, but not driven to despair. We are hunted down, but never abandoned by God. We get knocked down, but we are not destroyed" (2 Corinthians 4:8-9).

Why was Paul so resilient? He relied on God as the source of his power.

Our problems may be different from Paul's, but we all struggle with life at times. To make it through the turmoil, we must be plugged in to a source of power that is greater than what we can generate on our own. Pretending we are strong only leads to frustration and pain. But relying on God for our power allows us to live fully and resiliently in the midst of our ups and downs.

ASK YOURSELF

» Can you think of times when you tried on your own to "be strong" in painful or difficult situations? What was the outcome?

» What are some practical ways you can "plug in" to God as the source of power in your life?

ASK GOD

Jesus, I want you to be my power source. I surrender my own powerlessness to your care and lean on your strength. Give me the courage to more consistently surrender my will to your will.

Believe without Seeing

The angel of the LORD appeared to him in a blazing fire from the middle of a bush. Moses stared in amazement. Though the bush was engulfed in flames, it didn't burn up.

EXODUS 3:2

There was Moses, standing in the very presence of God. The experience was so real that he had to cover his face. He knew without a doubt that God was speaking to him. And yet when God told him to go to Egypt and help his people, Moses actually argued. He couldn't believe God was choosing him.

We like to think that if we experienced something tangible and miraculous like a burning bush, we would never doubt God again. But the truth is that even those who witness amazing miracles can have trouble believing. We need to hear again what Jesus said to Thomas after the Resurrection: "You believe because you have seen me. Blessed are those who believe without seeing me" (John 20:29).

To take our lives back, we really don't need a burning bush. What we need is the courage to act on our faith even when we're not completely sure. And our loving God, who supplies us with everything we need, will take it from there.

ASK YOURSELF

> » Why do you think people so often wish for a sign from God but then struggle with belief even if they get one?

> » What does it mean to "believe without seeing"? Where does that kind of faith come from?

ASK GOD

Lord, so many people didn't believe even when they saw you do miracles. I confess that I have often been indifferent to your presence in my life. I don't want to be like that. I believe—help my unbelief.

Setting the Record Straight

Yes, what joy for those whose record the LORD has cleared of sin.

ROMANS 4:8

As we make our way through this life, a great deal of information follows us: birth records, academic information, medical history, driving record, work history, tax information, credit history, and so on. If all that information were good, no one would mind having it recorded. It's the negative information we have a problem with. We would prefer to keep it hidden or, better yet, have it erased. But have you ever tried to have a piece of negative information deleted from your records? Even if it's erroneous, getting it removed can be extremely difficult. It can follow you around, accusing you, for the rest of your life.

With that in mind, look again at what Jesus did to clear the record of your sin. Had he chosen not to die on the cross, your failures would have followed you around for eternity, and your sin would have separated you from God forever. Instead, because of Jesus' sacrifice, all record of your sin has been wiped clean. You can now stand holy and blameless before the Lord as though you had never sinned. It's that fresh start that ultimately makes it possible for you to take your life back!

ASK YOURSELF

> » Do you typically give much thought to the magnitude of what Jesus did for you on the cross? Why or why not?

> » In what ways can a new appreciation of your clean record with God help you move toward health and recovery?

ASK GOD

Dear Jesus, you have cleared all record of my sins and have given me a new start, and that is something I never wish to take for granted. Keep me mindful of how blessed I truly am.

Living Past Fear

*While Zechariah was in the sanctuary, an angel of the Lord appeared
to him, standing to the right of the incense altar. Zechariah was
shaken and overwhelmed with fear when he saw him.*

LUKE 1:11-12

Fear is an interesting emotion. The more we give in to being afraid, the more
afraid we tend to become.

When Zechariah saw an angel, his reaction was the same as Mary's reaction
when an angel visited her. Both were overwhelmed with fear. But in each case,
the angel's message to them was, "Don't be afraid" (Luke 1:13, 30). God does
not want his people to live in fear!

Often, when we give our lives away to the seeming needs of others, our basic
motivation is fear. We are afraid to be ourselves and afraid of others' reactions.
(If you struggle with such feelings, know that you are not alone.) God provides
what we need to live beyond these fears: "For God has not given us a spirit of
fear and timidity, but of power, love, and self-discipline" (2 Timothy 1:7).

Notice that Paul states this to his protégé, Timothy, as something that has
already happened. God *has given* us power. If we're still living in fear, we simply
haven't chosen to receive this gift.

ASK YOURSELF

» Describe a typical situation in which you feel fear. How could you move
against that fear?

» Memorize 2 Timothy 1:7 and repeat it to yourself whenever you are
faced with a fearful situation.

ASK GOD

God of power and love, thank you for your gift of power, love, and self-discipline.
Help me to trust you and face fearful situations in your power. Help me to hear
your voice saying to me, "Don't be afraid."

Changing the Way You Think

Don't copy the behavior and customs of this world, but let God
transform you into a new person by changing the way you think.

ROMANS 12:2

This Scripture passage presents us with a choice. We can either pick up the behaviors and customs of this world, or we can let God transform us into our true selves.

Stated that way, it doesn't seem like a hard choice. Who wouldn't want to be transformed by God? And yet most of us find it extremely difficult to resist the influence of the world around us. Almost without knowing it, we absorb ideas, attitudes, and habits that keep us stuck in our old, reactive ways.

Jesus says, "Don't worry." But we can't sleep because of anxiety.

Jesus says, "Love your neighbor." But we're concerned that the wrong sort of person has moved in next door.

Jesus says, "The truth will set you free." But we can't help thinking that little white lies can make everything easier.

The key point Paul is making is that transformation begins with changing the way we think. Our thoughts generate our feelings, and our feelings generate our behaviors. If we want to live and act the way God wants us to, we must begin by thinking differently.

ASK YOURSELF

> » What are some of the behaviors and customs you have picked up from the world?

> » Do you agree that our thoughts generate our feelings? Have you ever seen this work in your life?

ASK GOD

Dear Jesus, I want to become my true self—the person you created me to be. Give me discernment to recognize when I have picked up worldly thinking, and help me replace those thoughts with your thoughts.

God Will Guide You

I look to the LORD for help. I wait confidently for God to save me, and my God will certainly hear me.... Though I sit in darkness, the LORD will be my light.

MICAH 7:7-8

Are you feeling overwhelmed by the task of taking back your life? Have you been faced with a situation that just doesn't seem to be solvable? You sit and ponder, and it all seems dark to you.

It's time to turn to the Lord for help. Actually, it's past time to do that.

So often we turn to God as a last resort when he has been waiting to help us all along. He longs for us to lean on him daily, to develop a habit of turning to him in even the most minor situations, and to allow him to be a part of our healing process. When we do that, we'll also be in a better position to face crisis situations. Even in our times of overwhelming darkness, we'll be able to see his light.

ASK YOURSELF

» When you are faced with an overwhelming task, how does God fit in to your efforts to tackle the job? What can you do differently the next time you are in an overwhelming situation?

» What are some strategies for developing new habits of turning to God for help and guidance on a daily basis?

ASK GOD

O Lord, how I need you in the process of taking back my life. Yet I get so involved in my own efforts that I even forget to ask for your help. Help me develop new habit patterns that allow you to be my light in the darkness.

The Real, Feeling Jesus

He took Peter and Zebedee's two sons, James and John, and he became
anguished and distressed. He told them, "My soul is crushed with
grief to the point of death. Stay here and keep watch with me."

MATTHEW 26:37-38

If you were raised in the Roman Catholic Church, you may have seen images or statues of Jesus in agony on the cross. But if you were raised in a Protestant church—or no church at all—you may be more familiar with paintings of a very serene Jesus basking in a peaceful glow. So it may be hard for you to believe that this Jesus would ever have felt anger or sadness or dread. But he did.

The picture of Jesus we glean from the Gospels is of a man who was fully divine but also fully human. That means he felt what we feel. He was in anguish in the garden of Gethsemane. He was enraged that retailers outside the Temple were ripping people off. He wept when his friend died.

As you begin to become alive to your feelings, let the *real* Jesus be your guide.

ASK YOURSELF

» When you were younger, whether or not you attended church, did you imagine Jesus as a man with feelings?

» How does understanding that the real Jesus had feelings change your attitude toward your own emotions?

ASK GOD

Jesus, I thank you that you know what my life is like. As I picture your face—full of grief and joy and sorrow and elation—help me to become fully human, as you intended, by helping me learn to feel.

Keep on Praying

Work hard and serve the Lord enthusiastically. Rejoice in our
confident hope. Be patient in trouble, and keep on praying.

ROMANS 12:11-12

Are you excited about your recovery? Here Paul tells us to serve the Lord enthusiastically—or, as a footnote to the New Living Translation suggests, to "let the Spirit excite" us as we live for him. There *is* something exciting about taking our lives back. There's a sense of wholeness that we've longed for and an anticipation of what God is going to do next. There is a growing sense of hope that life can be different.

But sometimes our forward movement feels so slow. And there can also be setbacks, where it feels like we've moved forward a bit, only to reverse direction.

When that happens—and it will—Romans 12 tells us to do three things. First, we are to remind ourselves to rejoice in what we have been working toward and hoping for. Second, when trouble comes, we are to be patient—there's that word again—and not throw in the towel. And third, we must keep on praying. God never tires of our prayers, even when in our frustration we repeat ourselves. He loves to hear from us, so we need to keep on talking to him.

ASK YOURSELF

» Are you excited about your process of healing and recovery? If not, why not? If so, why?

» Describe your strategy for what to do when you get discouraged with the healing process.

ASK GOD

Patient Father in heaven, help me be more patient, especially with myself. And Holy Spirit, I ask you to excite me about the process of my recovery. Help me experience that confident hope.

Every Day Is a Gift from God

This is the day the LORD has made. We will rejoice and be glad in it.

PSALM 118:24

The psalmist reminds us that every day is a day that God has made. It is a gift from God himself.

But what about those days when everything seems to go wrong? What about those days when stress is almost overwhelming? Are those days a gift from God also? Are we really being asked to rejoice on those days? Yes.

Here's the apostle Paul's take on this: "We can rejoice, too, when we run into problems and trials, for we know that they help us develop endurance. And endurance develops strength of character, and character strengthens our confident hope of salvation. And this hope will not lead to disappointment" (Romans 5:3-5).

A friend said once, "Whenever a problem comes along, or a trial, I say to myself, 'Whoopee! God wants me to learn something new.'" The attitude he displayed—the one Paul describes—is an authentic and effective way to deal with life's stressors. It's God's way, in fact.

ASK YOURSELF

» What do you think Paul means by endurance? How does it relate to faith?

» Try it. How can you remind yourself that in spite of what's happening, today is God's gift to you—and rejoice in that?

ASK GOD

Dear God, some days seem so hard for me. I need your help to learn endurance. Help me see how endurance contributes to strong character and strong hope. And by the way, thanks for the gift of today!

Loving Yourself Is Not Selfish

To acquire wisdom is to love yourself; people who cherish understanding will prosper.

PROVERBS 19:8

This verse offers a good antidote to the pressure we often feel from others—and put on ourselves—not to be "selfish." Can loving ourselves really be the wise choice?

Many of us grew up thinking that caring for ourselves is the same as being as selfish or self-centered. But that's not true at all.

Think about it. When we love someone, we want that person to be healthy and cared for and to enjoy positive relationships. When we love ourselves, we want that love and care and health in our own lives—and we'll never get that by being selfish. Self-care actually frees us to relate appropriately and even unselfishly with others. When our needs are met, we're in much better shape to relate to others without placing undue demands on them. Self-care makes it possible for us to relate to them responsively rather than reactively.

Something else to note about this verse—there's a close relationship between developing wisdom and growing in understanding. The one leads to the other. Godly wisdom seeks to understand both ourselves and God. In so doing we develop healthier relationships with God, other people, and ourselves.

ASK YOURSELF

» Why do you think that loving ourselves is so often dismissed as being selfish? Has that been part of your experience?

» How hard is it for you to take care of yourself and show yourself the love you need? How can seeking wisdom and understanding help you with that?

ASK GOD

Father God, help me to seek your wisdom and to understand your ways better. Help me understand how much you love me. And out of your love for me, help me to love myself and others more.

God Is Here

They were all filled with awe and praised God. "A great prophet has
appeared among us," they said. "God has come to help his people."

LUKE 7:16, NIV

As Jesus, his disciples, and a great crowd of people were about to enter the city of Nain, they met a sizable funeral procession coming the other way. What a contrast between the excitement and joy of the people with Jesus and the sorrow of the widow and her friends, mourning that her only son had died. Luke tells us that "when the Lord saw her, his heart overflowed with compassion" (Luke 7:13). Then he went over and did what no one else could do. He told the dead boy to get up. And the boy not only sat up; he began talking. Jesus had raised him to life.

Imagine if you had been there. Suddenly your mourning would have been turned into unbelievable amazement. Jesus simply spoke, and the lad was alive.

What power! What compassion! Everyone who saw it was amazed. But the most powerful part of the people's response was their jubilant cry that "God has come to help his people."

It's still true today. God has come and is here with you. You can count on him to help you take your own life back.

ASK YOURSELF

> » What help do you need today as you work to take your life back?

> » Have you specifically asked Jesus for help in your recovery? If not, stop and do so now.

ASK GOD

Lord God, I see the power Jesus possessed while on earth and the even greater power he has today. Fill me with a sense of awe that never leaves me. Help me to surrender all of me to your most powerful Son.

Approved by God

Obviously, I'm not trying to win the approval of people, but of God.
If pleasing people were my goal, I would not be Christ's servant.

GALATIANS 1:10

Whose opinion matters the most to you? Your spouse's? Your parents'? Your boss's? Your best friend's? Your neighbors'?

There's nothing wrong with caring what people think of us or wanting to please them—*unless* ...

Unless we make their approval our primary focus.

Unless we have to put on a front or change who we are to win them over.

Or unless we care more about pleasing other people than we do about pleasing God.

The apostle Paul states directly that God is the one we need to please most: "A person with a changed heart seeks praise from God, not from people" (Romans 2:29). But Paul is not proposing an either/or solution. It's really a both/and—which means it's a matter of focus.

If our primary focus is seeking the approval of other people, we are doomed to frustration. There will always be those who don't like us. But God's approval is guaranteed as long as we are seeking to follow Jesus. In the long run, he's the one we need to please.

ASK YOURSELF

> » How would you describe the difference between seeking the approval of people and seeking the approval of God?

> » Have you ever lost the approval of someone important to you? Regardless of who was at fault, what was the result in your life?

ASK GOD

Lord, help my focus to be on seeking your approval. Help me find the balance of caring appropriately what others think while at the same time seeking to please you only.

God's Character Is Faithfulness

God is not a man, so he does not lie. He is not human, so he does not change his mind.
Has he ever spoken and failed to act? Has he ever promised and not carried it through?

NUMBERS 23:19

Fearing the Israelites would overwhelm his country, King Balak of Moab summoned the prophet Balaam. He sent for Balaam to put a curse on the Israelites. So Balaam obediently set off on his donkey to see the king. But along the way the donkey suddenly stopped dead in its tracks and refused to go forward. Balaam was furious. He even beat the poor donkey—until God allowed it to speak in its defense.

It turned out that the donkey could see what Balaam couldn't—that an angel was blocking the path. The angel told Balaam to obey God, not the king. He ended up blessing the Israelites instead of cursing them and gave Balak a message about God's faithfulness.

Sometimes we get frustrated and react badly when things don't go as we expect. But what Balaam learned is also true for us in our experience of God. We may not understand what's going on, but God knows what he's doing. God does not lie. He does not vacillate or fail to act. He always keeps his promises to us. God's very character is faithfulness.

ASK YOURSELF

» How do you typically react when there's a hitch in your plans?

» What's a better way to respond? What lessons about God can you draw from this story?

ASK GOD

Almighty God, forgive me for my impatience when things don't go the way I expect. Help me to remember that you are faithful and you know what you're doing, even when I can't see what's happening.

Are You Beating Yourself Up?

A fool's proud talk becomes a rod that beats him, but
the words of the wise keep them safe.

PROVERBS 14:3

In the 1997 movie *Liar Liar*, Jim Carrey plays a habitually dishonest man who is magically compelled to tell only the truth for one full day. During the course of that day, Carrey's character grows so frustrated that he takes to beating himself up in a public restroom. When another man enters the restroom and sees Carrey walloping himself, he stares in disbelief. Why? Because Carrey looks ridiculous.

This is how we must look to God when we are spouting prideful talk. The Bible says that "a fool's proud talk becomes a rod that beats him." Our prideful words, attitudes, and actions do nothing but make us look ridiculous—and eventually they'll trip us up.

Pride is easy to identify if you are looking for it, but it can be a tricky and deceptive adversary if you're not. It can disguise itself as independence, high standards, stubbornness, or even humility. Be sure you are always on the lookout for pride in your life.

ASK YOURSELF

» Think of a time when pride made you look foolish or tripped you up.

» How can you recognize pride in your life and change it?

ASK GOD
Dear Lord, how foolish I must look to you when I am full of pride. It is no wonder that you have no tolerance for it. Help me to recognize pride in my life before it has a chance to take hold and cause me to fall. I want to be a person who is humble in spirit, but I need your help.

The Wisdom of Learning

Intelligent people are always ready to learn. Their ears are open for knowledge.
PROVERBS 18:15

When you entered school as a five- or six-year-old, you may have seen at least a dozen years of school stretching out before you. In high school you probably looked forward to at least four more years of education until you were done. When you held that final degree in your hand, you may have assumed you were finished.

Think again.

You may well be finished with school. But living a healthy and hopeful life means you're never finished learning.

People in recovery pursue learning because we want to grow and live with wisdom beyond our years. We feed our minds with the Scriptures, with other literature, with classes and conversations. We ask questions, listen to other people, and pay attention to what our experiences are teaching us. Having our ears open for knowledge, we've come to enjoy the process of learning in the rhythm of our everyday lives. Recognizing the foolishness of believing we have nothing to learn, we continue to grow by seeking wisdom and truth.

ASK YOURSELF

» How have you always learned best—from classes? From other people? From experience? Has the experience of taking your life back opened your mind to different ways you can learn and grow?

» What opportunities to learn can you seize today? How do you challenge yourself to keep growing?

ASK GOD

God, quicken in me a desire to learn and to be transformed by your truth and wisdom. Please whet my appetite to learn, grow, and mature into the person you made me to be.

For Richer or Poorer

Enjoy prosperity while you can, but when hard times strike, realize that both come from God. Remember that nothing is certain in this life.

ECCLESIASTES 7:14

One of the most tragic mistakes we can make in life is to let our personal identity and self-worth get mixed up with our finances. Having an abundance of cash certainly makes daily life easier, but it's not a dependable source of security or happiness.

The Bible advises us to enjoy prosperity while we can because chances are we will not always be so prosperous. Life is filled with ups and downs, and our financial situation will probably change along with them.

But the Bible also reminds us that both prosperity and hard times come from God. If we really understand that he is using the state of our bank account to mold us and shape us, we will be in the best position to benefit from either feast or famine. When we reach the point where our happiness is not affected by the state of our finances, we will have arrived, knowing that whatever God has chosen for us at the moment is in our best interest.

ASK YOURSELF

» What kind of circumstances tend to make you feel happy and secure? What happens when those circumstances change?

» What are some of the things God has taught you through your finances? Do you tend to learn best in times of feast or famine?

ASK GOD

Dear Lord, I do not want to be emotionally tied to my bank balance or any other circumstance. Help me remember that everything I have comes from you. Thank you for loving me and for using my finances to make me into the person you want me to be.

Carry Your Own Load

Share each other's burdens, and in this way obey the law of Christ.... Pay careful attention to your own work.... and you won't need to compare yourself to anyone else. For we are each responsible for our own conduct.

GALATIANS 6:2, 4-5

Does this passage sound like a contradiction? How can we "share each other's burdens" and at the same time focus on our "own work"? The answer to this question holds an important key to taking our lives back.

Sometimes it's actually easier to try to help others than it is to look at our own issues. We use other people's problems as a distraction to keep from doing necessary but difficult work in our own lives. But to take our lives back, we must pay attention to our own stuff.

The way Paul used the word *burdens* refers to helping someone carry something that is too heavy for that person to carry alone. And we should absolutely help people who are overloaded—but not as a way of ignoring our own issues.

So Paul reminds us to avoid an either/or approach. We need to care for others when they truly need help, but our primary focus should be working on our own side of the street.

ASK YOURSELF

» Why do you think it is easier to work on someone else's "side of the street"?

» What is one personal issue you are going to work on today?

ASK GOD

Dear God, I admit I have thought that being a caring person meant taking care of others regardless of the need. Help me find the right balance of caring—helping those who need help, but also working on my own issues. Thank you.

God Gives His Peace

I am leaving you with a gift—peace of mind and heart. And the peace
I give is a gift the world cannot give. So don't be troubled or afraid.

JOHN 14:27

Based on Jesus' words, there are two kinds of peace we can experience. The world offers a kind of peace based on circumstances—an absence of difficulty or struggle. Peace in a nation is the absence of war. Peace in a community is the lack of civil conflict. (Police are often called peacekeepers.) Peace in a relationship means you get along and don't fight.

The problem, of course, is that this kind of peace never lasts. No matter how hard we try to keep the peace, someone is always stirring up trouble.

But Jesus says he will give us a peace that the world cannot give—an inner "peace of mind and heart." This is his gift for his followers. As we take our lives back, we will experience more and more of this inner peace, which will help us overcome our tendency to be troubled and afraid. Instead of stressing over what is going on around us or what others are doing, we will trust God to take care of us.

ASK YOURSELF

» How do you access God's gift of peace whenever you are troubled or afraid?

» How is Jesus' gift of peace different from what we often call our search for "peace and happiness"?

ASK GOD

Jesus, all too often I get caught up in the stress and anxiety of worldly conflict. Help me to focus on you more, especially at those times of stress, so I can enjoy the gift of your peace.

Have You Tuned Out?

All who listen to me will live in peace, untroubled by fear of harm.

PROVERBS 1:33

Have you ever been caught not paying attention? You appeared to be listening intently, but your mind wandered off in all sorts of different directions. And like a daydreaming child called on by the teacher, you were suddenly at a loss when you tried to refocus. You didn't have a clue what was going on.

That's an uncomfortable position to be in—the very opposite of peaceful. And that's what your life is like when you don't pay attention to what God is saying to you.

The Lord is talking to you throughout every day. But are you really listening to him? Do you give him your full and undivided attention and act on what he communicates to you through his Word and his Spirit? One sign that you are really listening and responding is a sense of inner peace. Your life won't be perfect, but it will feel "right." If that's not true for you, maybe it's time to refocus and turn your full attention back to the Lord.

ASK YOURSELF

» What needs, wants, and compulsions are most likely to distract you from what God is communicating to you?

» Do you have the peace in your life that God promises to those who listen to him? If not, what kind of changes can you make to help you pay closer attention?

ASK GOD

Dear Jesus, keep me focused on you and on your Word. Sharpen my ears to hear even your smallest whisper. I want to claim the peace that you have promised me and to live a life that exudes your presence. Teach me how to be a good listener, Lord.

A Chosen People

The LORD gives his people strength. The LORD blesses them with peace.

PSALM 29:11

Who are the Lord's people? According to Paul, we are.

"Even before he made the world," Paul writes in Ephesians 1:4-5, "God loved us and chose us in Christ to be holy and without fault in his eyes. God decided in advance to adopt us into his own family by bringing us to himself through Jesus Christ."

This means that if we have accepted Jesus as our Savior, we're part of God's chosen family. Because we belong to him, we can read a promise like we find in Psalm 29:11 and realize God is talking to us. The promise here is that he gives us strength for the tasks involved in taking our lives back. He also promises to bless us with his peace—again, because we're his.

The apostle Peter puts it another way. He reminds us that we're "a chosen people . . . royal priests, a holy nation, God's very own" (1 Peter 2:9).

If you ever struggle with how you see yourself or whether God loves you, this is the reminder you need. You are God's very own, dearly beloved child. He has chosen you.

ASK YOURSELF

» How does it feel to be one of God's people? What feels good? Does anything about that reality make you uncomfortable?

» When is it hard to believe that God truly loves you? Why do you think that is so?

ASK GOD

Gracious God, it's hard for me to believe that I am adopted into your family. Sometimes it's even harder to believe how much you love me. Help me to bask in your love for me until its reality soaks into my whole being.

Keep Pecking

May God give you more and more grace and peace as you
grow in your knowledge of God and Jesus our Lord.

2 PETER 1:2

Have you ever seen one of those chickens that "play" the piano? Their trainers use a system that releases feed every time the chicken pecks the keys. The more the chicken pecks, the more she receives what satisfies her.

We're not chickens, of course, and our relationship with our Creator is far more complex and wonderful than just doing certain things to get a reward. But one lesson from those musical chickens can help us experience God's grace and peace more richly.

The grace and peace of God are always available to us, but to receive these blessings in our lives we have to keep "pecking." The more we keep coming back to the Word, the more time we share with other believers, and the more we pray and just spend time in God's presence, the better we'll get to know him. And the better we get to know God, the more we'll experience his grace and peace in our lives.

ASK YOURSELF

> » What does the current condition of your life say about the depth of your knowledge of God?

> » What spiritual practices can you adopt (or renew) that will help you know God better?

ASK GOD

Dear Lord, I want to get to know you intimately and experience all you have to offer. Give me the self-control to persist in the disciplines that bring me closer to you. Fill my life with the peace and grace you have promised to those who love you.

The Blessing of Boundaries

Put on all of God's armor so that you will be able to
stand firm against all strategies of the devil.

EPHESIANS 6:11

In the first chapter of Job, the devil complains to God that Job, God's faithful servant, has been spared hardship because God has placed a wall of protection around him. Can you picture that protective wall? Paul's letter to the church in Ephesus exhorts believers to put on the armor of God as protection against the wily strategies of that same devil.

Personal boundaries serve a similar protective function in our lives. Their purpose is to create a safe and secure place for us to live. They are essentially rules for engagement, standards for interaction that we intend to follow and that we expect others to honor.

There will be moments in the heat of relationship when you find it extremely difficult to defend the boundaries you've set. In those moments you might visualize a wall, a suit of armor, or even (if it's more fun) a space suit—a protective barrier that is there for your good and the good of others. Your boundaries can be a blessing to you and a blessing to those around you.

ASK YOURSELF

» In general, do you have a sense that your boundaries are too weak or too firm? Is there a particular relationship in which you need really strong and healthy boundaries?

» How can your protective boundaries be a blessing to others as well as to yourself?

ASK GOD

Gracious God, I thank you that you are my Protector. Teach me to exercise healthy boundaries so that I might flourish and those around me might flourish as well. I trust you to guard my heart and guard my life.

Deeply Rooted

Christ will make his home in your hearts as you trust in him. Your roots will grow down into God's love and keep you strong.

EPHESIANS 3:17

When a plant is being established, it is crucial that the roots have the opportunity to extend deep into the soil. If the roots stay shallow or if they are not grounded in the soil, they will wither and the plant will die—or the first strong wind will knock it over. As a child of God, it is crucial to your spiritual health that you root yourself firmly in the Lord. You do this by grounding yourself in Jesus and placing your trust in him.

Regardless of whether you recently accepted Christ or you have been saved for years, your spiritual health will always be tied to how deeply rooted you are in God. Make sure that you are placing your trust in him and seeking his will in your life. Staying grounded spiritually is not difficult, but it does require that you remain conscious of your need for God on a moment-by-moment basis.

You have invited Christ into your heart. Now trust him with all that you have. In doing this, you will grow in the love of God and become strong.

ASK YOURSELF

» What practices and habits can help you put down deep spiritual roots? Are there any that you have been neglecting?

» Which of these practices are currently part of your life? Which ones do you tend to neglect?

ASK GOD

Dear Lord God, please show me, moment by moment, what I need to do to become stronger in my Christian walk. I want to be deeply rooted in you so that I can be used by you.

Don't Just Say It

Those who obey God's word truly show how completely they
love him. That is how we know we are living in him.

1 JOHN 2:5

How many times have you heard the phrase "Talk is cheap"? It certainly can be. Our words matter, but words that are not backed up by behavior have little lasting impact. Whether you are the producer of empty talk or find yourself on the receiving end of it, it is just that—empty.

Follow-through in relationships is critical to growth and stability. No one wants empty promises—not you, not the people in your life, and certainly not God. Good intentions are easy to come by, but it is what we actually do that changes things.

It is not your words that prove your love for another person. It's your acts of generosity and caring.

It's not someone's words that prove their love for you. It's their faithfulness and support.

It is certainly not words that prove your love for God. It's your obedience and your worship.

What matters most is not what you say, but how you live.

ASK YOURSELF

» In your personal and spiritual life, are you prone to empty talk, empty promises, or good intentions that never quite pan out? How could you change this tendency?

» Can the *lack* of words ever be a problem in relationships? Why or why not?

ASK GOD

Dear Lord, help me remember to back up the words that come from my mouth with loving and faithful behavior. Let those around me see the love you have produced in my life, and let them see my love for them and for you in both my actions and words.

How God Sees You

The LORD doesn't see things the way you see them. People judge
by outward appearance, but the LORD looks at the heart.

1 SAMUEL 16:7

God spoke these words to the prophet Samuel as Samuel prepared to anoint a replacement for King Saul. The sons of Jesse were prime candidates, so Samuel had traveled to meet them. As each brother was brought before him, Samuel found himself thinking, "Surely this is the LORD's anointed" (1 Samuel 16:6), only to have the clear sense that God had not chosen that particular young man.

Finally Samuel met the youngest son, who had been out in the fields. And this time Samuel sensed God's confirmation. David was definitely the one.

God wasn't concerned with the external appearance of Jesse's sons. He saw their hearts. And he knew David would grow up to be not only a great king, but a man after God's own heart (see Acts 13:22).

So much of our energy gets tied up in our efforts to "look good" to others. So many of our reactive behaviors have at their root a focus on appearances. But nothing drains our energy more than worrying about how things look. Instead, we need to focus on who we are inside—because that's who God sees when he looks at us. He sees and understands our hearts.

ASK YOURSELF

» Describe some situations where you typically worry too much about how others see you.

» Why do you think your outward appearance in those situations seems more important than the condition of your heart?

ASK GOD

Father God, help me to guard my heart so that you will be pleased with what you see there. Help me to shift my focus from the external, and free me from worrying so much about appearances.

God Is with You

When you go through deep waters, I will be with you. When you go through
rivers of difficulty, you will not drown. When you walk through the fire of
oppression, you will not be burned up. . . . For I am the LORD, your God.

ISAIAH 43:2-3

Every one of us, at some time, will face "deep waters" or "rivers of difficulty" or "the fire of oppression." It's part of life, and God never promises to protect us from life. Instead, he reminds us that wherever we go, whatever we experience, he is with us.

Is that hard for you to believe? It might be because you're expecting God to come to you in an experience that is separate from your daily life. And God does sometimes work that way. But just as often—perhaps more often—he works through other people. (He also works through us to help others.)

You may have good reasons for not trusting people. You have probably been wounded by others—who probably had been wounded themselves. But God works through wounded people! If you isolate yourself from others, you may also be isolating yourself from the saving work God wants to do in your life.

ASK YOURSELF

» Describe your issues with trust in general and with trusting God in particular. Where do you think these trust issues came from?

» How can you learn to trust God's work through others without setting yourself up to be hurt again?

ASK GOD

Dear God, help me when I find it difficult to believe you are with me. Help me sense your presence more and trust the way you work in my life through others. And remind me that you want to show your presence to others as well.

God Knows My Name

Do not be afraid, for I have ransomed you. I have called you by name; you are mine.

ISAIAH 43:1

Do you realize that if Jesus were walking on this earth today and he met you on the street, he would call you by your name? He is so intimately involved in caring about you that he already knows everything about you. We see an example of this when Andrew brought his brother Simon to meet Jesus: "Looking intently at Simon, Jesus said, 'Your name is Simon, son of John—but you will be called Cephas' (which means 'Peter')" (John 1:42). Jesus knew Simon Peter's name without a word being spoken, and he knows your name too.

A special intimacy exists when someone knows your name. In some ancient cultures, a person's real name was kept secret from all but his family and other trusted people. Everyone else knew only that person's "public" name—because it was believed that those who knew the real name would have power over the person.

The Jesus who knows our name does have power over us, but he would never use it against us. Instead, he gives us access to his power as well. All we have to do is call upon his name.

ASK YOURSELF

> » What does it mean to you that Jesus knows you by name?

> » Philippians 2:10 says that "at the name of Jesus every knee should bow." Why do you think Paul says this happens "at the *name* of Jesus"?

ASK GOD

Dear Jesus, it amazes me that you know me so intimately that you know my name. Help me to understand more what an incredible gift it is to me to be known by you.

Coming Out of Hiding

People who conceal their sins will not prosper, but if they
confess and turn from them, they will receive mercy.

PROVERBS 28:13

A little girl was playing with her grandfather's antique cuckoo clock when she yanked one of the chains too hard and it broke. Dropping the chain to the ground, she felt so ashamed that she ran away to hide, locking herself in the bathroom.

Too often this—hiding and clinging to our shame and guilt—is how we choose to behave as adults. We mistakenly believe that keeping our sins hidden will somehow save us. But the wise author of Proverbs reminds us that's just not the case.

We all sin. It's part of our nature in that we are born sinners. It's also human nature to attempt to conceal our sins. But if we do that, we will not prosper in any way. Our health will suffer. Our spiritual walk will suffer. Our relationships and even our work will probably suffer.

But confessing our sins changes things. It brings us out of hiding to a place where we can receive mercy and begin to heal. The little girl who broke the clock learned this when her kind grandfather sought her out—searching the house until he found her—and forgave her. God longs to forgive you, too, as you confess your sins.

ASK YOURSELF

» Think of a time when you hung on to a sin longer than you should have before confessing it. What happened?

» How did it feel to admit your wrongdoing? What happened after you confessed your sin?

ASK GOD
God who forgives, I long to be set free from my sin. Thank you that you are faithful to forgive and to heal when I confess my sin to you.

A Healthy Fear

His unfailing love toward those who fear him is as great
as the height of the heavens above the earth.

PSALM 103:11

When the Bible talks about the "fear of the Lord," it is not referring to the kind of fear that we feel when watching a scary movie or walking alone in a strange part of town. The type of fear God wants us to have toward him is more like a deep respect for or awe of his holiness. You can be close to him, wrapped in his arms, and still fear him in this reverent way.

The experience is similar to what a child might feel about a loving or responsible earthly father. She knows he loves her. She has no doubt he will take care of her. She even enjoys playtime with him. But when she crosses a line that should not be crossed, she fears her father appropriately because she knows he will discipline her. It is his way of directing her onto the right path.

This is the relationship that God wants to have with us. Loving. Trusting. But respectful of who he is and his appropriate role in our lives.

ASK YOURSELF

» Can you relate to the parental illustration above, or does your relationship with an imperfect earthly parent make this kind of healthy fear problematic for you?

» What are some possible strategies for relearning an appropriate relationship with your heavenly Father?

ASK GOD

Father God, I want to have a healthy fear of you, a fear that is consistent with your holiness. Keep me aware of your deity and remind me to show you the reverence that you so deserve.

Embrace Your Emotions

Fear of the LORD is the foundation of true knowledge,
but fools despise wisdom and discipline.

PROVERBS 1:7

"Don't trust your emotions." "Don't let feelings fool you." "Feelings are dangerous."

Perhaps, like us, you've heard warnings like these, even in the church. Although we've been warned to distrust feelings, God actually gave them as a gift. They make us aware of what's good in the world, and they also signal us to areas that need our attention. Guilt leads to godly sorrow. Joy signals God's goodness. Anger can alert us to danger and reveal bitterness or resentment in our hearts. And as the author of this proverb declares, even fear can be a gift. Fear of the Lord leads us to know God better and to trust him more fully.

God invites us to *feel* our feelings and to learn from them instead of denying them. That doesn't mean we need to act on every feeling we have! That's where wisdom and discipline come in. But if you've been wary of embracing your emotions, ask God to guide you on the journey to a new fullness of life.

ASK YOURSELF

» What messages did you hear about feelings as you were growing up?

» What do you think is a healthy balance between "feeling your feelings" and letting them inappropriately guide your life?

ASK GOD

Father, thank you for creating me with the ability to feel and to grow from those feelings. As I welcome my emotions as a good gift from you, I seek your wisdom and guidance in handling them appropriately.

The Fruit of Having a Plan

Good planning and hard work lead to prosperity, but hasty shortcuts lead to poverty.

PROVERBS 21:5

Think of prosperity as the wealth of character we receive through the process of taking our lives back. If we give up or insist we can never change—or if we impatiently insist on doing things our own way—we may well end up spiritually and emotionally impoverished, which is not what God wants for us at all. But with planning and hard work—not to mention loads of grace—we will eventually prosper. All we have invested will pay off as we learn to live the way God intended for us.

But how exactly does planning fit in with the process of taking our lives back? For one thing, it allows us to understand our priorities and keep ourselves looking forward. It's not some rigid, legalistic approach where we map everything out to the last detail and then beat ourselves up for not following it perfectly. It is simply choosing to listen to God, set some priorities and determine some strategies, and then do our best to move ahead while keeping our eyes on Jesus.

ASK YOURSELF

> » Where do you struggle in following a plan? Do you tend to map out your course too rigidly or fail to look ahead? What are the pitfalls of each approach?

> » What happens when your plans don't seem to be working or your priorities need adjusting? What (or who) will keep you moving toward spiritual and emotional prosperity?

ASK GOD

Lord, I want to lead a rich life in you. Be with me and guide me as I plan for my recovery and work toward healing. Help me focus on your priorities and do those things that really matter in the long run.

Progress, Not Perfection

Don't you know that this good man, though you trip him up seven times,
will each time rise again? But one calamity is enough to lay you low.

PROVERBS 24:16, TLB

Moroccan weavers believe that creating a perfect rug is blasphemy—because only God is perfect. So they purposely weave a mistake into every one of their creations as a way of fighting their perfectionist tendencies.

That's something to keep in mind in your recovery. You will inevitably fail at some point and to some degree. And if perfection is your focus, that "calamity" will be "enough to lay you low." You may feel hopeless, but ideally you will eventually "rise again" and get back on track. Either way, you will be better off if you focus on *progress* instead of *perfection*.

There's a reason the proverb speaks of being tripped up seven times. In the Bible, seven is the perfect number. It symbolizes completeness. The implication is that no matter how many times we fall, we must get up again each time. The key is to persevere regardless of the circumstances and regardless of how many times we have failed. That's part of why those of us in recovery call our stumbles relapses instead of failures.

ASK YOURSELF

> » How do you tend to react when things don't go right for you? Does perfectionism make it harder for you to go on?

> » What could you do in order to "rise again" more quickly from your stumbles?

ASK GOD

Dear Lord, help me focus on perseverance, not perfection. I don't want to give up when things don't go as planned. Teach me how to persevere and how to get up quickly if I stumble. Thank you!

What Is Good?

The LORD has told you what is good, and this is what he requires of you:
to do what is right, to love mercy, and to walk humbly with your God.

MICAH 6:8

God's people just didn't get it.

He had spent centuries loving these people, providing for them, and explaining to them what he cared about, but they persisted with their own ideas of how to please him. What about burnt offerings? Gallons of oil poured on the altar? Sacrificing children? God must have been really shaking his head at that point. So he sent Micah to explain once more.

What God wanted was not over-the-top worship, Micah explained, but simple obedience. He'd taken great pains to teach them what was right. Now he wanted them to do it—but with the right attitude. They were to value compassion, forgiveness, gratitude, grace, and forbearance just as he did. And they were to stay humble—remembering who they were and not inflating their importance. That way they could stay in right relationship with God.

Much, much later Jesus would summarize God's law as loving God and loving other people (Matthew 22:37-40)—basically the same message as Micah's.

Who knows? Maybe someday we'll finally get it.

ASK YOURSELF

» What are some of the ways you have tried to please God? What do you think he wants from you today?

» What does "humbly" mean to you, especially in the context of how you relate to God and others?

ASK GOD

Dear Lord, I do want to please you. Help me to remember that what you want most from me is obedience, a loving attitude toward others, and a humble opinion of myself. Thank you for loving me enough to keep reminding me.

Let People Be People

Love prospers when a fault is forgiven, but dwelling on it separates close friends.

PROVERBS 17:9

We all know that being human means being fallible. And yet the perfectionist in us sometimes requires that those around us be perfect or else. The sad fact is, we all have faults. The sooner we learn to be accepting of the faults of others, the sooner we will find peace in our lives and in our relationships.

Do you tend to place impossible expectations on others or hold them to standards that no one could ever maintain? When was the last time you found yourself irritated by someone's behavior? Did you let that irritation turn into anger and then hold on to that anger for all you were worth?

If we want healthy, fulfilling relationships, we must allow the people in our lives to be flawed. When we truly accept both the good and the bad in others, then we will see our relationships start to bloom.

ASK YOURSELF

» Who in your life tends to annoy or irritate you most? Whose flaws and failures do you find it hardest to accept?

» Are you holding on to any past grievances that are hurting your relationships? What would it take for you to let go of these?

ASK GOD

Dear Lord, I want to have rich, meaningful relationships with the people in my life. I do not want to be always looking for the flaws in others. Help me to recognize the failures of those around me simply as proof of their humanness and not as something they have done to agitate me. Teach me to be more like Jesus, in whose name I pray.

It Will Work Out

We know that God causes everything to work together for the good of those
who love God and are called according to his purpose for them.

ROMANS 8:28

Life is a mix of the good, the bad, and the boring! No one has control over every aspect of it, and there are certain to be things in our lives that we will not understand. Fortunately, God has made us a promise. He assures us that no matter what we come up against in our lives, he will ultimately use everything (even the bad experiences) for our benefit. All we have to do is keep on loving him and following him. He'll take care of everything else.

Have you gone through things that have left you shaking your head in confusion, wondering how they could possibly be a part of anything good? It's important to realize that you don't need to understand the how—you simply need to trust that God will do what he has promised. Try thanking God for your next trial instead of letting yourself be frustrated or afraid. Ultimately, every problem will be just a memory, and in the end you will be better for having experienced it.

ASK YOURSELF

» If God causes *everything* to work together for good, is there *anything* in your life that is worth stressing over? Why do you think we continue to worry?

» How can understanding God's promise help you respond appropriately to your problems instead of just reacting to them?

ASK GOD

Dear Lord, I desperately want to learn how to trust you in times of trouble. Your Word promises me that you will cause everything in my life to work together for my good if I love and follow you. Help me, Lord, to cling to this promise when things get tough.

Getting Busy for God

Work willingly at whatever you do, as though you were working for
the Lord rather than for people. Remember that the Lord will give you
. . . your reward, and that the Master you are serving is Christ.

COLOSSIANS 3:23-24

Taking your life back isn't easy. It takes time and hard, consistent work. Paul reminds us that there are rewards for those who work willingly, especially when we keep our motives straight. (We are working to please God and become the people he created us to be, not to impress others.) But it won't happen immediately—which is why we need *patience* as well as willingness.

Patience must have been a challenge for Paul, for he refers to it often in his letters. It's listed in Colossians 3:12 as a personal quality we should work for, and it's also mentioned in Galatians 5:22-23 as a "fruit" the Holy Spirit grows in our lives.

Patience is also a huge challenge for most of us. We want results now. We want healing now. But patience is what it takes to work willingly for the Lord and for our healing. The good news is that God, who rewards our work, can also help us grow the fruit of patience.

ASK YOURSELF

» What is the most difficult or frustrating challenge for you in taking your life back?

» How can you grow in your ability to be patient with God's healing process?

ASK GOD

Lord God, how I wish I could just take my life back without all the hard work. Help me be patient and remember that the work itself is part of my learning and healing process—and the work will be worth it.

Anchor Yourself

Evil people try to drag me into sin, but I am firmly anchored to your instructions.
PSALM 119:61

If you have ever been out on an oceangoing vessel, you understand the importance of having an anchor. Without one, you would drift with the tide or the current and could quickly find yourself lost or in danger. But once you have dropped anchor, you know you will be firmly locked in that location because your boat is tied to a heavy weight that holds it in place.

Being anchored to God's instructions works in a similar way. When you stay attached to the weight of his Word, you're not likely to be carried into areas of spiritual danger. The danger comes when your attachment weakens. Without that anchor you are bound to drift, and even if you move slowly, the result is the same. Eventually you'll end up in a place you never intended to be.

Don't allow yourself to drift into sin by floating aimlessly through life. Tie yourself to God, stabilize yourself through his Word, and avoid dangerous waters.

ASK YOURSELF

> » Have you ever found yourself in dangerous waters when it came to your spiritual well-being? How did that happen? How were you able to get back on course?

> » Practically speaking, what does it mean to anchor yourself in God's instructions? What's the best way to do that?

ASK GOD

Dear God, I know that you are my Stabilizer and that only you can keep me on course. Help me stay connected to you at all times so that I do not drift into areas that could be harmful to my spiritual health.

The "I Want" Cycle

*Enjoy what you have rather than desiring what you don't have. Just
dreaming about nice things is meaningless—like chasing the wind.*

ECCLESIASTES 6:9

Do you ever get caught up in wishing that you had more—more money, more
friends, a more expensive automobile, nicer furniture, a bigger house, the lat-
est electronics? It is easy to get caught up in the cycle of "I want," but it is not
a healthy place to be.

There is nothing wrong with having nice things, but if we're more focused
on what we don't have than on what we do, we are headed for trouble. We'll be
so much happier if we make the decision to simply enjoy what God has given
us instead of always wishing for something new or different.

The Bible likens an unhealthy focus on "nice things" to "chasing the wind." It
is a complete waste of time and energy and sets us up for dissatisfaction. Why
would we do that to ourselves?

Thank God daily for all that you have and enjoy his provision. When you
have a need, give it to God and let it go. Chasing material things will only steal
the joy that is available to you now.

ASK YOURSELF

» What is usually on your "I want" list? What does this tell you about
yourself?

» What circumstances tend to trigger your "I wants"? What would help
you choose contentment instead?

ASK GOD

Dear Lord, I know I do not show you the gratitude you deserve. I'm sorry that
I take your provision for granted. Help me to recognize all that you have done
for me, to keep my eyes on all that I have and not to be always looking for more.

Who Needs a Doctor?

When Jesus heard this, he said, "Healthy people don't need a doctor—
sick people do. . . . I have come to call not those who think they
are righteous, but those who know they are sinners."

MATTHEW 9:12-13

Picture a medical center full of healthy people waiting to see a doctor—because they've been told they need to. But when the doctor asks, "How can I help?" they all reply, "Oh, you can't help me. I'm fine."

The obvious question would be why these patients are there in the first place. If a person is perfectly healthy—or claims to be—a doctor can't do much to help.

The same is true of our relationship with Jesus. If we were totally healthy, we wouldn't really need him. But the truth is, no one is completely healthy. Every one of us is infected by sin and in need of the Great Physician.

The Lord doesn't expect us to be perfect. But he wants us to be aware of our "sin sickness" and to ask for his help. Only then can we begin to find the healing we need.

ASK YOURSELF

> » Are you quick to protest, "I'm fine" when confronted with the possibility that you might not be fine at all? Why do you think you do this?

> » Why is forgiveness a necessary part of healing?

ASK GOD

Dear Lord Jesus, sometimes I strive so hard to lead a life that is pleasing to you that I don't see the areas where I am failing. Open my eyes to any sin in my life. Teach me that it is okay not to be perfect. Remind me that I can always come to you to be forgiven and restored.

Follow God's Lead

The commandments of the LORD are right, bringing joy to the heart.
The commands of the LORD are clear, giving insight for living.

PSALM 19:8

You're driving way out in the country and suddenly realize you have no idea where you are. There are roads but no road signs. Your phone isn't picking up a signal. Even your GPS seems confused. That's truly a sinking feeling. The choices you make from this point until you (hopefully!) reach your desired destination will be filled with anxiety.

As we work to take our lives back, we need a dependable source of guidance. The good news is—we have one. The Bible tells us that "the commands of the LORD are clear" and give "insight for living."

We can follow God's lead with confidence. The more time we spend in his Word, the better able we will be to discern his voice and his instruction about what to do in a given situation. His guidance will be in line with Scripture (because he never contradicts himself), and it will feel "right" in our souls. If we obey the commands and the insight he gives us, we can be sure of eventually finding the way.

ASK YOURSELF

> » How do you usually discern God's guidance for your decisions? Has he ever guided you in a way you didn't expect?

> » Are you following the road that God has set for you, or do you tend to insist on finding your own way? What do you think would happen if you stayed on his path?

ASK GOD

Dear Lord, I know you will never lead me astray. Thank you for caring enough to give me direction in my life. Help me learn to recognize your voice and to follow where you lead.

A Love That Never Fails

*No one is abandoned by the Lord forever. Though he brings grief, he also
shows compassion because of the greatness of his unfailing love.*

LAMENTATIONS 3:31-32

A little girl we'll call Sarah was born to an addicted mother who was unable to
care for her. When Sarah was two, she went into her state's foster-care system,
and she was eventually adopted when she was five. Her parents were thrilled
to welcome Sarah into their family as the daughter they'd always longed for,
and Sarah was happy to finally be in a permanent home. But something in
her remained wary. Deep inside, she believed her new parents would fail. She
assumed they would eventually abandon her.

Sarah's skepticism was natural. How could she expect unconditional love
and acceptance when she had never experienced it? But over time she would
learn that her new family's love was different from what she'd received in her
early years—and that God's love was even better. God was the one who would
never abandon Sarah. Because of his steadfast compassion and unfailing love,
she could always count on him.

ASK YOURSELF

> » Based on your earliest experiences, what do you tend to expect from
> God and from others?

> » Have you experienced God as one who never abandons you? If you
> have difficulty trusting that truth, what would make it more real
> to you?

ASK GOD

Compassionate God, you have shown yourself to be the one who never abandons or forsakes your children. Lord, may this truth move from my head to my
heart and from my heart into my bones. Thank you that your love never fails.

Bulletproof Protection

The LORD is my strength and shield. I trust him with all my heart. He helps
me, and my heart is filled with joy. I burst out in songs of thanksgiving.
PSALM 28:7

Police officers who go out in the line of duty are well protected. They wear
body armor or riot gear, drive vehicles that are designed to protect them, and
carry a variety of weapons to defend themselves. If they were forced to go on
duty without these protections, they would find it hard to do their work with
confidence. In fact, such an order would cause so much stress that it would be
hard to staff a police force. No one would want the job.

You have protection, too, as you go about your life. Knowing the Lord is
your shield and your strength should give you not only confidence but joy.
Start your day by acknowledging God's protection. Thank him for watching
over you, trust that he has your back in every situation, and watch your level
of joy increase.

ASK YOURSELF

» Do you really believe that God is always there to protect you? What
  form do you think this protection takes?

» Can you look back and think of a time when you know that God protected you mentally, emotionally, or even physically? How does this
  knowledge increase your trust, confidence, and joy?

ASK GOD

Dear Lord, I want to live my life full of the confidence that you intend for me
to have. Help me trust in the protection that you provide for me day in and
day out. Make me aware of your presence, and let my life exhibit the joy I can
find when I fully trust you.

When God Seems Absent

God heard their groaning, and he remembered his covenant promise to Abraham,
Isaac, and Jacob. He looked down on the people of Israel and knew it was time to act.

EXODUS 2:24-25

By the time Moses grew up to be a prince in Pharaoh's household, his people—
the Hebrews—had been enslaved in Egypt for four hundred years. For centuries they'd endured abuse and humiliation, forced to perform grueling labor
for their captors. It's difficult to imagine what they suffered and how it affected
their bodies, minds, and hearts. And they had to have wondered where God
was. Hadn't he made promises to their ancestors, Abraham, Isaac, and Jacob?
Didn't he know what was happening to them now?

When we suffer, it's easy to believe the lie that God doesn't see us, God
doesn't hear us, and God doesn't care what is happening to us. And yet Scripture
announces that God did hear the groaning of his people. God was not absent
from his people in Egypt, and God is not absent from our suffering today. In
the darkest moments of our lives, God bears witness to what we've endured.
And when the time is right, he will act on our behalf.

ASK YOURSELF

> » Either now or in the past, have you struggled to recognize God's stead-
> fast presence with you in suffering? Describe your experience.

> » How can you find assurance of God's presence when you are in pain?

ASK GOD

Father God, remember your covenant promise to the Hebrews and your covenant with me through Jesus Christ. I belong to you, Lord, and I cry out for
your mercy. Trusting in your faithfulness, I wait to be relieved and redeemed.

Be Careful What You Crave

The love of money is the root of all kinds of evil. And some people, craving money,
have wandered from the true faith and pierced themselves with many sorrows.

1 TIMOTHY 6:10

Cravings are powerful desires. The more we try not to think about them, the stronger they become, and they cannot usually be overcome by conscious effort or willpower. What you crave is usually what you love most. It's always on your mind, and it feels more like a need than a want.

The Bible warns specifically against a common craving—the love of money. Money isn't a bad thing in itself. But when we value it too much, it can take a wicked hold on our hearts. We feel the need for more and more of it, but it never really satisfies.

How can we break the power of unhealthy cravings? A hint comes from those who study food cravings. When a "sugarholic" substitutes healthy foods for the sweet stuff, the sugar cravings quickly disappear—because real nutritional needs are finally being met.

Freeing ourselves from other unhealthy cravings works much the same way. Developing a taste for the healthy and satisfying things of God is the best way to short-circuit unhealthy, obsessive, and unproductive desires.

ASK YOURSELF

» Are there desires in your life that feel more like needs? What are they?

» What are some strategies for replacing worldly cravings with godly ones?

ASK GOD

Dear Lord Jesus, help me evaluate my desires to see if they are leading me in the right direction. Please don't allow anything in my life to become more important to me than it should be, and help me to focus on what will nourish me and bring me closer to you.

Finding Rest

Come to me, all of you who are weary and carry heavy burdens,
and I will give you rest. . . . You will find rest for your souls. For
my yoke is easy to bear, and the burden I give you is light.

MATTHEW 11:28-30

Which makes you wearier over the long haul—physical exertion or mental and emotional stress?

Hard physical labor can certainly tax the body (although it also makes it stronger). But inner stress almost always takes a greater toll. We plan, we seek to please, and we carry a heavy burden of worries and anxieties. And this is why we desperately need the kind of rest Jesus offers us.

Rest for our souls.

Jesus cares about the demands we are making on ourselves, so he offers another way. A single, simple responsibility. The law of love that applies to all believers is that we are to love one another as Christ has loved us (see John 15:9-17). If we follow Jesus, we are to follow the law of love—a light burden.

That's not to say loving is always easy. It's not—not on our own. But if we are following Jesus, we aren't on our own. We have the Holy Spirit living in us. Jesus' burden of love is light because he does all the heavy lifting!

ASK YOURSELF

> » What burden is wearing you out these days? How would you go about handing that burden over to Jesus?

> » Who in your life is hard to love? Why?

ASK GOD

Father, thank you for your offer of rest for my soul, and help me see that what is required of me is not to worry but to love. Guide me as I seek to obey Jesus' commandment.

Stop Fighting

God blesses those who patiently endure testing and temptation. Afterward they will receive the crown of life that God has promised to those who love him.

JAMES 1:12

Are you fighting an ongoing battle, one that seems like it should have come to an end long ago but hasn't? God promises to bless us if we "patiently endure testing and temptation"—with *patiently* being the key word here. If you are fighting something, you are not being patient. Only when you stop fighting a situation can God reveal what he wants you to learn.

It is easy to lose perspective in the midst of our problems because we are simply too close to the situation. When we stop trying to solve the problems on our own and patiently look to God for the answer, then we can back up and take an objective look at what we are facing. Often God is simply waiting for us to do this so he can solve the problem or show us how to solve it. He is not going to fight us for control. But when we take a step back, he will move in and show us what to do next.

ASK YOURSELF

» What is the difference between waiting patiently and just giving up? How do you distinguish what God wants to do for you and what he wants *you* to do with his help and guidance?

» What are some strategies for developing patience and perspective in the midst of problems?

ASK GOD

Lord, how many trials have dragged on in my life because I stubbornly tried to fight them in my human strength? Forgive me for fighting the battles I should have immediately turned over to you. And please, Lord, develop patience in me.

Repairing Our Boundaries

Hezekiah worked hard at repairing all the broken sections of the wall.... Then Hezekiah encouraged [the people] by saying: "Be strong and courageous! Don't be afraid or discouraged because of the king of Assyria or his mighty army."

2 CHRONICLES 32:5-7

The kingdom of Judah was under attack by the king of Assyria. The Assyrians had not made it to Jerusalem yet, but they were on their way. So King Hezekiah set out to shore up the city's neglected boundaries. He repaired the shattered city walls and then built another wall to create a double barrier. But he was well aware that the new boundaries were not enough in themselves. As he told his people, "There is a power far greater on our side! [The Assyrian king] may have a great army, but they are merely men. We have the LORD our God to help us and to fight our battles for us!" (2 Chronicles 32:7-8).

We have the same assurance as we seek to rebuild and repair the personal boundaries that our reactive living has destroyed. All we need is a willingness to allow God to help us and fight our battles for us.

There will always be people to whom we can't say no and situations in which we feel pressured to give in to another's desires. Boundaries are rebuilt as we learn to say no and still stay connected to the other person.

ASK YOURSELF

» What makes saying no difficult for you? What are you afraid of?

» Who are the people to whom you have trouble saying an appropriate no? How can God help you develop the ability to do this in a kind way?

ASK GOD

Dear God, help me to remember that you are more powerful than anyone I fear, and that you will give me strength and courage. I need both now, and I want to act in a way that brings honor to you. Restore my broken boundaries, I pray.

The Freedom of Contentment

Be satisfied with what you have. For God has said, "I will
never fail you. I will never abandon you."

HEBREWS 13:5

Do you ever feel dissatisfied with your position in life? Does it seem that the "treadmill of achievements" is going faster each day?

It's easy to stay busy looking for material security and seeking after "things"—things that will make us happy, things that will make us feel complete, things that will show others we have arrived. And it's *very* easy (in this world) to get caught up in a state of discontent.

God knows how much precious time can be lost seeking after things. He also knows how much peace and pleasure can be found in a state of contentment. That's why he encourages us to be satisfied with what we have. Contentment is a skill to be perfected.

Did you know that God has promised to supply all of your needs? Not just some, but all. He wants you to experience the freedom of being happy with where you are and what you have. This doesn't mean you shouldn't have goals or desires. It simply means you should not let them dictate your happiness or control how you spend your time.

ASK YOURSELF

» What in your life right now (if anything) tempts you to be discontented or dissatisfied?

» What are some ways you can "perfect" the skill of contentment in your life?

ASK GOD

Dear Lord, please help me learn to be content with what I have. Make me aware of your provision and thankful for everything you have given me.

God Never Fails

Do not be afraid or discouraged, for the LORD will personally go ahead of you. He will be with you; he will neither fail you nor abandon you.

DEUTERONOMY 31:8

Moses spoke these words to Joshua as Joshua was about to lead the Israelites into the land that God had promised them. And Joshua needed the encouragement because he and his people would face all kinds of setbacks. Battles would be lost. Petty rivalries would break out among the tribes. Again and again, the people would fail to be obedient. But through it all, God would remain the same, just as he does today.

We all have times when we are tempted to give up on God. Things aren't going the way we think they should, so we assume he doesn't care. But that's us trying to play God, telling the Lord what to do and then getting upset when he doesn't follow our orders.

We, like Joshua, have to learn that regardless of the circumstances, God is with us in the process. He will never fail nor abandon us, and the way things look at any given moment doesn't change that reality. That's an important lesson for us as we seek to take our lives back.

ASK YOURSELF

> » How much of your ability to trust God is dependent on his doing what you ask him to do—in just the way you expect him to?

> » How do you hold on to the promises that God will be with you when circumstances say otherwise?

ASK GOD

Father in heaven, forgive me for sometimes doubting that you care about me. I know you do. Help me to hold on to that promise when I'm faced with difficult situations. Please make yourself more real to me at those times.

You've Got What It Takes

May you experience the love of Christ, though it is too great to understand fully. Then
you will be made complete with all the fullness of life and power that comes from God.

EPHESIANS 3:19

Do you ever feel like you just aren't good enough? Like you're never going to have what it takes to navigate this life? When you find yourself feeling that way, chances are you're looking at yourself apart from God.

When you accepted Christ as your Savior, you became a child of the King. So isn't it silly for you to keep trying to prove yourself? What prince or princess would ever do such a thing?

When you are loved by the living God, he gives you everything that you need to take your life back and live as a strong, loving, productive human being. Don't be deceived into thinking otherwise. Instead, trust in his love and do whatever you need to do to live into your inheritance.

ASK YOURSELF

» Are you living with the confidence that a child of the King should have? If not, what do you think gets in your way?

» When you feel insecure, how can you remind yourself that because of what Christ has done for you, you are already complete and worthy?

ASK GOD

Dear Lord, I sometimes feel empty and insecure. I know that this is not the way you want me to feel. Help me to call upon you when I feel like this, to draw upon your love and the fullness of life that you have already set apart for me as your child. I know that in you I am complete already. Please make that real to me every day.

The Light of God's Truth Dispels Shame

I prayed to the LORD, and he answered me. He freed me from
all my fears. Those who look to him for help will be radiant
with joy; no shadow of shame will darken their faces.

PSALM 34:4-5

Shame tells lies about who we are. It whispers that we don't measure up to others, so we try to hide what's lacking or different. Then we isolate ourselves to preserve our secret. Until we deal with it, shame drains us of life and joy. But God's truth is the antidote for shame. It declares the reality about who we are as people God loves. It reminds us that because we've already been accepted by God, through Jesus, we can accept ourselves. God's truth sets us free from our prisons of shame and fear and puts us back into right relationship with God and with others. As we tip our faces toward God, the psalmist says we will be "radiant with joy." So when others see us and interact with us, they'll no longer see the shadow of shame.

ASK YOURSELF

> » List one or more lies you've believed about who you are. How has that lie (or lies) affected the way you live?

> » What does the truth of God's Word tell you about the area of your life in which you feel shame?

ASK GOD

God of glory, the truth of your Word shines in the darkness and dissolves the shadow of shame. Let my face reflect your radiance as you set me free from darkness. Today I choose to believe your truth and live in your light.

It's Okay Not to Fit In

The world would love you as one of its own if you belonged to it, but you are no longer part of the world. I chose you to come out of the world, so it hates you.

JOHN 15:19

Like-minded people tend to congregate together, often to the exclusion of those they deem unworthy. This can be exhilarating if you are one of the chosen but painful if you're among the excluded.

If you're a new Christian, you might notice you don't fit in with your friends the way you used to. In accepting Christ, you have "come out of the world." You are different now, and the unbelieving will sense that and relate to you in a new way. You should still reach out to everyone as God directs you, but it is important to understand that it is okay not to fit in.

Taking your life back can also give you that sense that you don't fit. You relate to other people differently than you did, and that can make all of you uncomfortable. That's okay too! In the long run, you'll find that all your relationships—including your relationship with God—are healthier and more positive.

ASK YOURSELF

> » Have you changed recently in ways that make you feel like an outsider? How can you handle the discomfort positively?

> » How can you reach out to the world without being a part of it?

ASK GOD

Dear Lord, I know that I am a new creature in you and that you are still in the process of changing me for the better. Keep me from gauging my worthiness by what others think. Show me who I am in you, Lord, and cause me to shine so that the world sees you.

Confession Is Healing

Confess your sins to each other and pray for each other so that you may be healed.

JAMES 5:16

In recovery we are asked to confess our failings—our sins. Why is this so important? Because we can't begin to heal until we get honest about what is making us sick—the guilt and shame that cut us off from God, from others, and even from ourselves. So in order to take our lives back, we must admit our sins to ourselves, to God, and to another person. But confession isn't easy, especially when we're stuck in reactive behavior patterns.

Confessing to ourselves can be tricky because most of us hate to admit our failures. Confessing to God is a little easier, since he already knows about our sin. But confessing to another person can be downright terrifying. What if that person rejects us or—worse—tells someone else?

According to James, however, that's when the healing occurs. That act of admitting our failures to another human brings our reality out into the open so that it can be changed.

ASK YOURSELF

> » What in your life would you find most difficult to confess to another person? That's probably what is blocking your efforts to take your life back.

> » Who is a safe person in your life to whom you could confess? If you don't have one, who could become such a safe person for you?

ASK GOD

Loving Father, the thought of confessing my sins to another person scares me to death. It's hard enough to confess to you. Give me the courage I need to find healing through confession.

Your Image Is Not Your Worth

You rescue the humble, but your eyes watch the proud and humiliate them.

2 SAMUEL 22:28

Have you ever noticed how awkward it is when people try to elevate themselves, to hold up their accomplishments for all to see? No one is comfortable in a situation like this. These people have confused their worth with their image.

Being humble doesn't mean that we are empty or have nothing to offer. In fact, those who are humble often have more to offer the world than those who flaunt their achievements.

Self-promotion will not give you the feeling of accomplishment you are hoping for. Do things that are praiseworthy without seeking recognition, and let the Lord lift you up. He values you for who you really are, not for your inflated self-image.

When you become comfortable with who you are in Christ, others' opinions of you will lose their importance, and your need to be recognized by them will disappear. Knowing that true fulfillment comes from God's recognition and not from that of other people will keep you from developing a prideful nature.

ASK YOURSELF

» Do you have a tendency to promote yourself and advertise your accomplishments? Why do you think you feel the need to do this?

» Can pride take forms other than obvious self-promotion? What else can it look like?

ASK GOD

Dear God, sometimes I find myself seeking admiration and acceptance from others more than from you. Help me to keep my priorities straight, to be humble, and to grow into the person you desire for me to be.

What Fear?

How joyful are those who fear the LORD and delight in obeying his commands.
. . . They are confident and fearless and can face their foes triumphantly.

PSALM 112:1, 8

We've all seen movies or TV shows where a mobster puts out a "hit" on some-one he wishes to harm. But have you ever seen one where the mobster puts out the hit on himself? Of course not. And yet many of us do something similar every day when we give in to fear. Fear's only power exists in the mind. So entertaining fear is basically like hiring your own attacker.

Entertaining fear is not the same as being scared in the face of danger. That's an involuntary response, and there's nothing wrong with it. In fact, it can save your life. The problem comes when you hold on to the fear and let it become part of your thinking.

If you have been attacking yourself by holding on to fear—giving the ugly monster its teeth by empowering it with your thoughts—you can reduce its in-fluence. When you choose to trust that God has your back, fear loses its power. So place yourself firmly in God's hands and watch as your confidence grows.

ASK YOURSELF

» What kinds of thoughts and assumptions tend to empower fear in your mind?

» What are some of the ways you could reduce the power of fear in your life by changing the way you think?

ASK GOD

Dear Lord, sometimes I allow myself to get caught up in the what-ifs that are generated by fearful thoughts. Help me recognize that the only power fear has is the power that I give it. Teach me to rely fully on you and to trust that you will always be there to keep me safe.

Give It Back to God

Those who love their life in this world will lose it. Those who care
nothing for their life in this world will keep it for eternity.

JOHN 12:25

Have you ever decided to give something over to God, only to take it back a short time later? You may take it back in such little bits and pieces that you don't even realize what you're doing. But before you know it, God is in the backseat and you're driving again.

Why does this happen? Perhaps you feel it is your responsibility to keep everything in your life on track. Or maybe you are overly attached to something or someone, and that clouds your vision.

It is human nature to want to be in control of our lives and to invest too much in certain people, objects, or situations. But God is ultimately in charge of everything in our lives anyway, so it makes sense to just let him "drive." Why hang on to things that take away from our peace and from our relationship with him?

ASK YOURSELF

» Are you currently holding on to something that you should be giving over to the Lord—including control of your life? What is it?

» What system could you develop to alert yourself when a relationship or attachment has taken on a life of its own?

ASK GOD

Dear Lord, teach me to discern when I have taken back control of my life or am giving too much of my time or my emotions to a situation or a person. Show me how to turn these things over to you and then trust you to see them through.

Specks and Logs

Why worry about a speck in your friend's eye when you have a log in your own? How can you think of saying to your friend, "Let me help you get rid of that speck in your eye," when you can't see past the log in your own eye?

MATTHEW 7:3-4

Have you ever noticed that brothers and sisters love to point out each other's failings? A little girl might point in disgust to her brother's dirty socks strewn about the den but not even notice her backpack left on the floor beside them. That same brother might tattle about his sister's cereal bowl on the living room table but somehow fail to notice his soccer cleats just three feet away.

Jesus knew that this is how we humans are—children and adults alike. He pointed out that we're usually quick to see the sin in someone else's life but much slower to recognize our own sin. We might even obsess about other people's minor transgressions—the "specks" in their eyes—while completely ignoring much larger sins ("logs") in our own lives.

Jesus' advice? We need to stop concerning ourselves with other people's sin. Instead, we should work to "see" and conquer our own sin and let God worry about the other people.

ASK YOURSELF

» Why do you think it's so tempting to focus on someone else's short-comings and ignore our own?

» Do you think Jesus was saying we should *never* point out another person's sin? Why or why not?

ASK GOD

Gracious God, you have forgiven all of my sins through the life, death, and resurrection of Jesus. Thank you. Father, give me eyes that are quick to recognize my own sin and slow to recognize the faults of others.

A Kind No

Let us run with endurance the race God has set before
us. We do this by keeping our eyes on Jesus.
HEBREWS 12:1-2

For those of us with reactive tendencies, running the race God has set before us may include confronting our habit of saying a reluctant or resentful yes when we really want to say no.

Imagine, for example, that someone pressures us to do something we don't have time to do. God wants us to be comfortable saying no to such unwelcome requests—if for no other reason than that our ability to say a kind no gives meaning to our willing yes. But for those of us who are dependent on pleasing others, saying no can feel almost impossible.

The writer of Hebrews gives us great insight into how we can learn to say no appropriately: "by keeping our eyes on Jesus." *No* becomes easier when we focus our minds on what—and who—matters most in our lives. The more we say yes to him as we run our race, the easier it becomes to say a kind and appropriate no.

ASK YOURSELF

» It seems God doesn't like reluctant yeses. Instead he looks for willing yeses. How would you describe the difference?

» How can you become more aware of the difference between pleasing people and pleasing God?

ASK GOD

Lord Jesus, it's so hard to break old patterns of behavior. Help me break free from reactive yeses and learn how to say a kind and appropriate no. Help me better understand why I do what I do, and deliver me from my reactive lifestyle.

Fighting against Yourself

Let the peace that comes from Christ rule in your hearts. For as members
of one body you are called to live in peace. And always be thankful.

COLOSSIANS 3:15

A host of autoimmune diseases afflict people today—lupus, multiple sclerosis, and rheumatoid arthritis are just a few. These diseases occur when the immune system sees another part of the body as an invader and begins to attack it. The results can be devastating.

The body of Christ often experiences an autoimmune disease of sorts. Christians attack one another, tear each other down, and even destroy each other. These attacks within the church body, often carried out by people who are living reactively, can be devastating to local congregations and destructive to the church as a whole.

To cure this "autoimmune disease," it is imperative that Christians recognize that we are all part of the same body. When we attack one another, we are attacking ourselves.

You would not wish an autoimmune disease on your physical body, and it is crucial that you do not become involved in inflicting it upon the body of Christ either.

ASK YOURSELF

» Think about your interactions with other believers over the past weeks. When have you criticized or quarreled with other Christians, and when have you built them up?

» What can you do to remind yourself that all Christ followers are a part of the same body?

ASK GOD

Dear Lord, I want to be someone who seeks to lift up others, but I don't always succeed at doing that. Please teach me to see you when I look at other believers, to see the body as a whole and to realize that I am just a small part of something much bigger than myself.

Don't Forget to Sign In

The LORD must wait for you to come to him so he can show you his love and compassion. For the LORD is a faithful God. Blessed are those who wait for his help.

ISAIAH 30:18

Imagine you've walked into a crowded restaurant, given your name to the hostess, and waited for a table. You might have to wait a bit, but eventually your turn comes and someone seats you.

Now imagine you walk into the same restaurant but don't bother to check in. You can wait and wait, but your number will never be called.

Why? Because you neglected to make that first connection.

This is a great picture of the relationship some people have with God. It's not that we have to wait our turn to be with him. But we do need to reach out to him. Our God is a respectful God, and he does not force himself upon us. Instead, he waits patiently for us to bring him our needs and our concerns so that he can help us. So if you are feeling neglected, alone, or unloved, consider: Have you forgotten to "check in"?

ASK YOURSELF

» Do you sometimes expect God to just take care of your needs without your reaching out to him? Do you think he ever does this?

» What can you do to get into the habit of asking God for his presence and his help in your life, moment by moment?

ASK GOD

Dear Lord, help me remember to seek you each minute of my day. Keep me aware of the times when I shut you out or simply forget to ask for your help.

Know Who You're Talking To

Don't bother correcting mockers; they will only hate you.
But correct the wise, and they will love you.

PROVERBS 9:8

Have you ever found yourself deep in a passionate discussion with someone, only to realize the other person is not listening to a word you say? The more you talk, in fact, the more stubborn and resistant the other person becomes. This is the time to remove yourself from the conversation.

This dynamic intensifies if you need to correct or admonish someone. If the correction is appropriate and you share it in love, a wise person will receive it in the spirit you intend. If what you are sharing is *not* well received, you must look first at yourself. Is it your place to correct the other person? Do you have his or her best interests at heart? Is the correction really necessary?

If your answer to any of these questions is yes, then you should also consider who you're talking to. If the other person is arrogant or argumentative, you could talk until Jesus returns and he or she would still turn a deaf ear to your message.

When you encounter angry "mockers," turn them over to the Lord. Pray for them, but don't be drawn into their negative world.

ASK YOURSELF

» Under what circumstances would it be appropriate for you to correct or admonish someone else? How could you make sure your corrections are done in a spirit of love?

» Are there people in your life you should be praying for instead of debating with?

ASK GOD

Dear Lord, please give me the wisdom to know when it is not my place to correct, and help me to show compassion and love when it is.

Manage Your Emotions

Don't turn your back on wisdom, for she will protect
you. Love her, and she will guard you.

PROVERBS 4:6

One of the things wisdom teaches us is to manage our emotions. Too often it's the other way around—our emotions manage us. Many times we just react blindly to what we feel and then regret our reaction later.

Managing our emotions begins with the ability to name what we are experiencing. There are four basic emotions that give us trouble: fear, anger, sadness, and disgust or shame. There are also two positive emotions: joy and surprise.

Once we can put a name to our emotions, we can begin to manage them. It's important to understand what we feel, but we must also recognize that feelings are not always reliable. They shouldn't be denied or repressed, but they do need to be tested for accuracy. Most important, we must bring them to God. That's wisdom's way of protecting us.

ASK YOURSELF

» Which of the four difficult emotions tends to give you the most trouble? Why do you think that is?

» What is the difference between reacting blindly to emotion and denying or repressing it? What problems can each reaction raise? How can you learn, with God's help, to manage your emotions instead of reacting to them or denying them?

ASK GOD

Lord, you know how I struggle to handle my difficult emotions and the toll they sometimes take on me. Help me to slow down so I can test what I am feeling and bring it to you before I react unwisely. Thank you, God.

All the Wrong Places

Seek the Kingdom of God above all else, and live righteously,
and he will give you everything you need.

MATTHEW 6:33

Have you heard the old joke about the guy who is looking for his car keys in the refrigerator?

"Why do you think they would be in there?" his wife asks.

"I don't," he replies. "I dropped them outside. But the light is better in here."

Corny, yes, but it does illustrate a point. Don't fool yourself into looking for meaning and purpose in places where it can never be found.

It's easy to keep yourself busy seeking gratification in places that appear to provide fun or freedom or satisfaction—or, as in the joke, where there is better lighting. But even if you look and look, you won't find what you're seeking there.

Jesus himself said, "Seek the Kingdom of God above all else . . . and he will give you everything you need." Why keep looking for what you need in places where it cannot be found? Walk with God, seek him first, and the light will move with you.

ASK YOURSELF

» What are some of the disappointing places you've looked for purpose or meaning or tried to get your needs met?

» How does seeking God's Kingdom first shine light on all the other areas of your life?

ASK GOD

Dear Jesus, I tend to make my life so much more complicated than it needs to be. Teach me to look to you first and then trust you to give me everything I need. Show me the peace that comes from living a life where you are number one.

No Reason to Fear

The LORD is my light and my salvation—so why should I be afraid? The LORD is my fortress, protecting me from danger, so why should I tremble?

PSALM 27:1

Have you ever allowed yourself to be overcome with fear? The more attention you give it, the more it grows. As your body reacts to the fearful feelings, you experience another level of anxiety, even panic. Fear can consume you if you allow it to. But you don't have to allow it.

When you accepted Jesus as your Savior, God's Holy Spirit came to live inside of you. God is your security. He is your light in the darkness, your eternal salvation. God's protection surrounds you, and because he knows all, he handles many threats before you are even aware of them. By the time you start to worry or to feel fear, the Lord already has a plan for your ultimate safety. If you will remember this at the first sign of fear, you will save yourself a great deal of discomfort, stress, and worry.

ASK YOURSELF

» Under what circumstances are you likely to let fear grow in your life instead of claiming God's protection?

» Does God's protection and presence mean you will never be physically hurt? If not, what do you think it means?

ASK GOD

Dear Jesus, I know you are always with me. I know you will protect me from harm. And yet I still allow fear to creep into my life. Teach me that I have nothing to fear and help me to trust in you always.

What's Your Motivation?

Give me an eagerness for your laws rather than a love for money!
PSALM 119:36

What gets you out of bed every morning? Is it your work? Your family? A desire to prove yourself by making money or earning praise? A thirst for adventure? Whatever that motivation is, examine it closely because it will tell you a great deal about the condition of your soul.

The things that motivate us, the things we give our energy to, are the things that will shape us. So we must be careful what we allow to become our motivation, because the things of this world cannot shape us for eternity.

While we are on this earth, we will have responsibilities, attachments, and goals, and that is healthy. The key to living in the fullness to which we were called is not allowing these temporal goals to take on greater importance than they deserve.

Keep your eyes on the real prize: the Kingdom of God. If you ask the Lord to bring your daily motivations in line with his eternal plan for your life, he will.

ASK YOURSELF

» What *is* your motivation for getting out of bed? This isn't as simple as it sounds. You may need to peel away several layers before you find your true motivator.

» How can you keep a healthy balance between your spiritual goals and your earthly responsibilities?

ASK GOD

Dear Jesus, I know that as long as I live on this earth, I will be driven by necessary responsibilities, goals, and requirements for my survival. Help me to keep these earthly demands in the proper perspective. Keep me always focused on my eternal destiny.

Shameless

I can never escape from your Spirit! I can never get away from your presence!
If I go up to heaven, you are there; if I go down to the grave, you are there.

PSALM 139:7-8

Have you ever seen a toddler run naked through the house before bath time? The little streaker is *shameless in the very best sense of the word.* But a decade later, that same child is probably much more modest. Being naked now makes him or her feel embarrassed and vulnerable.

When Adam and Eve realized their nakedness, their impulse was to *hide from God.* And that's our impulse as well—not just when we're physically naked, but when we feel vulnerable or exposed. We cover up. We hide.

The psalmist announces the truth that despite our best efforts to flee—to the east or to the west, to the heavens or toward the grave—we can never escape God's loving presence. In fact, God wants to receive all of who we are. In the process of healing our shame, as we embrace godly sorrow, God gently woos us out of hiding and toward himself.

ASK YOURSELF

» What are some of the ways you try to hide from God?

» What would it take for you to trust God with all that you've done and all that you are? What is holding you back?

ASK GOD

Lord, forgive me for trying to hide from you. I believe you are inviting me out of hiding to be fully seen and known by you. Grant me the courage to stop covering up and trust you to be my Healer.

Pray for the Troublemakers

I love them, but they try to destroy me with accusations even as I am praying for them!

PSALM 109:4

Are there people in your life who are not happy unless they are causing trouble or making someone else miserable—including you? If you encounter people like that, don't try to hurt them back. That will just escalate the situation. Don't try to win them over or appease them. That's sure to undermine your recovery. And don't attempt to change them. That's God's job, not yours.

So what can you do instead?

First, love them. Love them with no expectation that they will become nicer. Love them regardless of whether or not they appear to change. Love them from a distance if you can, but love them nonetheless.

Second, pray for them. Set aside a time each day to bring them before God, asking that he will reveal himself to them and change their hearts. You might be surprised what happens when you do that. Prayer is powerful, and God does some of his finest work in our times of deepest discomfort.

ASK YOURSELF

» What are some ways you can respond in love to those who seem to be against you—without compromising your recovery?

» Who are the people in your life that you should be showering with prayer?

ASK GOD

Dear Lord, right now I'm handing the haters in my life over to you. Let your love shine through me to them, and let me be a beacon to all those who are filled with hate.

When It's Good to Be *Slow*

*The LORD is compassionate and merciful, slow to get
angry and filled with unfailing love.*

PSALM 103:8

What attributes do you look for in a friend or companion? If you could order the perfect person, what character traits would he or she have? What about compassion, mercy, and unfailing love? If any of us could have just one of those attributes, the world would be a better place. But God, our perfect role model, embodies all three—plus another very important one. He's "slow to get angry."

In this fast-paced world, we tend to think of *slow* as a bad thing. We gobble down fast food or nuke our meals in a minute, snap up products that offer quick weight loss, and search for medical clinics that offer quick care. But when it comes to God's anger, slow is definitely good! If he had a quick temper, most of us would be in *big* trouble.

So the next time you find yourself frustrated because something is taking too long, turn that thought into an opportunity to thank God that he is slow with his anger and to ask for more patience.

ASK YOURSELF

> » Under what circumstances are you slow to anger? When are you quick to anger?

> » How can you slow your angry reactions toward others?

ASK GOD

Dear Lord Jesus, I appreciate the fact that you do not lash out in anger when I displease you. You are so patient and gentle in your correction, and I want to have more of those character traits in my life. Make me conscious of the times when I am short-tempered with others, and teach me to be more patient on a daily basis.

Forgiving Others

Forgive us our sins, as we have forgiven those who sin against us.

MATTHEW 6:12

You've heard it a million times: "Forgive and forget." If you find that aphorism a little annoying, don't worry. It *is* annoying, even when offered with the best of intentions. More important, it's bad advice. It implies we can jump straight from injury to healing. But trying to do that just short-circuits the healing process.

Before we can forgive the wrongs that have been inflicted on us, we must *notice and acknowledge* them. If we don't own our pain, our forgiveness will have little meaning. God's Spirit opens our eyes and guards our hearts as we do this necessary prep work for forgiveness. Only then can we move forward and truly forgive.

Even then, it's not realistic to think we'll forget a deep hurt quickly—if ever. We may need to hand the matter over to God many times before it loosens its grip on us. But healing will happen if we keep on doing the work of facing the truth and giving it to the Lord. Forgiveness is just one of the many gifts that enable us to take our lives back.

ASK YOURSELF

» Why is it so tempting to jump straight to "forgive and forget" when someone has wronged us? Why do you think people give that advice?

» Who makes your "top five" list of those you need to forgive? Where are you now in the process of forgiving and releasing them?

ASK GOD

God, you have graciously forgiven all of my sins, and you invite me to forgive the sins of others. Give me courage this day to face the wrongs done to me and then to forgive those who wronged me.

He Will Never Let You Fall

I cried out, "I am slipping!" but your unfailing love, O LORD, supported me.

PSALM 94:18

Have you ever had one of those half-awake dreams where you find yourself free-falling? You hurtle toward the ground, arms and legs flailing, and have absolutely no control over what is happening to you. What an utterly helpless feeling!

Life approached in our own strength can be much like this. We're moving along, confident and carefree, and we think we've got everything under control. Then something unforeseen happens, and suddenly we're slipping—free-falling, with no way of saving ourselves.

As Christians, we never have to worry about that free fall. God is always there to catch us when we cry out to him. This doesn't mean we will never have that momentary panic when we feel ourselves start to slip. But we can be certain that his loving arms will quickly envelop us and place us safely on solid ground.

ASK YOURSELF

» If you can, describe a time when you felt your life slipping out of control. What did it feel like? What was the outcome?

» What are some of the ways you have tried to save yourself before calling out to the Lord for help?

ASK GOD

Dear heavenly Father, I always want to have a confident attitude, an assurance that everything will be okay in my life, but I want to base it on you. Keep me mindful that it is only because of your presence in my life that I can have any confidence at all. Keep me from being full of myself, and teach me to call out to you instantly when I feel myself starting to slip.

No Bragging Rights

*Salvation is not a reward for the good things we have
done, so none of us can boast about it.*

EPHESIANS 2:9

Does the fact of having received salvation make any of us better than anyone else? Of course not. God gives salvation as a free gift, and the fact that we have received his gift does not give us reason to gloat. We have done nothing to earn it.

It is important to keep our focus on God at all times. Everything in our lives comes from him, and he is the only one with "bragging rights."

We have received a gift that we did not deserve from a God who loves us.

Does that make us fortunate? Yes.

Does it make us special? No.

When we consider what God has done for us, the only sensible response is gratitude. We should thank God every day for his amazing love and grace. And we should let everyone else know how much we appreciate the fact that while we were still sinners, Christ died for us (see Romans 5:8). He did all of the work, and he should get all of the glory!

ASK YOURSELF

» Have you ever been guilty of taking your salvation for granted? Why do you think this happened?

» How could you express your gratitude to God for the gift of your salvation? Why not thank him now?

ASK GOD

Dear Jesus, I am sure I do not say thank you often enough. My salvation is something I do not deserve and I could never earn on my own. Help me to share this gift with others, and don't ever allow me to become boastful or proud.

Déjà Vu

The faithful love of the LORD never ends! His mercies never cease.
Great is his faithfulness; his mercies begin afresh each morning.

LAMENTATIONS 3:22-23

Wouldn't it be amazing if your bank account renewed itself every day? If no matter how much you had spent the day before, you always woke up to a full account the next morning? What would it feel like if you could not spend or give away enough of your resources to make a dent? Imagine what you could accomplish. Imagine how the stress in your life would be reduced.

This is exactly what God's love is like. It is limitless and never-ending. The Lord can give and give and give some more, but he will never run out of love and mercy.

How many times have you wondered if God has had enough of you and your troubles? Perhaps you are trying to comprehend how he could bear to watch you fail time and again without giving up on you. It's because of his limitless "love account" that refills itself daily. Whenever you find yourself thinking you have pushed God to the limit, just remember that is impossible. Every morning, his love and patience for you is set back to full.

ASK YOURSELF

» Describe a time when you wondered if you had pushed God too far or exhausted his "love account." How did it happen—and what happened next?

» Do you have trouble believing that God's love and mercy are truly limitless? Why do you think this is hard for you to accept?

ASK GOD

Dear Lord, I long to understand the nature of your love better. Help me to trust in your never-ending mercy. Forgive me when I stumble time and again, and thank you for always being there for me.

The Only Opinion That Counts

Do not remember the rebellious sins of my youth. Remember me in
the light of your unfailing love, for you are merciful, O LORD.

PSALM 25:7

Isn't it amazing how some parents tend to see their children through rose-colored glasses? They always seem to focus on the good and overlook the bad. To many mothers and fathers, there is no one more perfect than their child, and no amount of persuasion will alter their opinion.

This is exactly how God looks at us because of what Jesus did on the cross. Our heavenly Father does not remember our past sin, and he does not focus on our faults and failures. Although he knows our weaknesses, they never define us in his eyes. Instead he looks at us and sees his beloved children, made perfect by the sacrifice of our Savior. He also sees our future success and our final destination.

God looks at us always through "eternal glasses"—and with the eyes of love.

Can you learn to look at yourself (and others) the way God does and to accept his opinion as the ultimate authority? It is his opinion, after all, that really matters.

ASK YOURSELF

» What would it take for you to see the same value in yourself that God sees in you?

» How can you learn to look at the bigger picture when you are evaluating your progress in life?

ASK GOD

Dear Lord, I know that I am far from perfect, but I thank you that you see the good in me. Help me to be diligent in my pursuit of you and to respect the eternal opinion you have of me. Cause me to draw nearer to you each day so that I may be used by you.

Think *Before* You Speak

The tongue can bring death or life; those who love to talk will reap the consequences.

PROVERBS 18:21

Have you ever blurted out something that you didn't even mean—and hurt someone deeply? Have you ever been the victim of careless gossip or malicious lies? If you have, you know the damage words can do. And once they have been unleashed, they cannot be retracted.

But words can also express love and create beauty. They can speak forgiveness and instill wisdom. They can be tools of encouragement and agents of salvation.

Never underestimate the power of words. And never forget that you are accountable for the way you choose to use your words—which is why controlling your tongue should be a priority.

It helps to make a habit of pausing before you speak, just enough to think about what you want to say. As you practice responding intentionally instead of just reacting with your words, you'll gain better control over one of the smallest yet most troublesome parts of your body.

ASK YOURSELF

» Do you tend to think before you speak? How has this reactive habit affected your relationships?

» How can you use your words to be a blessing to those who hear them?

ASK GOD

Lord, help me to always be aware of the content of my words before I let them out of my mouth. Keep me conscious of the effect my words have upon those who hear them.

A Stable Foundation

Let your lives be built on him. Then your faith will grow strong in the truth you were taught, and you will overflow with thankfulness.

COLOSSIANS 2:7

Have you ever watched as a building was being constructed? There are many phases to the process, but all of them are dependent upon a stable foundation. Imagine looking at a fabulous home, decorated impeccably, with every upgrade and option that one could desire. Now imagine that this beautiful home was built for display only and had no real foundation beneath it. As good as it looks, it is not going to support real life—and it is not going to be around for the long haul. Something can look good from the outside but not withstand the test of time.

It is important that your life is built on a foundation that will support you for eternity. Don't worry about what your life looks like on the outside—looks can be deceiving. If you build a strong foundation for your life based upon godly principles, everything else will fall into place.

ASK YOURSELF

> » Do you tend to make life choices based on what looks good or what others will think? Why do you think you have that tendency?

> » What can you do if you realize your foundation is shaky? What are some ways to shore it up?

ASK GOD

Dear God, I want to be a strong, stable Christian. Teach me how to build my life with you as the foundation of everything I do.

Choose Wisely

A bowl of vegetables with someone you love is better than steak with someone you hate.

PROVERBS 15:17

Necessity often draws people together, especially in the workplace. But most of the time we still have a choice about our close associates. Are you choosing wisely? Are the people in your life there for the right reasons?

The most fulfilling relationships you will have in life are those that involve mutual respect. They are built upon what each person has to offer the other, not what one can gain from the other. Both parties give of themselves and both receive. Do your best to avoid relationships where this is not the case.

But what if you don't have a choice? For professional, family, or other reasons, some people are difficult to avoid. If that is true, your best strategy is, first, to give the situation to the Lord and, second, to do your best to behave honorably and peacefully. Limit your interactions with difficult people if you can, try to learn from the situation, and trust God to either remove you from the relationship in his time or to show you how to thrive within it.

ASK YOURSELF

» What (if any) relationships in your life would you consider problematic or unhealthy? What makes these relationships difficult? Do you have a choice about whether to spend time with these people?

» What is one thing you could do this week to build healthier relationships with the people in your life?

ASK GOD

Dear Lord, please draw the right people into my life—those who help me grow closer to you. Shine your light upon my unhealthy relationships and make clear what I should do about them. And remind me always that even the people I don't get along with are still people you love.

Staying on the Right Path

The king trusts in the LORD. The unfailing love of the
Most High will keep him from stumbling.

PSALM 21:7

When we're hiking on a marked trail, why do we follow the posted signs? Usually it is because we assume that whoever posted them did so for our benefit—to keep us safe, to direct us to special areas of interest or beauty, and to help us get where we want to go.

God's Word states that he will keep us from stumbling and keep us on the right path. And yet how often do we ignore his loving direction and his prodding? What will it take for us to fully trust in the Lord? Perhaps we simply need to step out in faith and do what we think he is asking us to do. Even if we make a mistake, we can trust him to get us back on track.

Our job, always, is to trust him. If we do, he will be faithful to keep us from stumbling and make sure we arrive safely.

ASK YOURSELF

> » What are some of the "trail markers" God has laid out for you in the past? How did God communicate this direction to you?

> » Is there a step you feel God wants you to take right now? What holds you back from taking it?

ASK GOD

Dear Jesus, deep in my heart I know that you always have my best interests in mind as you direct me along life's path. Keep me constantly aware of your presence, and help me not to doubt the instruction that you give me.

Great Misery

The lush produce of this land piles up in the hands of the kings whom you have set over us because of our sins. . . . We serve them at their pleasure, and we are in great misery.

NEHEMIAH 9:37

When the Persian Empire conquered Babylon, the Jewish people who had been living as exiles there were allowed to return home. But many years later, the city of Jerusalem was in a mess. The city walls—rebuilt by Hezekiah centuries before—were once again in rubble. The Law of Moses was practically forgotten. And the people were at the mercy of incompetent or oppressive overseers. No wonder they were "in great misery."

Word of this situation got back to Nehemiah, a Jew who served the Persian king Artaxerxes. Concerned for his people, Nehemiah turned first to God in prayer and fasting. Then he convinced the king to send him to Jerusalem as governor. He repaired the walls, called the people to repentance, and made great strides in delivering them from their misery.

Often we are in the same miserable position as those people in Jerusalem. Our lives are chaotic and controlled by others. That's when we need to turn to the only one who can put things right—Jesus Christ, our higher power.

ASK YOURSELF

» What specific "misery" tends to spoil your life? How can you best find help for it?

» Nehemiah depended on God, his higher power, but he also needed human help. Name at least one human person you can count on for help.

ASK GOD

Lord Jesus, I want you to be the higher power in my life. I want to focus on you, lean on you, trust you, obey you, and love you. Help me to act in your power and authority as I also learn to lean appropriately on other people.

A Structured Peace

On the first day of each week, you should each put aside a portion of the money
you have earned. Don't wait until I get there and then try to collect it all at once.
1 CORINTHIANS 16:2

Structure and planning are essential to living a successful life. Whether you are looking at finances, daily actions, or long-term goals, you need to have a map and follow it, or you will find yourself scrambling to catch up when you should be at the finish line.

This is especially true when it comes to money. Those who are self-employed know the challenge of coming up with the income tax they owe if they haven't budgeted for it throughout the year. But even those whose taxes are taken care of through withholding at work can get in financial trouble without proper planning and structure. It is very easy to misspend and end up in a panic that takes your focus off everything else.

Life is simply more peaceful and productive if you have a plan and follow it. When you don't, you'll most likely find yourself being controlled by the things that you should be in control of.

ASK YOURSELF

> » Do you have enough structure in your life—financial or otherwise? If not, why do you think structure is a challenge for you? What are some concrete steps you could take to provide more?

> » Some people actually overdo planning and structure. Do you think this is an issue for you? Where is the line between helpful structure and rigid overcontrol?

ASK GOD

Dear Jesus, I want to have ultimate peace in my life. And in order to do that, I know I must have structure. Help me to be responsible and to plan ahead, especially when it comes to my finances. Show me how to take control of the things that would like to control me, and free up my mind to focus on you.

Breaking Generational Patterns

Those of Israelite descent . . . confessed their own sins and the sins of their ancestors.

NEHEMIAH 9:2

As Nehemiah prepared his people to dedicate the rebuilt walls of Jerusalem, he invited them to confess the sins of their ancestors. But why? Surely they weren't responsible for bad things other people had done in the past.

Nehemiah understood—as we must understand—that if the past hasn't been resolved, it is still active in our present. It can even become a "generational pattern," in which we consciously or unconsciously act out the negative attitudes and behaviors of those who came before us. So before we can leave the past behind and take our lives back, we need to be intentional about facing past sins and giving them to God.

This could mean sins we ourselves have committed, sins done against us (perhaps by a parent), or even destructive patterns from past generations (addiction, racism, dishonesty) that haunt our present. One key to taking our lives back is to acknowledge the damage that has been done in the past and ask specifically for the Lord's restoration.

ASK YOURSELF

» Make a list of negative generational patterns that might be affecting your life today. How do you think these generational sins hold you back?

» Share the patterns you've listed with someone you trust. The purpose here is not to blame. It's to name and forgive. How can such confession help you move forward?

ASK GOD

Father, as you have forgiven me for my sins, give me the ability and the willingness to forgive those whose past sins affect me today. Help me draw strength from your love to resolve past issues and move forward in confident faith.

Your Most Dependable Helper

Don't put your confidence in powerful people.... When they breathe
their last, they return to the earth, and all their plans die with them.
But joyful are those who have the God of Israel as their helper.

PSALM 146:3-5

When we feel our weakest, it is human nature to look to other people to help us or to keep us safe. But this is *not* the first place God wants us to look. He puts other people in our lives as a support, but he wants to be our first source of help. After all, those other people are human too, which means they are fallible and limited.

When you are feeling vulnerable or overwhelmed, you will want to reach out to those positive people in your life—and you should, but *only after* you've had a chat with the Lord. Talk to him just as you would talk to anyone else. He's listening. He wants to be involved in your everyday life. And he's the most dependable Helper you could ever find.

ASK YOURSELF

» Is God the first person you seek out in times of trouble, the one in whom you confide most readily?

» Do you have fellow humans you can confide in as well? How can you balance trusting them with knowing they are fallible and limited?

ASK GOD

Dear Lord, my Helper, thank you for the gift of human companions and advisors, but please teach me to reach out to you first. Help me to place my strongest confidence in you.

What If?

Rejoice in our confident hope. Be patient in trouble, and keep on praying.

ROMANS 12:12

Do you ever find yourself getting caught up in what-ifs? *What if I can't pay my rent? What if I don't pass that test? What if my vehicle falls apart?* What if . . . what if . . what if. Life can be full of them if you allow it, but why would you?

What-ifs are worry in disguise, and worry will rob you of valuable time. It will steal your joy, and the stress that worry creates will take its toll on your physical body.

Here's an idea. Each time your mind entertains a what-if, stop and pray about that situation. Consciously turn it over to God. Do this over and over as the worries return. This practice will help you turn your worry into hope. The hope will then give you the patience to either work out the problem or to wait it out. And this in turn will give you confidence that God is going to take care of everything.

I promise you, this is a treadmill you want to run on, a cycle that will add much joy to your life. "What if" you gave it a try?

ASK YOURSELF

» What varieties of what-if thinking tend to bother you most? What fall-out does this kind of worry have in your life?

» Have you ever tried challenging your what-ifs with prayer? If so, what was the result?

ASK GOD

Heavenly Father, so often I allow my mind to wander and to worry, but I don't want to. Cause me to recognize the what-ifs in my life and convert them to prayer. Let me focus on the hope I have in you and the confidence it gives me. Let me be filled with the joy that comes from trusting in you.

Not Your Problem!

Why worry about your clothing? Look at the lilies of the field and how
they grow. They don't work or make their clothing, yet Solomon
in all his glory was not dressed as beautifully as they are.

MATTHEW 6:28-29

Are you a worrier? A perfectionist? Has anyone ever accused you of overcontrol or micromanaging?

There's nothing wrong with caring about details and planning ahead. But worry, overcontrol, and perfectionism are time killers. They can rob you of the peace God intends for you to have.

How many times have you come to the end of a day and wondered where all the hours went—with so much left to do? How many times have you lamented the "what-ifs" of things that never came to pass? How often do you wear yourself out trying to orchestrate the perfect outcome in a situation?

If you even suspect that this is a problem for you, ask yourself this question: *Do I really trust God?* If you genuinely believe that God is in control and has your best interests at heart, why would you ever worry about anything? And if you trust him in the big things, why not trust him for the details as well?

ASK YOURSELF

> » Why are worry and perfectionism such a waste of time?

> » What holds you back from trusting God in every aspect of your life? What do you fear will happen?

ASK GOD

Dear God, I know that you are the Creator of the universe. You make the sun rise and set. You make my heart beat. And yet I still think that I need to be in charge of every detail in my life. Teach me, Lord, to let go. Teach me to trust you in everything.

Who's the Pilot?

If you reject discipline, you only harm yourself; but if you
listen to correction, you grow in understanding.

PROVERBS 15:32

Can you imagine the disaster that would occur if an airplane rejected the correction of its autopilot or, even worse, its pilot? No one would make it from point A to point B. Why is it that machines will accept correction from the one who designed them, but humans have the hardest time with it? We insist on being in full control, all the while fighting the gentle correction of our Maker, who intends to keep us on the right path.

Do you have a hard time accepting correction? If so, you should ask yourself why. It could be ego, pride, embarrassment, power, status, or one of many other frailties we humans are subject to. But any one of these is a poor excuse for refusing admonishment or discipline that could keep us on the right path. Remember that God sees the complete picture and knows your final destination. Who could be better equipped to direct your path than your Maker, the Master of the universe?

ASK YOURSELF

> » What are some of the ways God has given you correction in the past?
> How have you typically responded?

> » Do you resist correction from other people as well? Why do you think
> this is so hard for you?

ASK GOD
Dear Lord, I know that I am often stubborn and willful. Often I ignore your direction because I want to show that I have everything under control. Help me to realize that you are the best Captain of my life, and cause me to trust that you are in the best position to lead me.

Are You Stuck in Neutral?

The Spirit of the LORD is upon me, for he has anointed me to bring
Good News to the poor. He has sent me to proclaim that captives will
be released, that the blind will see, that the oppressed will be set free.

LUKE 4:18

Imagine you've just acquired a beautiful, powerful new car, and you're ready to get on the road. You fuel it. You get into the driver's seat. You start the engine and step on the gas. The engine gives a powerful roar, but the car does not move.

What's wrong? The vehicle is stuck in neutral. That car has the potential to get you where you need to go, and yet it does nothing.

Have you ever felt that God was prodding you to do something, but you hesitated to obey? You know what God has asked you to do. You have what it takes to get it done. You are in the driver's seat. And yet you do not move. How we all must frustrate God at times!

Today it's time to shift gears. Move forward in faith and see what God can accomplish through you.

ASK YOURSELF

» Why are you sometimes hesitant to act upon the prodding of the Holy Spirit?

» What can you do to become more in tune with God's leading in your life?

ASK GOD

Dear Lord, give me the faith necessary to step forward and act upon the things that you want me to do. Help me develop a spirit that recognizes your voice, and give me a willingness to do what you ask.

Are You Full of It?

The Holy Spirit produces this kind of fruit in our lives: love, joy, peace,
patience, kindness, goodness, faithfulness, gentleness, and self-control.

GALATIANS 5:22-23

How would you react if someone told you, "You're full of it"? Would that accusation make you feel good? Probably not. The phrase doesn't have the most positive connotation in the English language. But as a child of God, you should *want* to be "full of it" in one particular sense—to be full of the Holy Spirit.

Are you experiencing everything that God has made available to you—the peace, the joy, the goodness? If not, you probably need more of the Spirit in your life.

God refers to his Spirit as "the Comforter"—your companion in this world. Galatians 5 says he's the source of a fruitful, fulfilling life. And if you are a Christian, the Holy Spirit already lives inside of you. But you decide how much influence he has.

Your life is a living testament to the one who is in charge of it. If you have given control over to the Holy Spirit, it will be obvious to you and to those around you because your life will be full to overflowing with good spiritual fruit.

ASK YOURSELF

> » What does it mean in practical terms to give the Holy Spirit control of your life?

> » What are some signs that you have taken back control of your life?

ASK GOD

Dear God, I want to be filled to the brim with the good qualities your Spirit makes available to me. Teach me how to open myself to your Spirit's control so I will always be "full of" you.

Deny Myself?

*If any of you wants to be my follower, you must give up your
own way, take up your cross daily, and follow me.*

LUKE 9:23

For many of us, this passage in Luke may have been a barrier to taking our lives
back. When we read in many English translations of the Bible that we must
"deny" ourselves, we took it to mean that we must see ourselves as nothing. But
the New Living Translation offers an important clarification: "you must give
up your own way."

Jesus doesn't want us to believe we are nothing. He wants us to let go of our
own self-centered agendas in order to follow him.

What is "our own way"? It is when we demand our rights at the expense
of others. It is when we try to fix something broken in us by "fixing" someone
else. It is when we live reactively—isolating ourselves from others or lashing out when someone triggers our insecurities—instead of choosing to live
responsively.

Giving up our own way means moving against our fears, our anger, and our
shame so we can truly follow Jesus as disciples who have experienced inner
healing.

ASK YOURSELF

> » How have you interpreted the familiar translations that claim we are to
> "deny ourselves"?

> » Make your own list of what "selfish ways" could mean. Are any of them
> really appropriate forms of self-care?

ASK GOD

Lord, I get so confused about what is really selfish and what is self-care. Please
make the distinction clear to me and help me care for myself so that I can
authentically care for those I love.

Exposing the Devil's Lies

The devil . . . has always hated the truth, because there is no truth in him. When
he lies, it is consistent with his character; for he is a liar and the father of lies.

JOHN 8:44

There are different kinds of lies, and some are easier to spot than others. We probably won't be tempted to believe someone who insists he's a billy goat. But when the lie is rooted in a real moment of our experience, it may be harder to shake off.

If we were relinquished at birth, for instance, we might be tempted to believe we're not worth sticking around for. If a parent left us when we were young, we might be prone to believe we're not worth loving. If we were hurt during childhood, we may believe we weren't worth protecting.

Every one of those treacherous lies—and a thousand more like it—has been authored by the devil, who is the father of lies. And when we agree with any of them, we self-induce shame we don't deserve. Such lies can be hard to root out because they have almost become part of us. But the more we immerse ourselves in the truth of the gospel, the more obvious the devil's lies will become.

Don't fall for the whoppers that liar tells you about yourself and your worth. Listen to God instead.

ASK YOURSELF

» Have any falsehoods about your past become imbedded in your belief system? How can you tell?

» What are some truths from God's Word you can use to expose these lies?

ASK GOD

Lord, you said that you are the Truth. Send your Spirit to dispel the enemy's lies that have taken root in my life, and quicken my heart to cling to what is true.

Comforted to Comfort

He comforts us in all our troubles so that we can comfort others. When they are
troubled, we will be able to give them the same comfort God has given us.

2 CORINTHIANS 1:4

When Paul wrote to the early church in Corinth, he was addressing a group of people who were hurting and in need of hope. He sent them words of comfort and reminded them that God was the actual source of their comfort. And then he exhorted them to be agents of God's comfort to others as well.

That message applies to us, too. Everybody experiences pain and trouble from time to time—a ruptured relationship, a difficult diagnosis, a business failure, poor choices made by someone we love. And those of us who have known God's comfort are in a unique position to share that same comfort with others.

How has God comforted you in the past? Maybe he encouraged you with a particular Scripture passage. Maybe he buoyed your spirits by meeting you in prayer. Perhaps a pastor, a counselor, or a friend reached out to offer God's kindness and comfort. You can do that too. Even if your own situation isn't perfect, you can still comfort others.

ASK YOURSELF

» What are some specific ways you have experienced God's comfort?

» Do you know someone who might be in need of comfort today? How can you reach out to that person?

ASK GOD

God of grace, you have been steadfast and faithful to me. You've helped me and soothed me during my darkest days. You've given me hope to keep going. So today I offer myself as an instrument of your grace. Show me those who need comforting, and allow me to share the hope you've given me.

Mind Control

*Letting your sinful nature control your mind leads to death. But
letting the Spirit control your mind leads to life and peace.*

ROMANS 8:6

In every facet of life, the people who are placed in a position of authority determine the success or failure of their task. Where they lead, others follow. And for better or worse, the followers arrive at the same place.

This is why it is so important that we guard the "leadership" of our minds and be mindful of who we put in authority. The Bible says that allowing our sinful nature to be in charge will lead to death and that letting God's Spirit lead will result in life and peace. So it makes sense to ask ourselves each morning: *Who will I put in charge of my mind today? Will I allow my thoughts to wander to places that will eventually cause me pain, or will I give the Holy Spirit full control, knowing that he will lead me to life and peace?*

If we consciously make this choice every day, the decision is an easy one. It's the days when we don't ask the question that we are likely to be led astray.

ASK YOURSELF

» Who takes the lead most often in your mind and your thoughts?

» Are you willing to take a moment each morning to give God authority over your mind? What would this change in your life?

ASK GOD

Dear Lord, I want to live the life that you intend for me, and a big part of that involves my thoughts. Help me to be aware of who is in charge of my mind at each moment of every day. I want to give the Holy Spirit full control of my life, and that includes my thoughts.

Decide, Defend, Develop

God blesses you who are hungry now, for you will be satisfied. God
blesses you who weep now, for in due time you will laugh.

LUKE 6:21

In order for our lives to be satisfying and fulfilling, we must step into three crucial roles:

» *Decider*, making healthy choices
» *Defender*, standing up for justice and protecting ourselves from negative situations and people
» *Developer*, supporting and encouraging growth

You may have trusted others in the past to fill these roles for you, but they let you down. In response, you developed reactive lifestyles that hurt your relationships and hindered your growth. Now, as you take your life back, you're learning to do these things for yourself—making responsible and life-affirming choices, standing up for yourself and your recovery, and saying yes to new opportunities instead of holding back out of fear.

Ultimately, of course, it is God who guides you, protects you, and encourages our growth. He is our ultimate Decider, Defender, and Developer.

ASK YOURSELF

» What are some ways you have been hurt by those who made choices for you, failed to protect you, or stood in the way of your growth?

» Name at least one success you've had in learning to be your own decider, defender, or developer. How can you succeed more often?

ASK GOD
Father, thank you for all you do to guide my choices, protect me from evil, and help me flourish in my new life.

Learning to Feel Again

When Jesus saw her weeping and saw the other people wailing with her, a deep anger welled up within him, and he was deeply troubled. "Where have you put him?" he asked them. They told him, "Lord, come and see." Then Jesus wept.

JOHN 11:33-35

Sandra grew up in a home with an alcoholic father. She, her mother, and her four siblings suffered as a result of her father's dangerous and frightening behavior, but no one ever admitted there was a problem. When Sandra tried to talk to her mother about it, her mother ignored her daughter's fear and assured her that everything was fine. So Sandra learned to ignore her feelings. Eventually she learned not to feel much of anything—although her buried emotions often drove her to react inappropriately to experiences. For her—and for many of us—taking her life back meant uncovering her buried emotions and learning to feel them again.

Thankfully, we have the witness of Jesus, which helps us know what it is to be fully alive. When Jesus heard that his friend Lazarus had died, he *felt* something. He was disturbed, and he wept along with others who were sad. As you begin to take your life back, being able to feel is a life-giving sign of health.

ASK YOURSELF

> » What in your past may have caused you to avoid feeling?

> » As you heal, are you learning to experience your feelings in ways that are life-giving?

ASK GOD

Lord, you know the most tender places in my heart. Continue to heal me so that I might be fully alive and might experience the feelings that you gave to bless me and others.

Guard Your Heart

Guard your heart above all else, for it determines the course of your life.

PROVERBS 4:23

If there is one place you do not want to be, it's at sea in a boat without a rudder. The rudder steers the boat and directs it to the desired destination. Without the rudder, the boat will drift aimlessly and possibly never arrive.

Our hearts are the "rudders" of our lives. If they are not working properly, we may drift aimlessly and never arrive at the place that God has intended. That's why God's Word warns us to guard our hearts carefully. Whether we are going in the right direction or the wrong one, our hearts will be steering us there.

So how do we guard our hearts effectively? First, by soaking them in the protective Word of God. And second, by being alert to anything that might damage the "steering mechanism"—sinful inclinations, erroneous thinking, negative influences. The more quickly we can deflect these threats, the more successful we'll be at keeping our "rudders" in good working order.

ASK YOURSELF

> » Practically speaking, how does your heart—the seat of your mind and emotions—steer your life? How do your thoughts and responses determine your direction?

> » How alert do you tend to be to the condition of your heart? What kind of potentially damaging influences do you need to guard against today?

ASK GOD

Dear Jesus, please make me aware of those times when I am heading in the wrong direction and correct my course. Keep me always conscious of the condition of my own heart so that I can steer straight in the way you want me to go.

It's Not Just about You

*The human body has many parts, but the many parts make
up one whole body. So it is with the body of Christ.*

1 CORINTHIANS 12:12

If you have ever looked under the hood of an automobile, you realize that a car is constructed of many individual parts. Each one has a specific purpose, and all of them are interrelated.

If you put a substance other than gasoline into the fuel tank, you can destroy the entire motor. If you disconnect one battery cable, the entire car will be disabled until you correct the problem. All of these individual parts, on their own, have little value. It is only when they are connected and working properly that they reach their full potential.

The moment that you were "born again," you became a part of something much bigger than yourself. You became a part of the body of Christ. Everything that you do now has an effect on the body as a whole. It is important that you realize not only your individual value but also your significance to the body.

ASK YOURSELF

» As a Christian, how do you see your life intertwined with the entire body of Christ?

» What does it mean to look beyond yourself and make decisions for the good of the entire body? Does that mean you should stop loving yourself or caring for yourself?

ASK GOD

Dear Lord, so often I focus only on myself. I think, *How does this affect me? What do I want? Am I happy?* On and on it goes. I do not want to be that way. Help me live in a way that benefits the body as a whole.

Be Bold

God has not given us a spirit of fear and timidity, but of power, love, and self-discipline.

2 TIMOTHY 1:7

Do you ever find yourself in a situation where you feel so powerless and confused that you are unable to move forward? Do you ever become so paralyzed by fear that you lose your sense of direction and the ability to cope? This is not what God wants for you. He desires that you walk in his power so that you can face your problems head on. Let fear be your alarm, an alert that you are relying upon your own strength and not that of the Lord. When you try to go it alone, situations will overpower you and take you off course. Fear, timidity, and a lack of discipline are indicators that you are not living through God's power.

When you first sense fear or apprehension about any issue in your life, stop immediately and ask for the Lord's guidance. Call out to him and admit you cannot handle things on your own. When you do this, the Spirit of the Lord will come upon you. He will guide your steps and ease your fears.

ASK YOURSELF

> » What kinds of circumstances tend to make you fearful or anxious? How do you typically react to such circumstances?

> » How can you condition yourself to recognize fear as a sign that you are living in your own power?

ASK GOD

Dear Lord, I don't want to live my life feeling fearful and overwhelmed; I want to live in the boldness of your Spirit. Help me to recognize my anxiety as a signal that it's time to redirect my path and depend more fully on you.

Love, Not Grudges

Do not seek revenge or bear a grudge . . . but love your neighbor as yourself.

LEVITICUS 19:18

The famous feud between the Hatfield and McCoy families of Appalachia began during the Civil War and extended into the 1890s. Various causes have been cited—the war, land disputes, even the ownership of a pig—but pride, anger, and revenge kept the dispute going. Before it finally fizzled out, at least sixteen people were dead and seven were serving life sentences.

Few of us are involved in feuds of that magnitude, but pride and anger can get the best of anyone. When they do, common sense goes out the window and people get hurt—which is why God tells us specifically not to "seek revenge or bear a grudge" against others. Then he goes one step further—a *big* step. He tells us to love our neighbors as much as we love ourselves.

Think about it. Who is your primary concern in life? Who do you most want to keep happy? It's *you*. So if you "love your neighbor as yourself," everything else will fall into place.

ASK YOURSELF

» Do you tend to hold grudges when you feel you have been wronged? What's the best way to release that anger without harming yourself or others?

» Do you think it's really possible to love other people as much as you love yourself? How can you manage it?

ASK GOD

Dear Lord, teach me how to love instead of holding grudges and to look out for others the way I look out for myself. Allow me to see where I fall short of this command, and help me to change.

Growing Strong

The godly will flourish like palm trees and grow strong like the cedars of Lebanon.

PSALM 92:12

Do you ever feel like your growth as a Christian has stalled? Do you wonder what it will take to get you growing again? You might find it helpful to compare your spiritual growth to a child's physical growth.

Children don't usually grow in steady, measured increments—a little bit every day. Instead, they alternate periods of little perceptible change with times when they seem to "shoot up" overnight. But they still need to eat well every day! If parents only fed their children when they thought they might be getting ready to "shoot up," the children would never have what it takes to become healthy and strong.

In much the same way, you need daily nourishment from Scripture in order to grow spiritually. If you are partaking of God's Word only when you feel like you need it, you are probably missing out on the nutrition you need to flourish. Dig into the Word every day, bring your concerns to the Lord in prayer, and watch how quickly you start to grow again.

ASK YOURSELF

» Describe a time when you felt like you weren't growing as a Christian. How did that feel? Do you think there was a correlation between that lack of growth and your daily habits?

» What signs of spiritual growth have you seen in your life recently? Are there any changes you need to make in order to flourish?

ASK GOD

Dear Father God, I know my spiritual growth lags when I neglect my need for your Word and my time with you. Help me to make my spiritual condition a priority in my life.

It's Tough Being Human

I don't really understand myself, for I want to do what is right, but I
don't do it. Instead, I do what I hate. . . . I want to do what is good, but
I don't. I don't want to do what is wrong, but I do it anyway.

ROMANS 7:15, 19

These verses sound so familiar. They describe one of the most common struggles of being human. We all struggle to some degree with our lower nature, and we're always disappointing ourselves. As Paul reflects on this frustrating situation he ends up depressed, and he says at the end of Romans 7, "Oh, what a miserable person I am!" (verse 24). How can we ever know joy if all we have is an ongoing—and losing—struggle with the worst in us?

But that's not where it ends. The solution is in Romans 8:1, where Paul states that "there is no condemnation for those who belong to Christ Jesus." No condemnation! That means that when we belong to Jesus, nothing in our behavior—really nothing in the universe—can condemn us.

Being human can be tough and frustrating. But when we belong to Jesus Christ, we enter the "no condemnation" zone. And there is no better place to be.

ASK YOURSELF

» Sometimes we condemn ourselves more than anyone else does. What are some things you tend to condemn yourself for?

» How could taking the "no condemnation" principle seriously help you take your life back?

ASK GOD

Lord Jesus, it's hard to believe that when I belong to you, there is literally nothing that can condemn me. What freedom that brings. Help me to live out that truth today.

Fruits of Your Labor

Those who plant in tears will harvest with shouts of joy.

PSALM 126:5

Sometimes when we're struggling with a problem, we find it difficult to see anything else. Troubles seem to take over our lives, and we begin to doubt that we will ever come out on the other side.

Problems are part of the sad reality of life on earth. And God never promises that we will be completely free from affliction. But he does promise that our affliction won't go on forever—and that it will eventually bring us to something better. In fact, he says that what we "plant in tears," we will someday "harvest with shouts of joy."

Just knowing that promise should make it much easier to get through the rough times. So the next time trouble comes your way, why not lean into God's promise and look beyond the problem, knowing you are on your way to something very good in your future.

ASK YOURSELF

» Can you think of a time in your life when you just couldn't see a way out of your difficulties? Name any problems that threaten to steal your joy right now.

» Do you believe it's always true that pain leads to joy? Does what we do in the midst of our suffering make a difference?

ASK GOD

Father God, teach me to look beyond my problems and trust that you will increase the joy in my life through them. I don't want to wallow in my difficulties. So please help me to look forward and focus on following you rather than allowing my troubles to suffocate me.

The Perfect Parent

Don't leave me now; don't abandon me, O God of my salvation! Even if
my father and mother abandon me, the LORD will hold me close.

PSALM 27:9-10

Greeting cards, charming books, and heartwarming movies show countless images of perfectly loving mothers and fathers—especially around Mother's Day and Father's Day. But those images aren't *real*. In fact, the reality of most families is that mothers and fathers fail, in small ways or large, to be the parents their children need. Parents, like all human beings, are fallible. They are sinners. Even with the best of intentions, they let their children down or even actively harm them.

But we all have access to the one Parent whose love never fails. That's the point of today's Scripture. The psalmist writes as someone who has felt the sting of having imperfect parents. But he affirms, even in the midst of heartache, that the Lord holds him close.

We need to remember this as (former) children and possibly as parents ourselves. Parents make mistakes. Some make big, awful mistakes, and their children pay the price. A good part of recovery, in fact, involves dealing with the fallout of parental failures. But in the midst of it all, we can know our heavenly Parent will never abandon us and never let us go.

ASK YOURSELF

» Where in your life have you felt the sting of your parents' failure?

» How can you forgive your parents for their human imperfections while being honest about the damage their failures have done to you?

ASK GOD

Abba, Father of Jesus, I thank you that you have also called me your child. I run to you, the perfect Parent who will never fail me. Hold me near your heart this day.

You Are Loved

No power in the sky above or in the earth below—indeed,
nothing in all creation will ever be able to separate us from the
love of God that is revealed in Christ Jesus our Lord.

ROMANS 8:39

Regardless of how often we fall short, take the wrong path, or allow ourselves to be distracted from God's plan, we will always be surrounded by his love. He is always beside us. But that does not mean we will always be able to *feel* his love and his presence.

Feelings fluctuate. Many factors in life influence them. And while they can give us important clues about ourselves, they can also be unreliable. So we should learn not to depend on feelings as our primary measurement of reality. Instead of reacting to our emotions, we must learn to respond to life according to the truth of God's Word.

Thankfully, God's love is not based upon our worthiness, but rather upon what Christ did for us on the cross. Perhaps it is because we humans put conditions on our love that we assume God functions the same way. But he does not.

God looks at you through Jesus. Because of this, nothing you do or fail to do will ever cause God to abandon you. And nothing that you feel or don't feel will change that reality.

ASK YOURSELF

» Do you tend to view God's love for you as conditional? If so, why?

» How can you learn to depend more on God's Word and less on your feelings?

ASK GOD

Dear Lord, so often I am deceived by my feelings. Teach me to depend on your Word and not my emotions. Make me aware that you are always beside me and that your love is not based on how well or how poorly I behave.

Bought and Paid For

I will shout for joy and sing your praises, for you have ransomed me.

PSALM 71:23

Movies often rely on a hostage/ransom scenario to create tension and build a fearful energy in their plot. The bad guy takes something that doesn't belong to him and refuses to release it to the rightful owner unless a price is paid. Often that "something" is a person—a hostage whose future depends upon whether he or she is more valuable to the good guy than the ransom being demanded.

God's Word says that he has ransomed you. He paid the price to set you free from sin—and this price was not a small one. The fact that God ransomed you with the blood of Jesus, his only Son, shows just how much you are worth to him.

If you ever feel that you are insignificant, that you are worthless, or that taking your life back is a waste of space and time, think about the value God places on you. You are priceless to him, and you honor him when you value yourself the way that he values you.

ASK YOURSELF

» In what specific areas of your life do you tend to feel unworthy or insignificant? (It's not uncommon to feel confident in one area while feeling unworthy in another.)

» What changes in your thinking would help you see yourself the way God sees you in *all* aspects of your life?

ASK GOD

Dear loving Father, there are times when I feel so worthless, as though I have nothing to contribute to this world. Help me see myself through your eyes and recognize the value you have placed on me. Thank you for paying the ransom that I might live and for finding in me something worth saving.

Why We Serve

The greatest among you must be a servant. But those who exalt themselves
will be humbled, and those who humble themselves will be exalted.

MATTHEW 23:11-12

Jesus calls all leaders to be servants. But being a servant in Jesus' eyes isn't just about what we do for others. He's interested in our motivation as well.

If serving were just about doing good works, the religious leaders of Jesus' day would have been the best servants of all. But Jesus called them hypocrites, blind guides, blind fools, even whitewashed tombs—because everything they did had to do with receiving praise from others. They made sure they were known for good works, but on the inside they were greedy and even lawless (see Matthew 23:13-28).

Before we take our lives back, many of us resemble those religious leaders. So much of our behavior—even our loving, caring, serving behavior—is done to win the approval of others. Yes, we care about others to a point, but we care even more about filling the empty places inside of us.

When we take our lives back, however, these motivations change. We still care and serve, but we're doing it for Jesus' sake. The approval we're really seeking comes from Jesus himself.

ASK YOURSELF

> » Our motivations are always going to be mixed. How do you discern when you are seeking the approval of others and when you are seeking to please Jesus?

> » What's the key to serving with genuine humility?

ASK GOD

Dear Lord, check my motives for serving others and caring for others. I want to serve humbly and patiently—not to impress other people or make myself feel better but to show my love, obedience, and gratitude to you. Teach me to care for others appropriately and to take care of myself as well.

Help! I'm on Overload

O God, listen to my cry! Hear my prayer! From the ends of the
earth, I cry to you for help when my heart is overwhelmed.

PSALM 61:1-2

Feeling overwhelmed is a signal that we are losing touch with our lives. We can easily recognize the stress and overload, but often we don't know how to regain control.

David, the author of this psalm, knew about stress. He spent twenty years running for his life with King Saul on his heels, determined to kill him. But David knew what to do when he was on overload.

O God . . . lead me to the towering rock of safety,
    for you are my safe refuge. . . .
Let me live . . . safe beneath the shelter of your wings!

PSALM 61:1-4

God is indeed our refuge. He provides a place where we can safely unwind, and David depended on that. But David also needed the support of friends who could be honest with him. They, too, were part of his "towering rock of safety."

Like David, we need to take the time to pray, and we also must have friends we can lean on, friends who will support us as we take our lives back. We just can't do it on our own.

ASK YOURSELF

» Think today about God being your safe refuge. What makes him safe?

» Who are the safe people in your life today? If you can't think of someone, who might become a safe person in your life?

ASK GOD

God, help me to experience life beneath the shelter of your wings. Help me to experience more of you and less stress in my life today. Please show what I can do today to take my life back.

Exercise Your Spirit

You know that when your faith is tested, your endurance has a
chance to grow. So let it grow, for when your endurance is fully
developed, you will be perfect and complete, needing nothing.

JAMES 1:3-4

Do you ever think that the various trials in your life are a form of punishment? They aren't. Trials are the means by which we develop trust in God, and developing that trust is the foundation for spiritual health. In a sense, trials are our spiritual exercise, and if we trust God through them, we will build our endurance and our faith.

That's not easy to remember when we're grappling with a problem—a financial crisis, a relational conflict, or a period of deep grief or emotional turmoil. It's easy to become so consumed by the issues at hand that we lose sight of the bigger picture. But even the most painful trial can be an opportunity for growth if we trust the Lord.

When you encounter trials, try not to let yourself be sidetracked. Make the healthiest decisions you can, grit your teeth if you must, and keep on trusting. You may not see the growth when it's happening. But afterward you'll be amazed to look back and see what God has done.

ASK YOURSELF

> » Do *all* difficulties in life help us grow? What difference do our personal choices make in this dynamic?

> » Why do you think it's easier to see spiritual growth in retrospect?

ASK GOD

Dear Lord, I'm so quick to complain when my life gets difficult. Please keep me mindful of the spiritual growth each trial can bring rather than wallowing in the difficulty itself. Develop in me an unwavering faith so that I can endure every trial, knowing that you are my support.

How to Care for Others

We urge you to warn those who are lazy. Encourage those who are timid.
Take tender care of those who are weak. Be patient with everyone.

1 THESSALONIANS 5:14

Sometimes, as we seek to take our lives back, we find we must adjust our typical interactions with others, especially our need to take care of them or fix them. But this can leave us confused. Are we supposed to be hard-hearted or uncaring? Of course not. Paul suggests several ways we can care for others appropriately.

For one, we can warn those who need to step up their game—not taking responsibility for them, but simply sharing our observations. (If we find we can't do this with love and humility, it's better not to say anything.)

Second, we can offer encouragement to those who need it. Encouragement can be a powerful gift indeed.

Third, we can "take tender care" of the weak. It's totally appropriate to help those who cannot help themselves.

The hardest part of this verse is the instruction to be "patient with everyone"—including ourselves . . . and God. Our hurry-up world does not count time as God does. So we need to be patient as we work and wait for things to change.

ASK YOURSELF

> » How hard is it for you to limit your caring to what others can't do for themselves? Why is it so difficult?

> » Having patience in tough circumstances helps us experience God's faithfulness. Why is that so hard to do?

ASK GOD

Lord Jesus, help me learn more appropriate ways of caring for others. Help me to trust your faithfulness and to slow down so I can experience the gift of patience more fully.

Who's Calling the Shots?

We may throw the dice, but the LORD determines how they fall.

PROVERBS 16:33

People who think they're in charge of anything are guaranteed to be frustrated. The owner of a trucking company can dictate a route, but she can't control traffic conditions and detours. A teacher can map out a dynamic lesson plan, but he can't control which students will learn and which will not. A surgeon may perform a perfect operation, and still the patient may not recover. Being in charge (or feeling that we *should* be in charge) brings so much pressure and stress. Why do so many insist on it?

You would be wise to acknowledge God's control in your life because he has the final say anyway. Make your plans and do what you can to accomplish them, but don't make the mistake of believing you call the shots. God is in control. He decides the outcome of every situation.

This doesn't mean you have no responsibility or no power to choose, only that you should not be surprised when things do not go exactly as you planned. Your plan is not the deciding one.

ASK YOURSELF

> » How do you typically react when things don't go exactly as you have planned? What does this tell you about yourself?

> » In what areas of your life do you have trouble letting God take the lead?

ASK GOD

Dear Lord, I often get frustrated when things don't go my way. I sometimes get angry when you choose an outcome that's different from what I had envisioned. Help me to see that you are the one who determines what happens in every situation in my life. Give me the wisdom to let you do what you do best.

Like a Child

Anyone who becomes as humble as this little child
is the greatest in the Kingdom of Heaven.

MATTHEW 18:4

The disciples had just asked a pointed question: "Who is greatest in the Kingdom of Heaven?" In response, Jesus called a small child to him (Matthew 18:1-2) and used the little one as a visual aid to explain that God's expectations for us are completely different from what we usually think. He wants us to be like children.

What are children like? Jesus refers to a child's humility. Children naturally know how powerless and dependent they are, so they're not proud or arrogant. They live relatively simply and freely—unburdened by the worries and responsibilities of adulthood. And they typically live in the here and now—with few worries about tomorrow or regrets about yesterday. Picture a carefree child skipping down the sidewalk. That's the kind of spirit God wants us to have.

And no, not all children are like this. What we've just described are children who know they are loved and cared for. And that's the way God wants us to live in relation to him. It's not that he wants us to be irresponsible or immature. But he does want us to live more simply and freely because we know our limitations and trust our heavenly Father completely.

ASK YOURSELF

» Describe some of the worries and concerns that make your life feel complicated. Is there one place where you could simplify so you could feel freer and more childlike?

» How does a person become childlike without being irresponsible or childish?

ASK GOD

Dear God, I long to live as a carefree child in your presence. Help me deal more effectively with the complexities of my life. Give me the courage to trust you and simplify.

Weighed Down with Worry

Worry weighs a person down; an encouraging word cheers a person up.

PROVERBS 12:25

"He looked like he was carrying the weight of the world." Have you ever heard that said about someone? If so, chances are that person was a worrier. Because "heavy" is exactly what worry feels like. It's a weight that pushes us further and further down into a valley of despair.

To worry is to expend time and emotional energy on future troubles that may never come to pass. Once we give worries a home in our heads, they can take on a life of their own.

But believe it or not, worry is a choice, which means we can keep it from weighing us down. If we refuse to give our worried thoughts space in our minds, they will dry up and blow away because they are nothing without our attention.

Refuse to make room for worry. Cast it out of your mind the moment it appears. Recognize it for the empty waste of time and energy that it is, and that overwhelming heaviness will gradually disappear.

ASK YOURSELF

> » Do you tend to focus on things that may never come to pass as though they were already happening? How does this worry change the way you live?

> » How can you stop your worrisome thoughts and keep them from weighing you down?

ASK GOD

Dear Jesus, I know it is a foolish waste of my time and energy to be concerned with things that may never happen. Show me how to recognize this worry habit for what it is—an empty threat that only gets its power when I breathe life into it. Help me not to do this.

Set Free to Share

All the believers met together in one place and shared everything they had. They sold their property and possessions and shared the money with those in need.

ACTS 2:44-45

Have you seen one of those reality shows about hoarders—people who collect mountains of belongings in their homes, to the point that normal life becomes impossible? They cling to each item even when it's obvious that they are jeopardizing their health and relationships.

Very few of us will actually become hoarders of this magnitude. (Many people featured on the shows have some form of mental illness.) But the dynamic of holding on to what we have too tightly is familiar to many on the road to recovery. We have felt so needy and deprived that we've kept a death grip on everything we have—not just our material possessions but our gifts, our talents, and our love.

But when we trust God enough to let go a little, we can discover the joy and fulfillment that comes with sharing. When he is our source of security, we are set free to give and to meet the needs of others.

ASK YOURSELF

> » Do you relate to the hoarding mentality at all? Do you suffer from a tendency to want more and more and have difficulty letting go of what you have? How can you break this pattern and take your life back?

> » How can you give—from your material resources or from the other gifts God has given you—to help meet someone else's need today?

ASK GOD

God, I thank you for the witness of the early believers who shared everything they had. And I thank you for offering to set me free from all I hold so tightly.

Don't Give Up on Love

Give thanks to the LORD, for he is good! His faithful love endures forever.

PSALM 106:1

It is easy to take for granted the things in our lives we count on most. God's love is one of those foundational blessings that often goes without recognition or thanks. Like spoiled children who expect their parents to cater to their every need, we children of God come to accept our heavenly Father's love and provision as our due.

Are you ever guilty of taking God for granted? Do you quickly point out the things that he chooses *not* to provide you with but fail to show your appreciation for the amazing gifts he showers upon you daily? Don't let yourself become numb to the awesomeness of God's unfailing provision. He isn't going to shun you because of your ingratitude, but it is in the act of thanking and praising him that you will find true joy.

ASK YOURSELF

» When was the last time you specifically thanked God for his love and his provision in your life? How did this bring you joy?

» In addition to verbal prayers, what are some tangible ways you can express your gratitude to God for all that he does for you?

ASK GOD

Dear Lord, thank you, thank you, thank you! I know that I do not say this enough. Forgive me for taking you for granted. Keep me aware of everything that you do for me on a daily basis. May I never grow tired of praising you.

The Safety of Integrity

He grants a treasure of common sense to the honest.
He is a shield to those who walk with integrity.

PROVERBS 2:7

Is it ever okay to tell a lie—maybe the "little white" kind intended to protect our driving record or someone else's feelings? As tempting as it is to bend the truth on occasion, God's Word makes it pretty clear that it's better to be honest.

God says he "grants a treasure of common sense" to the honest. Being consistently transparent with others and with ourselves helps us assess our lives clearly and accurately. Good judgment becomes almost an instinct—which is a good way of describing common sense.

God also says he "is a shield to those who walk with integrity." The more we align ourselves with what is real and true in life, the closer our walk with God will be—and the safer we'll be as a result.

If you have not yet reached the level of honesty and integrity you wish to have in your life, it's not too late. Ask the Lord to nudge you whenever you stray from the truth so that you can correct yourself. You may be surprised at how often you get nudged, but in the end you will win the prize.

ASK YOURSELF

» Is there any particular area in your life where you are especially tempted to be dishonest? Why do think this area is a challenge to you?

» Is there more to honesty and integrity than just refraining from lies? How would you describe these qualities?

ASK GOD

Dear Lord, I want to be someone others can trust—and to be able to trust my own judgment. Teach me that there is never a good reason to be less than honest.

Prevent Contamination

Your boasting about this is terrible. Don't you realize that this sin is
like a little yeast that spreads through the whole batch of dough?

1 CORINTHIANS 5:6

That old saying, "A little goes a long way," can be applied to many things. A small seed grows into a gigantic tree. A handful of popcorn kernels produces a bucketful. A tiny bacterium multiplies into billions. And a little sin can corrupt the whole world.

The Bible compares sin to yeast. A very small amount will increase in volume and cause dough to double in size. Once the yeast has done its job, there is no hiding it. You can easily see the effect of the yeast in the dough. Sin spreads in much the same way. When you tolerate a little sin in your life, it is sure to multiply and can spread to those around you. Thus, a little lie becomes a deceptive lifestyle. A little pride becomes a stronghold. A "harmless" flirtation grows into a full-blown affair.

The best precaution against the growth of sin in your life is to deal with it as soon as you are aware of its presence. Do everything you can to make your life a "sin-free" zone!

ASK YOURSELF

» Why is it so tempting to tolerate "just a little" sin in your life?

» How can you learn to recognize sin when it's small and eradicate it before it can grow?

ASK GOD

Dear Jesus, I do not want to give sin a foothold. Show me how to recognize it while it's little, and give me the discipline to confront it and remove it before it can grow. Help me to be vigilant and not to tolerate even a little sin in my life.

If It Ain't Broke . . .

How foolish can you be? After starting your new lives in the Spirit, why are you now trying to become perfect by your own human effort?

GALATIANS 3:3

Have you heard people say, "If it ain't broke, don't fix it"? That's good advice. For some reason, many of us like to meddle with things that don't need to be fixed. We'll even try to fix things we have no qualifications to work on, like our spiritual growth.

Remember when you first accepted Jesus as your Savior? You were so in tune to God's Spirit, and you allowed him to do whatever was necessary in your life. You didn't try to help him work because you had no idea what needed to be fixed.

But then you learned a little and decided to help God out. So you tried to be "holy." You worked at looking right on the outside. You tried, in your flesh, to become the perfect Christian, and you failed miserably.

Why? Because Jesus is the only one who is qualified for that job, and he has already done the work for you on the cross.

ASK YOURSELF

» In what ways do you sometimes try to do God's work for him or to fix yourself without relying on him?

» What work *are* you qualified for when it comes to taking back your life?

ASK GOD

Dear Jesus, it is so easy to get caught up in trying to do all the right things and look like a "good Christian." Please keep me from trying to do the work that Jesus has already done. Show me how to step aside and allow the Holy Spirit to do his work in me.

You Choose

*If you become wise, you will be the one to benefit. If you
scorn wisdom, you will be the one to suffer.*

PROVERBS 9:12

Life is full of choices, but none is more important than whether or not we choose wisdom. Wisdom is what keeps us on the right path when the wrong path seems like a nice diversion. It is what keeps us focused on doing what is right rather than on what might be easy or expedient. True wisdom takes the long view, the view of eternity.

In this world, you will be faced with the choice between wisdom and foolishness every minute of every day. Godly wisdom is foreign to the world at large, which tends to look for quick fixes and instant benefits rather than take the eternal view. But such worldly thinking is folly. It's reactive living at its worst.

In the long run, focusing on what "what works right now" instead of what is right just results in more suffering and more difficult choices down the road. Truly wise choices, however, lead to long-term benefit.

ASK YOURSELF

» Have you ever been tempted to ignore the voice of wisdom in your life to meet an immediate need or desire? What happened?

» Think about a decision you are facing right now. How can seeking an eternal perspective help you decide? How can you gain such a perspective?

ASK GOD

Heavenly Father, I need your eternal perspective and your wisdom every day of my life. Help me avoid shortsighted folly and make right choices that lead to benefit rather than suffering.

God's Mighty Weapon

We use God's mighty weapons, not worldly weapons, to knock down the
strongholds of human reasoning and to destroy false arguments. We
destroy every proud obstacle that keeps people from knowing God. We
capture their rebellious thoughts and teach them to obey Christ.

2 CORINTHIANS 10:4-5

Some folks in the early church accused Paul of being timid when speaking to them in person and more forceful when writing to them. His second letter to the church in Corinth is certainly bold—a powerful exhortation that reads like a declaration of war. He claims that God's weapons knock down whatever stands in the way of our knowledge of God.

One mighty weapon that you and I have in our godly arsenal is the stronghold-destroying power to "capture . . . rebellious thoughts." God's powerful weapon of truth is able to clear minefields, unearth any rebellious thoughts, and pull our minds back into submission to Jesus Christ.

There are many kinds of rebellious thoughts. One person might doubt God's promises. Another might be furious about perceived injustices. Yet another might have feasted on unhealthy images that now occupy his or her mind.

Whatever your form of rebellious thinking, the Holy Spirit can help you notice and capture your thoughts, replacing them with God's truth.

ASK YOURSELF

» What rebellious thoughts tend to occupy your mind?

» What is the most effective way you have found to knock down obstacles and conquer those thoughts?

ASK GOD

Lord, I know there's a battle being waged in heavenly places for my heart and mind. I submit myself to you and ask for your Spirit to illumine any of my thoughts that are not yet obedient to Christ. Replace them with the truth of your Word.

Extreme Protection

Then you will experience God's peace, which exceeds anything we can understand.
His peace will guard your hearts and minds as you live in Christ Jesus.

PHILIPPIANS 4:7

Many cities have gated communities designed to keep out those who do not belong. These communities have varying levels of security, from electronic gates that require passwords for entrance to physical guards who allow or deny access based on the residents' instructions. Regardless of the method, they all prevent unwanted visitors from gaining easy access.

This is what the "peace of God" does for your heart and mind if you ask.

As you take your life back, it is through prayer and trust in God that you will gain his peace. His peace will guard your heart and your mind from attack.

The key here, just as in the gated community, is that you, the resident, must make your request known. Communicate with God daily, present your needs, express your fears, and ask your questions. Thank him for the things he has already done for you, and trust him to guide you. The peace that this daily interaction provides is instrumental in forming the protection you will need to move confidently through life.

ASK YOURSELF

>» Are you leaving your "gate" open to intruders? How could you enlist the protection that is available to you through Jesus?

>» Are your heart and mind currently filled with God's peace? If not, what changes could you make this week to draw closer to him?

ASK GOD

Dear Lord, I want to know your peace every minute of every day. Teach me how to communicate with you moment by moment. Teach me to trust you fully and to express my thanks for the things you have done in my life. Fill me with the peace that only you can provide.

Trade In and Trade Up

I will turn their mourning into joy. I will comfort them
and exchange their sorrow for rejoicing.

JEREMIAH 31:13

Is there anything in your life that is keeping you down—something that seems to steal your joy day in and day out? Perhaps it's a job . . . or a house . . . or a familiar way of thinking and acting. It may have served you well at one time, but now it's a source of frustration and sorrow.

If that's true for you, take heart. You don't have to just live with your unhappiness. You can trade it in.

Think of trading in a vehicle that gives you grief on a daily basis for one that is dependable and makes you smile. God is ready and willing to take your sorrows and replace them with rejoicing.

Why would anyone decline such an offer? Usually it is because they have no idea that they're in a position to rid themselves of the "lemons" in their lives. The unhappiness seems like a part of them. They don't know how to let it go.

Well, now you know better. Your upgrade is ready and waiting for you. Trade in the old. Enjoy the new.

ASK YOURSELF

» Is anything in your life stealing your happiness? Are you ready to trade it in for the joy of God?

» Is trading in your problems the same as giving up on people or abandoning responsibilities? Why or why not?

ASK GOD

Dear Lord, I do not want to hold on to aspects of my life that are holding me back. Help me to recognize these for what they are and give them to you so that you can replace them with joy.

Serving in Joy and Freedom

You have been called to live in freedom, my brothers and sisters.
. . . Use your freedom to serve one another in love.

GALATIANS 5:13

Service can take many different forms. If you've dined in a fine restaurant, you may have been served by a waiter who wasn't overworked, could take his time reciting the specials of the day, and went home at closing with a wallet full of generous tips. If you stopped at a roadside diner, though, you might have been served by a weary waitress who was harried by too many demanding customers and who struggled daily to make ends meet.

Before we begin to take our lives back, we might be serving others, but our service resembles that of the diner waitress—frazzled, worried, overworked. We serve because we're dependent on the opinions of others and the obsessions and compulsions that run our lives. How much better it is to serve from a place of peace and freedom—not because we're compelled to, but because we sense God calling us to service and we know he will take care of us.

We have the power and freedom to choose service that is rewarding rather than stressful or joyless. And in the Lord's service we always receive back more than we could ever give.

ASK YOURSELF

> » What does it feel like when you serve under compulsion? What specific motivations force you into "service"?

> » How does it feel to serve with joy and reward? Are you there yet?

ASK GOD

God, I thank you for the gifts you've given me to serve others. Help me break free from compulsion and obligation so I can serve you freely and joyfully. Let me show others your goodness in my actions today.

Feeling Guilty?

Fools make fun of guilt, but the godly acknowledge it and seek reconciliation.

PROVERBS 14:9

If we're wise, we'll always check the fuel level in our cars before venturing out on the road. If the gauge indicates we're running on low, we'll be sure to make a stop at the gas station. None of us looks at the gauge hoping to buy fuel. We look at it because we know the information provided is important. If we ignore it, we might end up stranded.

As much as we abhor the feeling of guilt, it can be a blessing if we acknowledge it and try to understand it. Guilt feelings draw our attention to something that is not as it should be. If we have hurt someone or broken a law, we need to face the consequences, seek forgiveness, make restitution, and do what is necessary to avoid repeating the transgression. If we are feeling guilty about something that wasn't really wrong, we need to examine the situation and let go of our false guilt.

Just as ignoring the *E* level on the fuel gauge can put us in a bad place, ignoring guilt will certainly have negative consequences in our lives.

ASK YOURSELF

» What are the benefits of using a guilty conscience as a catalyst for change?

» How can you know the difference between real guilt and false guilt?

ASK GOD

Dear Lord, I want to be in tune with my conscience and listen to the message my guilt is trying to convey. Prevent me from turning a deaf ear to guilt simply because it makes me feel uncomfortable. Teach me to act upon these feelings and to bring myself into perfect alignment with you.

Just Be Willing

*Don't worry in advance about what to say. Just say what God tells you at
that time, for it is not you who will be speaking, but the Holy Spirit.*

MARK 13:11

When we are preparing for something, be it a business meeting, a speech, a
test, or anything else where we are called upon to perform, it is easy to panic.
When this happens, we procrastinate, we fail to complete the task, or—worst of
all—we run and hide. Whether we are well prepared or not prepared at all, we
stand a much better chance of success when we actually do *something*. Then,
even if we fail, we will be moving forward and able to learn something.

When God calls us to a task, we are in an advantageous position because
he sends the Holy Spirit to help us accomplish it. The only obstacle that can
prevent us from completing God's task is us. If we try to do God's work on our
own, we are sure to fail.

So allow the Holy Spirit to work through you. Don't worry about what needs
to be done or what the outcome will be. Simply be willing to do as he instructs
you, and you will succeed.

ASK YOURSELF

> » In what ways are preparation, trust, surrender, and obedience linked?
> Which of these are more challenging for you?

> » How can you tell the difference between being called by God to a task
> and doing it for your own reasons?

ASK GOD

Dear Lord, your ways are so far above anything that I can fully understand.
Remind me of this daily. Make me receptive to the prodding of your Spirit so
that I can be used by you. Teach me to discern your leading and be willing to
step up when you call upon me.

The Great Equalizer

We are made right with God by placing our faith in Jesus Christ. And
this is true for everyone who believes, no matter who we are.

ROMANS 3:22

In this world, people are ranked by status. Power and privilege provide advantages to some that others will never know, and respect is usually based on position rather than on character. It's not fair. And that shouldn't surprise us. It's a fallen world, after all.

But there is one place where we are all equal, and that is in the eyes of God. Being right with him is the key to eternal life, and the way to get right with God is the same for everyone.

Jesus came to earth and taught us how to live. He took our sin upon himself and carried it to the cross. He died and then he defeated death. And he did all this so that every person on this planet would have access to God the Father.

Faith in Jesus is what makes us right with God, and that's available to everyone. Jesus is the great Equalizer.

ASK YOURSELF

» How does realizing we are all equal in God's eyes change the way you view other people? How does it change your view of the power struggles and injustice you see around you?

» How often do you reflect on the sacrifice Jesus made for all of us? Have you placed your faith in Jesus?

ASK GOD

Dear Father in heaven, help me to realize the depth of your love for me and to return that love in the way I live. Thank you for making the path to eternal life so accessible and for making it available to all people, no matter who they are.

Before You Lose It

Don't sin by letting anger control you. Think about it overnight and remain silent.

PSALM 4:4

Have you ever gotten so angry about something that you lost control? There is nothing worse than speaking or acting in anger and knowing you cannot take those words and actions back.

Being angry is not a sin, but allowing anger to control you is. The next time you become angry, why not use the experience as an opportunity to grow in self-knowledge and self-control? Here are some suggestions:

First, admit your anger, especially to yourself. Don't try to pretend you're not angry when you are.

Second, take a step back and ask yourself *why* you're angry. Usually it's because you feel frustrated or threatened in some way. But have you really been harmed?

Third, do your best not to lash out at those around you. Instead, take a walk, wash the dishes, or find some other way to discharge the extra energy the angry feelings generate.

Fourth, after your anger has subsided and you have had time to assess the situation, decide whether you need to do or say something in response. If so, do it as honestly and as calmly as you can.

ASK YOURSELF

> » Do you have a tendency to lash out when you are angered? How has this hurt you and others in the past?

> » Why is it important not to deny your anger?

ASK GOD

Dear Jesus, I don't want to deny my honest feelings of anger, but I also don't want my anger to control me. Help me learn to be angry without doing or saying something I regret.

Be Careful What You Wish For

Desire gave you renewed strength, and you did not grow weary.

ISAIAH 57:10

Desire is a powerful thing, and your mind is just as powerful in its quest to help you acquire the object of your desire. Have you ever noticed how your subconscious picks up on your desires? Think about the last time you wanted a new car. Once you clarified the make and model, you saw that vehicle everywhere. Why? Because your mind was focused on your desire and was seeking to help you acquire it.

The prophet Isaiah describes a time when desire gave people "renewed strength." In this case it was a desire for ungodly things, and it got these folks into trouble. But desire can also give us strength to pursue good things. Both good and bad desires create an energy that will push us forward when we might otherwise give up, and it will likely continue until that desire has been satisfied or quenched. This is why it is so important that we keep our minds focused on the things of God.

Entertaining ungodly desires is a dangerous thing. Once we start that wheel in motion, it is not easily stopped.

ASK YOURSELF

» What godly and ungodly desires have driven you in the past?

» What can you do to weed out the ungodly thoughts that cross your mind?

ASK GOD

Dear heavenly Father, my mind is a busy place. My thoughts come and go at a rapid pace, and not all of them are good. Help me to filter my thoughts and to question the nature of my desires before they take on a life of their own. I need your help to stay on the right track.

Renewable Energy

*Those who trust in the LORD will find new strength. They will soar high on wings
like eagles. They will run and not grow weary. They will walk and not faint.*

ISAIAH 40:31

Strength comes from many sources. Emotional energy creates a strength of
sorts, and we can build physical strength from conditioning our bodies. But
both kinds of strength have their limitations. If we live in our strength, we'll
eventually give out.

The strength we can always count on comes from the Lord. As we build
our trust in God, we find we have constantly renewed energy to face what this
world throws at us. God's strength can get us through anything.

Do you ever feel that you have come to the end of your ability to cope?
When you feel defeated by life, let that be an indicator for you to step aside so
God can take over. When you place your trust in him, something amazing happens. He will give you the strength to continue what you're doing or to choose
a different path.

This is no great mystery. The more you trust in God, the more you will be
able to handle.

ASK YOURSELF

» How can you take advantage of the strength that is available to you
through the Lord?

» Why do you think trusting in God and being energized by him are
related?

ASK GOD

Dear Jesus, when I feel that I cannot go on, when I feel defeated and worn
down, remind me to call upon you for renewed strength and energy. Keep me
from trudging along in my own power when you are so ready to give me the
strength that I need if I will only ask.

Rugged Enough to Thrive

I am like an olive tree, thriving in the house of God. I
will always trust in God's unfailing love.

PSALM 52:8

An olive tree is an unbelievably hardy plant with a root system that spreads deep and wide. An olive tree will find a way to thrive in almost any location and is rugged enough to survive the encroachments of other plants, excessive pruning, punishing storms, and even the extraction of a large part of its root system. Is it any wonder that the psalmist compares those of us who have a thriving relationship with God to olive trees?

Have you rooted yourself deeply in the Lord? Are you feeding on his Word and letting yourself be watered with his thirst-quenching Spirit? These things are necessary for growing a strong root system, which is essential to your spiritual growth and survival. You can't take your life back without it. To weather the storms of life, you must be deeply rooted so that you cannot be swayed. When you are firmly planted where God has placed you, you will thrive. And there is no joy anywhere that compares to the joy of "thriving in the house of God."

ASK YOURSELF

» What can you do to make sure your spiritual roots go deep?

» How can you be sure you are "thriving in the house of God"? What are some signs of spiritual health?

ASK GOD

Heavenly Father, I do not want to go through life being twisted and torn by every storm that crosses my path. I want to be firmly rooted, just like the olive tree. Help me to invest in my spiritual foundation by reading your Word and spending time communicating with you daily. Show me the things I should be doing to have a healthy and strong relationship with you.

Building Up One Another in Love

Let us aim for harmony in the church and try to build each other up.

ROMANS 14:19

If you're a parent, you've probably experienced the shock of hearing your little ones parrot your own words back to you. Perhaps there's a snarl in traffic, and the child shouts angrily at the other drivers—sounding uncannily like Mommy or Daddy. Or a child playing house scolds her stuffed animals with painfully familiar language and tone.

Ouch! It's a strange feeling to realize what we really sound like.

What would you hear if an actual parrot took up residence in your home or if someone installed secret cameras? Would you hear bickering and criticism? Or would you hear words of encouragement that build others up?

Encouragement is the standard of communication to which the apostle Paul calls us in his letter to the Romans. We are meant to use our words to promote harmony and to build each other up in love. Give it a try this week by intentionally speaking positive, uplifting words to those who share life with you.

ASK YOURSELF

» Are you naturally more likely to build others up or tear them down? How can you become more encouraging in your interactions with others?

» Whom can you commit to building up in love this week?

ASK GOD

God, you spoke the world into being with your words, and you sent your Son, the Word made flesh, to save us. Teach me how to honor you by building others up with my words for the sake of your church and for the spreading of your Kingdom.

You Are Never Alone

If I go up to heaven, you are there; if I go down to the grave, you are there.
If I ride the wings of the morning, if I dwell by the farthest oceans, even
there your hand will guide me, and your strength will support me.

PSALM 139:8-10

There are times in life when we feel alone, isolated from the rest of the world. We may feel that no one understands what we are going through or that those closest to us are shying away. And whether this is true or imagined, it feels the same—very lonely.

When this happens, there is a way to extricate ourselves from the pit of loneliness. We can call upon the Lord. His Word makes it clear that he is everywhere. Even in those times when we feel alone, he is close at hand. He never leaves us for a moment. All we have to do is hold on to his promises, ask for his guidance, and allow him to support us.

Feelings are fickle and cannot always be trusted. But God's Word is always dependable. The Lord will never leave us or let us down.

ASK YOURSELF

» How do you typically seek comfort or support when you feel alone? How healthy and effective are these strategies?

» What are some practical ways to remind yourself of God's steadfast presence in your life?

ASK GOD

Dear ever-present Father, sometimes I feel like I am all alone in this world. Sometimes my problems seem so overwhelming that I lose sight of the fact that you are always with me. Help me remember to call on you when I feel alone and burdened. Never let me forget to thank you for your faithful, loving presence.

Your Secret Weapon

Who can win this battle against the world? Only those
who believe that Jesus is the Son of God.

1 JOHN 5:5

Let's face it, living in this fallen world can be extremely challenging. It's hard enough just to make it through our days and years—much less resist evil and stay focused on the things that are pure and good. Sometimes it feels like we're fighting a losing battle, and we're tempted to give up.

But here's the good news: As a child of God, you have what it takes to prevail against the evil in the world. When you are overwhelmed or sidetracked by the events of life, you can call upon the Lord, and he will help you. He is your secret weapon against evil.

But just having a weapon is not enough. You must also choose to use it. So pick up your sword (the Word of God—Hebrews 4:12) and your shield (your faith in him—Ephesians 6:16). And don't forget to call upon the Lord to help you fight the battle.

ASK YOURSELF

» What kinds of battles are you fighting at this time in your life? Do you feel fairly confident, or are you often overwhelmed and tempted to give up?

» How can you condition yourself to call upon the Lord for help in every situation?

ASK GOD

Dear Lord, I know you will help me fight life's battles and prevail against the evil I encounter. But sometimes I get so caught up in the issues at hand that I forget to ask for your aid. Remind me to call upon you at the first sign of difficulty in my life, and help me to trust that you will see me through.

Who Jesus Is

God in all his fullness was pleased to live in Christ, and
through him God reconciled everything to himself.

COLOSSIANS 1:19-20

The Bible says we can defeat this evil world through faith—specifically, through believing that Jesus is the Son of God (see 1 John 5:4-5). Sounds simple, and it is. But do we fully grasp how incredible Jesus is and what he has done for us?

Jesus existed before anything was created. In fact, according to Colossians 1:16, "he made the things we can see and the things we can't see." At a pivotal point in history, he chose to take on human form, to become "the visible image of the invisible God" (Colossians 1:15). As a man, he astonished people with his miracles—calming the wind and the sea, healing the sick, even raising people from the dead—and his teachings, which revealed God's astonishing love. He suffered a painful, humiliating death, but he turned it into victory through the Resurrection. And he did all this for our sakes. It is he who makes it possible for us to win this battle against the world.

ASK YOURSELF

» In what ways do you tend to take Jesus for granted or make him too much like you?

» Slowly read Colossians 1:15-20. How does this passage affect your understanding of who Jesus is?

ASK GOD

Lord Jesus, forgive me for forgetting how amazing you really are. It's incredible to think that everything I see and even what I can't see is made and sustained by you. Yet you know me, you love me, and you care about and for me. It's all too wonderful. Thank you.

Minute by Minute

Dear brothers and sisters, I plead with you to give your bodies to God because of all he has done for you. Let them be a living and holy sacrifice—the kind he will find acceptable. This is truly the way to worship him.

ROMANS 12:1

During the civil rights movement in America, Dr. Martin Luther King Jr. had much to say about forgiveness. In the face of repeated brutalization, he had learned that forgiveness needed to be ongoing. It "is not an occasional act," he exhorted. "It is a constant attitude." Dr. King was basically building on the words of Jesus, who urged his followers to forgive "seventy times seven" times (see Matthew 18:21-22).

Surrendering our lives to God is also an ongoing process. It is a daily exercise that starts in the morning, when we connect with God and offer him our day, and then challenges us all day long. Moment by moment we must resist the urge to wrestle control out of God's hands. Moment by moment we must make the choice to let him be in charge.

It's another one of those holy paradoxes: We take our lives back by surrendering them every day, all day long, to the one who gave us life.

ASK YOURSELF

» How can you forgive repeatedly and still protect yourself from ongoing damage?

» What is most challenging for you about surrendering to God? What is the most rewarding aspect of this surrender?

ASK GOD

Faithful God, today I offer you my body, my mind, my soul, and my spirit. Quicken my heart, moment by moment, to surrender myself to you in whatever way you ask, even if it's forgiving again and again.

Does Anyone Really Care?

All praise to God, the Father of our Lord Jesus Christ. God
is our merciful Father and the source of all comfort.

2 CORINTHIANS 1:3

There is no feeling more disquieting than that of being all alone in this world. We all need to know that if we really have the need, there is someone who will sit beside us and comfort us until we feel we can handle life on our own. As children of God, we have assurance.

The Bible tells us that God is the "source of all comfort." And since we have a direct link to the Source, we are never really alone. We have access to God's comfort through the Holy Spirit who lives inside us, through prayer to God the Father in the name of Jesus, and through other people who obey God and reach out to us.

As we move toward taking our lives back, it's important that we allow ourselves to draw upon the comfort the Lord offers us and that we become familiar with his voice. Once we get in the habit of letting him be our primary source of comfort, that sense of being alone and uncared for will dwindle.

ASK YOURSELF

» Do you often feel that you are all alone and that no one cares? What usually triggers these feelings?

» Do you have any hesitation about making God your primary source of comfort? What are your main concerns?

ASK GOD

Dear Lord, thank you for the many ways you extend comfort to me. Keep me focused on the reality of your presence in my life, and help me remember to turn first to you when I need comfort.

Why Argue?

Hatred stirs up quarrels, but love makes up for all offenses.

PROVERBS 10:12

Are you feeling the love these days? More important, are you spreading the love?

Everywhere we look, it seems, people are "standing up for their rights," pointing out the flaws in others, and making sure that they themselves are never being slighted. This contentious way of relating to each other is tolerated or even applauded, while gentleness and peacefulness seem to be equated with weakness.

An aggressive me-me-me focus is *not* the same as caring for ourselves or even loving ourselves. In fact, it's toxic to both individual relationships and society in general, and it won't help us take our lives back. Instead, we are instructed to love one other the way that God loves us (see John 13:34).

Godly love, shared freely, can overcome the effects that hatred and fighting have on this world. Do your best not to get caught up in quarreling and discord, don't be quick to take offense, and check your motives for hate and resentment. Strive to be an ambassador of love wherever you go, even as you work for healing in your own life.

ASK YOURSELF

» How do you usually respond to others when they approach you with an argumentative spirit?

» What habits can you form that will prevent you from being quarrelsome with others? How can you care for yourself and still be loving toward others?

ASK GOD

Dear God, I want to be a blessing to those I come in contact with. If there is anything in my spirit or my actions that would promote hatred or strife, please point it out to me and show me how to change. I truly want to be an ambassador of your love.

No Time to Waste

Teach us to realize the brevity of life, so that we may grow in wisdom.

PSALM 90:12

Have you begun to notice that the older you get, the faster the years seem to fly by? Life as a whole is a very brief experience, and there is so much to be accomplished. Why do you think time seems to pass so quickly as we grow older? Perhaps it is God's way of reminding us to keep focused and use our time wisely.

Are you making good use of the time you have been given on this earth? Do you ask the Lord to direct you each day so that you might accomplish what he would have you do? It is easy to become distracted with the wrong things, and time wasted can never be recaptured. Think about what you want to accomplish in this life. Try to give each hour of your day the respect it deserves, and ask God for the wisdom to discern what is really important in each moment.

ASK YOURSELF

» Do you have a sense of why you are here on earth and what you are meant to accomplish? If not, how can you get a better sense of what God has in mind for you?

» In what ways can you become more respectful of the time you have been given and use it more effectively?

ASK GOD

Dear Jesus, I know that life on this earth passes in the blink of an eye, and I want to make the time I have here count. Please help me to focus upon the things that will really make a difference, and don't let me get caught up in petty issues that steal the time I have.

Humble like Him

You must have the same attitude that Christ Jesus had. Though he was
God, he did not think of equality with God as something to cling to.

PHILIPPIANS 2:5-6

Imagine how differently the Bible would read if Jesus had been a glory hog.
What if he had instructed his disciples from the beginning to advertise his miracles instead of warning them not to talk about what they had seen? Or what
if he had said yes to Satan when the evil one offered him great earthly power?
Instead of being a chronicle of hope and redemption, the New Testament could
have been a "look at me" account that made everyone feel worse about themselves and doubt their future hope.

Though Jesus was God, he didn't throw his divinity in people's faces or
demand recognition. Instead, he humbled himself to reach each of us where
we are. The proper response to that is gratitude, not pride.

When you step out into the world today, remember that everything you are
is a gift from God—and live accordingly. If anyone should be full of himself,
it's Jesus—and he isn't. Pray to have the attitude of Christ in all that you do.

ASK YOURSELF

» Why do you think Jesus told his disciples not to broadcast news of his
early miracles?

» Why do you think the Bible talks so much about the sin of pride? Why
is it such a problem? What damage does it do?

ASK GOD

Dear Jesus, I want to learn from you. Show me how to have the attitude that
you had when you came to earth and lived among us. Teach me to be grateful
instead of being proud.

What Are You Bringing?

Wise words bring many benefits, and hard work brings rewards.

PROVERBS 12:14

Children tend to think that the things they count on for daily life just show up—that food, clothes, and toys just appear out of thin air, or that when we run out of money, we can simply go to the bank and get more. In their innocence, they often do not see the effort their parents make on a daily basis to ensure that all of their needs are met. But adults know all too well the effort and commitment necessary to provide our families with a comfortable life.

The fact is, everything we do in life leads to a benefit or a consequence, and the acts that create benefits will always require extra effort. But the energy is well spent. God identifies "wise words" and "hard work" as two ways that we can bring good things to our lives. Foolish words and laziness require less effort, for sure, but they also usually lead to unpleasant consequences. Putting extra effort into the right actions is always the right choice.

ASK YOURSELF

» In what areas of your life do you tend to take the path of least resistance?

» Should every aspect of life require equal effort? How do you prioritize where to focus your hard work?

ASK GOD

Dear Lord, I want to do the things that will bring good results in my life. Give me your wisdom, Lord, and show me the benefits of putting forth effort in all I do. Where I am slacking, show me what I should do.

Why the Angels Watch

Be truly glad. There is wonderful joy ahead, even though you must
endure many trials for a little while. . . . It is all so wonderful that
even the angels are eagerly watching these things happen.

1 PETER 1:6, 12

You already know that the road to joy and gladness is paved with many trials. But did you know that angels are eagerly watching as you encounter and overcome these trials? They watch because they are in awe of what Jesus and the power of his love have done—and will do—for you.

According to the author of Hebrews, future joy was a motivator for Jesus as he prepared to die on our behalf: "Because of the joy awaiting him, he endured the cross, disregarding its shame" (12:2). Our trials are nothing compared to his, of course. But his example of anticipating joy can help us as we struggle to take our lives back. Knowing that healing and recovery await us on the other side of our trials can help us endure whatever it takes to get there.

ASK YOURSELF

> » What good things do you anticipate on the other side of your trials?
> What do you think your healing and recovery will feel like?

> » Do you usually think of your current trials as just something you must
> endure in order to get where you want to be? How can they actually
> help in your recovery?

ASK GOD
Dear Jesus, I have already faced some trials, and I know there will be others ahead. Help me keep my eyes on you as I go through them, and remind me of the joy that is waiting for me as I endure each trial.

The Bright Side

We can rejoice, too, when we run into problems and trials.

ROMANS 5:3

When was the last time you thanked God for the troubles in your life? That is what he wants you to do. Why? He wants you to see the light at the end of the tunnel, the pot of gold at the end of the rainbow—the potential for him to bring joy from your sorrow.

The secret to finding the bright side of any seemingly negative situation is to hold on to the promises of God. He has promised us that the ultimate outcome of every situation in our lives will be for our good as long as we hold on to loving him (see Romans 8:28).

Think about that. We have a promise from the Maker of this universe. His Word tells us that he will take whatever Satan intends for evil and use it for good instead. If we believe this promise, nothing should be able to darken our days.

We already know the end of the story—we win!

ASK YOURSELF

» Do you ever find it hard to believe that God will use all the troubles in your life for your ultimate good? Why or why not?

» Does it feel odd or insincere to thank God for your problems? How could you get past that feeling?

ASK GOD

Dear Lord, I do not want to let the difficulties in my life overwhelm or sidetrack me as I pursue the life you have planned for me. Make your Word real to me, and remind me to give my problems to you instead of wasting my time with worrying.

Help My Unbelief

The father instantly cried out [to Jesus], "I do believe,
but help me overcome my unbelief!"

MARK 9:24

Have you ever left the house and then started second-guessing yourself? *Did I turn off the stove? Did I lock the door? Is the dog outside?* Such haunting doubts can ruin anyone's day. And those are just little doubts, the kind that simply waste time. What about bigger questions that occasionally plague the most faithful of us? *Does God really love me? Does he even exist?*

It is human nature to doubt, to double-check, to question. A little doubt can even be a good thing, causing us to examine our beliefs—or go back and turn off that stove. But doubt can also choke our confidence and drain our faith. It can keep us paralyzed, afraid to act. It can prevent us from accomplishing what is important to us and hamper our obedience to God.

So what can we do about our doubt?

Interestingly, one of the best ways to fight doubt is *not* to fight it. Instead of denying or banishing your questions, bring them to God. Be honest about your doubt and ask him for help. And then . . . do something. Act on whatever faith you do have. And Jesus, "who initiates and perfects our faith" (Hebrews 12:2), will give you more.

ASK YOURSELF

> » Do you tend to be a doubter? What kinds of questions are apt to occupy or overwhelm your mind?

> » How can you tell the difference between healthy, useful doubt and crippling doubt?

ASK GOD

Father in heaven, I don't want my doubts to paralyze or overwhelm me, so I'm giving them to you and trusting you to build my faith. Please help with my unbelief.

You Don't Have to Understand

*How great are God's riches and wisdom and knowledge! How
impossible it is for us to understand his decisions and his ways!*

ROMANS 11:33

Do you understand exactly how your smartphone or your computer works—
how surges of electricity and tiny little bits of plastic and metal translate into
words and pictures that can connect people around the world? Probably not.
But has that fact kept you from using your computer or smartphone? Again,
probably not. You don't have to fully understand all of the ins and outs of
something in order to benefit from it.

God gives you access to all of himself through Jesus. Will you ever fully
understand his majesty and all of his ways? Of course not. But that should
never keep you from trusting in him. The Lord counsels you not to "depend on
your own understanding" (Proverbs 3:5) because he knows that it's impossible
for us humans to comprehend the things of God.

When you are struggling with trusting God because you don't understand
how or why he would be willing to help you, remember how many things you
use every day that you could never explain with your limited understanding.
Shouldn't you place as much trust in God as you do in the technological miracles that you use but cannot wrap your mind around?

ASK YOURSELF

» When have you hesitated to put your trust in God because you could
not understand what he was doing?

» Is there any area of your life today where you are not trusting God
because of your limited understanding?

ASK GOD

Father God, your ways are so much higher than mine. Keep me mindful that
I don't have to understand everything you do in order for you to move in my
life. Teach me to rest in you.

Knowing Real Love

*This is real love—not that we loved God, but that he loved us
and sent his Son as a sacrifice to take away our sins.*

1 JOHN 4:10

Do you ever find yourself trying to measure how much another person loves you? It's human nature to wonder, but it's also a waste of energy. Even if we could measure another person's love for us, that love will eventually let us down.

God made us with the need for love and the capacity to love, and he commands us to love one another. But even the best-intentioned human love will always be flawed because humans are flawed.

As children of God, we have an unlimited source of real love—the selfless agape love of God. God's love is the only love we will ever receive that is not based at least in part on what we can give in return. It's okay to cherish the love and attention of our earthly companions, but we will be far happier if we make God our first source of emotional fulfillment.

ASK YOURSELF

» How much do you depend on other people for your sense of being loved and valued?

» What would it mean in practical terms to make God your first source of emotional fulfillment? How would that help you take your life back?

ASK GOD

Dear Lord, I know that you put other people in my life for love and support, but don't let me depend on them for my happiness. Cause me to look to you, first and foremost, as the supplier of real love in my life.

The Power of Good Judgment

Leave your simple ways behind, and begin to live; learn to use good judgment.

PROVERBS 9:6

Think of your "simple ways" as the time before you began the process of taking your life back. Living reactively was exhausting and painful, but it was also relatively easy. No judgment was required. You behaved this way for so long that your reactions were practically automatic.

But recovery requires you to use good judgment before responding to something that happens. That takes effort, especially when you encounter new challenges and attempt new behaviors.

Showing good judgment means you make an effort to discriminate between the choices available to you. In the past, your judgment may have been clouded by your need for approval or your feelings of unworthiness. But that's the old way of thinking. Now you can begin to ask questions like, *Am I acting in a caring way because of the wrong motives? Am I able to help this other person and still take care of myself? Am I offering to do something the other person needs to do for himself?*

The more you use good judgment, the more naturally it will come to you—and the faster your healing will progress.

ASK YOURSELF

» What reactive behaviors are still automatic in your life? What behaviors are based on good judgment?

» What other questions have helped you increasingly use good judgment?

ASK GOD

God, I want to grow in my ability to use good judgment and to base my choices on my relationship with you. Help me in that effort to grow and to take my life back. Thank you.

Being Present to the Present

Don't worry about these things, saying, "What will we eat? What will
we drink? What will we wear?" These things dominate the thoughts of
unbelievers, but your heavenly Father already knows all your needs.

MATTHEW 6:31-32

When Jesus taught his disciples and the crowd that had gathered on the side of a mountain, he described a way of living that blesses people: Ask for enough bread for today, don't be enslaved by money, trust God to meet our needs. Knowing how we are wired, that we're prone to anxiety about both the past and the future, Jesus urged us to focus on the present moment, reminding us that our "heavenly Father already knows all [our] needs."

When we trust that Father, we're able to stay present to our lives. As we reject distraction and obsession, we choose to trust God in the moment. Instead of mulling endlessly over the past or fearing for the future, we can now experience the joy of being where we are and engaging with those who are here with us. As we keep our focus on present reality, we can experience God's goodness as never before.

ASK YOURSELF

» Which do you tend to do more—rehash the past or fear the future?

» How can you balance living in the present and trusting God for the rest with appropriately facing the past and planning for the future?

ASK GOD

God, I confess that left to my own devices I am prone to obsess about my past and fear the future I can't control. Father, because you have shown yourself to be trustworthy, I release control to you and trust you to meet all of my needs.

Your Real Home

Dear friends, I warn you as "temporary residents and foreigners" to keep
away from worldly desires that wage war against your very souls.

1 PETER 2:11

If we are following Jesus, we live in two worlds. We live in this present world, but we're also acutely aware, as the old gospel song puts it, that "this world is not [our] home." In Peter's words, we live in this world as "temporary residents and foreigners" because our real home—where we are citizens—is heaven.

The problem is that we've lived in the world for so long, it *feels* like home. We've invested our time and energy in worldly "stuff." And even after we give our lives to Jesus, we still face a battle between our worldly desires and our desire to please God. The battleground is inside us, and we win only when we let our desire to please God overcome everything else.

As you work to take your life back, always remember where your real home is.

ASK YOURSELF

» Describe some of the worldly desires you struggle with.

» Are these desires bad in themselves, or do they represent a challenge to your putting God first? How can you tell?

ASK GOD

Lord, I know my real home is in heaven with you, but I have a hard time remembering that. I want to care about eternal values. Help me to keep my focus on pleasing you.

Renewed

I will give you a new heart, and I will put a new spirit in you. I will take out
your stony, stubborn heart and give you a tender, responsive heart.

EZEKIEL 36:26

God is talking here about the people of Israel, who had grown stubborn and stuck in their ways and refused to listen to him. He assured them that a day was coming when all that would change and their hardened hearts would be replaced.

These words are for us as well. As years go by, it's easy for us to get set in our ways and become resistant to change—even good change. We wear ourselves out doing things the same old way—people pleasing, hiding from our feelings, neglecting to care for ourselves—and we're frustrated when our lives and our relationships don't improve. What we need to understand is that taking our lives back means changing on the inside. Opening ourselves up to new possibilities. Changing our hearts.

But notice that God says, "*I* will give you a new heart." This change is a gift from God that comes as we turn our lives and our wills over to him. It isn't earned; it's a gift based on our choice to do things his way.

ASK YOURSELF

> » Are you willing to receive a new heart from God? What could that mean for your life?

> » What's scary about a new heart? What will you miss the most from the old heart?

ASK GOD

Dear God, I want to grow and heal, but I'm also set in my ways and afraid of change. Help me to remember that you give only good gifts, and that I won't be able to take my life back without the tender new heart you offer. I am willing to receive your gift.

Faithful in Darkness

*Even when I walk through the darkest valley, I will not be afraid, for you
are close beside me. Your rod and your staff protect and comfort me.*

PSALM 23:4

Can you recall, in your bones, what it's like to be alone in the dark and feel absolutely terrified? Perhaps you've experienced this terror when you felt like someone was following you in a dark alley or parking lot. Or perhaps you were in a more rural location and feared the bite of a snake or the jaws of a bear. Maybe as a child you felt afraid in your own home, even your own bedroom.

In Psalm 23 the psalmist affirms his confidence in God by comparing the Lord to a caring and protective shepherd. When a sheep finds herself in the darkness of a nighttime valley—the place where she is most vulnerable—she depends on her shepherd's rod and staff to fight off predators and preserve her life. And like that shepherd, the psalmist says, God is faithful to protect us.

In your own times of darkness, ask the Spirit to open your eyes to the Good Shepherd's nearness. God can be trusted to protect and comfort you when you're most afraid.

ASK YOURSELF

» Is there a fear that has hold of you today? Name it if you can.

» In what ways can you trust God to help you with your fears?

ASK GOD

Jesus, you called yourself the Good Shepherd, and you have promised to protect, comfort, and guide me when I find myself in darkness. I put my faith in you today.

True Worship

The time is coming—indeed it's here now—when true worshipers will
worship the Father in spirit and in truth. . . . God is Spirit, so those
who worship him must worship in spirit and in truth.

JOHN 4:23-24

Jesus said this in response to a question from the Samaritan woman he met at a well: *Should we worship in Jerusalem or at Mount Gerizim?* This was a major point of contention between Jews and Samaritans in that day. But like many worship questions—such as arguing over the music at church—it completely missed the point. Jesus countered with two life-changing points of his own about what matters in worship.

First, it's not *where* we worship that counts—it's *who* we worship. And second, true worship means being *truthful*. Instead of acting hypocritically or showing off for others, we approach God honestly. We are genuine. We stand before him with openness and vulnerability, aware that he knows our hearts.

This teaching on worship can be life-changing for us today. We can worship anywhere, but we need to be clear about who we're worshiping, and we need to worship with total honesty.

ASK YOURSELF

» As you worship God, are you transparently honest and open before him? If not, what tends to hold you back?

» Describe as many of God's characteristics as you can, and praise God for them.

ASK GOD

Almighty God, I worship you for who you are. You alone are worthy of my worship. Help me remember to be honest and transparent before you and to truly worship you with all of my being.

He Knows

*Worship and serve him with your whole heart and a willing mind. For
the LORD sees every heart and knows every plan and thought.*

1 CHRONICLES 28:9

Do you find it a little daunting that your phone and your computer know exactly what you have an interest in? With today's technology, few of us have many secrets. Data has been collected about our likes and dislikes, our shopping habits, our finances, our age, our health, and much more.

But this massive collection of information is nothing compared to what God knows about us. He knows the things that no one can track. He knows "every plan and thought" that we have. He "sees every heart," and he knows what is inside them. It's silly to even consider trying to hide something from him—yet many of us have tried. Perhaps we have believed God would punish us or abandon us if he knew what we were really like.

But God *does* know. That's the point. He's aware of every failure, every mixed motive, every moral shortcut—and he loves us anyway. Why would we ever want to hide from that love?

ASK YOURSELF

> » Is there something in particular about yourself that you wish no one knew—including God? Would you consider confessing that to him, knowing he is aware of it anyway?

> » How does it feel to realize that God knows all your thoughts and all your plans?

ASK GOD

Dear God, you know everything there is to know about me, and you choose to love me anyway. There are things that I hide from others, but I cannot hide them from you. Thank you for being patient with me as I struggle to become the person you have always intended me to be.

How Do You Measure Up?

No one can ever be made right with God by doing what the law
commands. The law simply shows us how sinful we are.

ROMANS 3:20

Standards are designed to show people where they are in relation to what is expected of them. For example, employers give sales representatives a monthly quota to measure their success or failure at work. Schools issue grades to help children evaluate where they stand in regard to their learning goals. And God's laws and commandments show what we need to do in order to please him.

But while salespeople and students do have a chance of measuring up to standards at work and school, not one of us has a chance of measuring up to what God requires. When we try, we fail miserably. None of us will ever be good enough on our own to meet God's standards and get into heaven.

That is why Jesus died on the cross. Jesus makes us good enough. When we stop trying to be good enough, do enough, and be nice or righteous enough and simply live our lives in Jesus and through him, that is when we will measure up to what God wants. That's part of taking our lives back.

ASK YOURSELF

» Have you ever fallen into the trap of trying to earn God's approval through your good deeds? What was the result?

» If you really believed that trusting Jesus makes you good enough for God, how would your life change?

ASK GOD

Dear Lord, I know that in my own strength I will always fall short of the standards you have set for righteousness. Thank you for sending Jesus to die in my place so that I can please you and someday live with you in heaven.

Go to the Source

I pray that God, the source of hope, will fill you completely
with joy and peace because you trust in him.

ROMANS 15:13

How many times have you suffered through trying times, stressed and depressed, simply because you went to the wrong place for relief?

When your car needs gas, where do you go? You go to the gas station because that is where the gas is.

When you are in need of groceries, you don't go to the library, do you? Of course not. You go to the grocery store because that is where the groceries are.

So where do you go when you are in need of peace, joy, and hope in your life? To God! He is the original source of all these good things. You can trust him to fill you up.

ASK YOURSELF

» Do you ever neglect to ask for the peace of God in your life when you need it? Where do you typically turn instead?

» Are there times when you seek to meet your spiritual needs with temporal fixes? Why do you think you do this?

ASK GOD

Dear heavenly Father, at times I struggle through the difficulties in my life and do not trust you to help me with them. I know that the peace and joy I so desperately need are only available from you, and yet I hesitate to ask you for them. Please help me remember to depend on you for my peace, joy, and hope.

You're Already a Winner

The God of peace will soon crush Satan under your feet.
May the grace of our Lord Jesus be with you.

ROMANS 16:20

What would happen if the outcome of a big boxing match was secretly determined beforehand—and only the predetermined winner knew? That boxer would walk into the ring with supreme confidence because he knew he couldn't lose.

Our spiritual lives are a lot like this. God's Word says that in the fight between good and evil, God will win and Satan will ultimately be defeated. He'll fight as hard as he can, but his defeat is already ensured. So the question is, are you walking around with confidence in what you already know?

"The God of peace will soon crush Satan under your feet." How powerful is this knowledge? No matter what you encounter in your day, no matter what the outcome may look like, no matter how it feels at the moment, because of what Jesus did on the cross . . . you will win.

ASK YOURSELF

» Do you approach your life with the attitude of one who knows he or she is on the winning side? If not, what do you think gets in your way?

» What is the best thing to do when fear or dread fills your mind?

ASK GOD

Dear God, thank you for defeating Satan and making him no more than a nuisance in my life. Keep me mindful of the power that I have through Jesus, and let me approach every day of my life with the confidence that comes from knowing I am on the winning side.

More than the Sparrows

Not a single sparrow can fall to the ground without your Father knowing
it. And the very hairs on your head are all numbered. So don't be afraid;
you are more valuable to God than a whole flock of sparrows.

MATTHEW 10:29-31

Has there been someone in your life who knew you intimately and received you exactly as you were? Perhaps it was a warm and gracious grandmother. Maybe it was a teacher or someone at church. If you've had just one person like that in your life, you're fortunate, because one of the deepest human longings is to be fully known and valued for who we are.

When he gathered up his disciples for a heart-to-heart talk, Jesus didn't teach them that all *people* are valuable, but that every *person* is known and valued by God as an individual. God keeps track of each teeny sparrow in a massive flock. And God keeps track of us, too, down to the individual hairs on our heads. Jesus insists that God knows each of us intimately and that we are precious to him as individuals.

ASK YOURSELF

» Is there a person who has let you know that you're uniquely valued? Have you ever thought of him or her as an extension of God's very personal love for you?

» In what other ways has God shown his personal love to you? Are there some ways you may have missed because you weren't looking for them?

ASK GOD

God who created heaven and earth, thank you that you know me inside and out and that you love all of me. Strengthen my heart today to know in my deep places that I belong to you and that you care for me as an individual.

Before Confession

You can't heal a wound by saying it's not there!

JEREMIAH 6:14, TLB

A critical part of taking our lives back is being honest with God, being honest with other people, and being honest with ourselves. That's really what the act of confession is about—facing the truth and acknowledging it. But before we can confess and receive healing, we have to do the hard work of *seeing* the truth. To do that, we must submit ourselves to the truth of God's Word and God's Spirit.

Just as we depend on a doctor to diagnose a physical ailment so a prescription for healing can be offered, we must allow the Spirit to identify our spiritual ailments. And then we must summon the courage to accept the diagnosis and submit to treatment. That's where the honesty comes in. We have to acknowledge what is wrong with us—the sins we have committed and the sins that have been committed against us. Once we do that, we can move on to confession.

ASK YOURSELF

» Have you ever delayed recognizing and treating the real cause of an emotional wound? What was the result?

» What practices can help open your eyes to wounds and sins you need to recognize?

ASK GOD

God who heals, I know I've shut my eyes to sins and situations I've not wanted to face. Open my eyes so that I might approach my life honestly, confess my sin, and find true healing.

No Shame

We know that our old sinful selves were crucified with Christ so that sin might lose its power in our lives. We are no longer slaves to sin.

ROMANS 6:6

Shame is a dreadful companion and a powerful adversary. Many people live with debilitating habits that are fueled by shame from their past. But it doesn't have to be that way. Just as the Lord took your sin and removed it "as far . . . as the east is from the west" (Psalm 103:12), he is ready to take the shame you bear and destroy the power that it has over you. But this requires an action on your part. You must give it to him.

You may feel that your shame has been well earned, that it is payment for the things you have done wrong and is your burden to bear. If Jesus had not died on the cross for your sins, you would be correct. However, since you no longer own the sin, why would you hold on to the shame associated with it? You need to consciously give your shame to God and let him dispose of it. You are carrying around garbage that belonged to "your old sinful self." Let it go.

ASK YOURSELF

» Are you still holding on to guilt and shame that are hindering your growth in Christ? Why do you think you have such a hard time letting go of these feelings?

» What remnants of your old self do you need to release to God?

ASK GOD

Dear God, I know I am a new creature in you. You made the ultimate sacrifice to remove my sins from me, and I don't want to belittle your sacrifice by holding on to shame and guilt from my past. Help me to look my old self in the face and then let it go.

God Is Orderly

God is not a God of disorder but of peace, as in all the meetings of God's holy people.

1 CORINTHIANS 14:33

Imagine you've been sent into the jungle in search of an exotic animal you've never seen before. You have no physical description or image you can refer to. How likely is it that you can find the animal? Not very.

But what if you were provided a list of the animal's habits and attributes—what the animal is like and what it is not like, how it typically acts and how it does not act? Now do you think you could locate the mystery animal?

That might be a farfetched analogy, but it tells us a lot about how we can recognize God at work in the world. The more we know about what he is like and what he isn't like, what he does and doesn't do, the better able we'll be to do that. And how do we learn what God is like? We should test everything against God's Word.

Today's Scripture gives an example: If we see chaos and misrule in a situation, we can be pretty sure God is not involved. Because God is "not a God of disorder but of peace."

ASK YOURSELF

> » Have you ever wondered whether a given situation was "of God"? What made you wonder? What did you conclude?

> » Are you willing to study God's Word to become familiar with all of God's attributes? Where will you begin?

ASK GOD

Dear Father, I want to see you. I want to know everything about you—what you like and what you detest. Help me to spend time in your Word so I can learn everything possible about you. Show yourself to me, Lord.

Checking Your Fruit

The Holy Spirit produces this kind of fruit in our lives: love, joy, peace,
patience, kindness, goodness, faithfulness, gentleness, and self-control.

GALATIANS 5:22-23

If you have an apple tree and the fruit is less than perfect, you can look at the growing environment to see why. The tree may not be getting the correct fertilizer or enough water. Perhaps it has been planted in the wrong climate or has been attacked by insects or disease. Whatever the reason, if growers are on the lookout for signs of trouble, they can correct the problems before the fruit is destroyed.

The fruit in your life is similar to the fruit of a tree. If you are consistently nourished by the Word of God and watered with the presence of the Holy Spirit, you will yield much good fruit. But even in the perfect environment, be aware that the enemy can send a barrage of attacks designed to destroy the good fruit that is growing in your life. Be watchful and take action when an attack presents itself. Call on the Lord to defeat the enemy. He will protect your fruit.

ASK YOURSELF

» Are you getting the nourishment that you need to produce good fruit in your life? If not, how could you get more?

» What can you do to be more proactive about the attacks on your spiritual life?

ASK GOD

Dear Lord, I sometimes wander through life with my eyes closed to the attacks of the enemy. Help me be aware of those times when my spiritual life is under attack, and remind me to call upon you for protection. I want to live a life that is full of the fruit your Spirit produces.

Know When to Run

Run from anything that stimulates youthful lusts. Instead,
pursue righteous living, faithfulness, love, and peace. Enjoy the
companionship of those who call on the Lord with pure hearts.

2 TIMOTHY 2:22

If you are on a diet, you don't sit in a pastry shop. If you are abstaining from alcohol, you don't go to a bar. If you are on a tight budget, you don't hang out at the mall. And if you don't want to be deceived by the enemy, you don't put yourself in situations where he hangs out.

If you give your mind just a little leeway, it can take an entire journey before you can catch up with it. This is why it is so important for us as Christians to know when to "run." Do not allow yourself to be placed in situations where you know you will be tempted to do things that are not in your best interest. More important, deliberately place yourself in situations and with people that build you up and bring you closer to the life God has for you.

ASK YOURSELF

» What situations have you placed yourself in that could cause you to stumble?

» Does the need to "run" from situations where you might be tempted mean that you should only spend time with people who believe exactly as you do? Why or why not?

ASK GOD

Dear Lord, I need your wisdom to guide my life. Help me know which situations I should avoid and which I should seek out. Cause me to spend time with those who will bring me closer to the life you want me to experience. Teach me when to run and when to stay.

Fair–Weather Friends

When you had eaten and were satisfied, you became proud and forgot me.

HOSEA 13:6

Have you ever had one of *those* friends? You know, the kind who come around only when they need something and who disappear as soon as their needs have been met? Although we may care about such fair-weather friends in spite of the way they treat us and may even give them what they ask for, such one-sided relationships can't help but be disappointing.

But isn't this the way we sometimes treat God? We hit him up when we need something. We plead for his help and make all kinds of empty promises. But once we have what we want, we more or less forget about him. And how do you think this makes him feel? He listens to us because he loves us, but our attitude must still hurt.

God desires an ongoing relationship with each of his children—when we are in need and when our lives are going just fine. If we want our relationship with him to flourish, we can't only turn to him when we have a problem and ignore him otherwise. We must make him a part of everything we do.

ASK YOURSELF

> » Have you ever been guilty of seeking God only when you needed something? Would you say you have this kind of unbalanced relationship now?

> » What changes can you make to develop a deeper relationship with the Lord?

ASK GOD

Dear Lord, sometimes I don't show proper appreciation for your love and provision. Once you have met my needs, I go about my life as though you don't exist. Forgive me for being a fair-weather friend, and show me how to stay close to you every minute of every day.

God Listens and Responds

I love the LORD because he hears my voice and my prayer
for mercy. Because he bends down to listen.

PSALM 116:1-2

An unidentified psalmist wrote about a time when he had hit bottom in his life and all hope seemed gone. He described the experience this way:

Death wrapped its ropes around me;
the terrors of the grave overtook me.
I saw only trouble and sorrow. (verse 3)

He knew his position was hopeless, but he knew where to look for hope. He turned his will and his life over to God's care—and God responded.

He has saved me from death,
my eyes from tears,
my feet from stumbling. (verse 8)

When we are worn down and feel that life is just too much, we can take a lesson from the psalmist, who prayed honestly to God and found that God stepped in and saved him. We may not be facing death, but most of us know what it's like to feel hopeless. Turning to God, we can use our low points to launch us into a new level of recovery and healing.

God bends down to listen and respond when we cry out to him.

ASK YOURSELF

» Think of a time when you sensed that God bent down and listened to you. What was different from other times when you talked to God?

» How do honesty and humility affect your sense that God is listening?

ASK GOD

Lord, help me to trust the reality that you listen to me when I call to you.

Cool, Calm, and Wise

A fool is quick-tempered, but a wise person stays calm when insulted.

PROVERBS 12:16

It is easy to be foolish. Just do the first thing that pops into your head! Foolishness takes no effort because it is human nature personified. It's also the essence of reactive living. Do whatever comes to mind with little thought for consequences, and you have mastered foolishness.

Being wise takes more effort. It requires some thought, some self-control, and a desire to be better than you are inclined to be. Wisdom is a treasure, but you don't find most treasure lying on top of the ground. You must dig for it. Wisdom does not come naturally, and acquiring it is more difficult for some than for others, but it is always worth the effort. It's also key to taking back your life.

Do you tend to speak before you think? Do you react rashly when someone is rude to you? Do you often have to go back and apologize after you've lost control or reacted badly? You can change—and your life will be better for it. Take a good look at your own behavior, and ask God to help you make the corrections required to live more wisely.

ASK YOURSELF

» Think about your actions and reactions on a recent day. If you were asked to graph these on a chart showing wisdom and foolishness, what would the graph look like? What kinds of situations tend to trigger unwise reactions in you?

» What strategies could you adopt to help you respond more wisely to what happens to you?

ASK GOD

Dear God, I want to live a life that is based on wise choices. Show me your ways, Lord. Teach me to think and pray before I act.

Unsafe Seeking

I will also turn against those who commit spiritual prostitution by putting
their trust in mediums or in those who consult the spirits of the dead.

LEVITICUS 20:6

It is tempting to want to know the future, to get a glimpse into a side of life that is not readily available to us. There is something compelling about knowing what is to come or what is on the other side. The desire for such knowledge can be a magnetic force that draws us in, but it is not something we should be drawn into. God's Word likens these activities to "spiritual prostitution."

If you have no interest in fortune-telling, mediums, and the like, good for you. If you are intrigued by such things, even as entertainment, be careful.

The Word of God was written to communicate with you. Every line was chosen carefully and purposefully. And like it or not, God means what he says. He makes it clear that attempts to see into the spirit world through any means other than what he gives you will cause him to turn away from you. If you really want to see into the world beyond, look in God's Word.

ASK YOURSELF

> » Are you drawn to spiritual "entertainment" that you should not be involved in? Why do you think this is so appealing to you?

> » Why do you think God warns against dabbling in the spirit world?

ASK GOD

Dear God, show me how to live the way you want me to. If I am involved in things that are harmful to my relationship with you, please make me aware of them so that I can change. Cause my spirit to be in tune with yours so that I do not stray into areas that are not good for me.

Getting Your Fix

You will keep in perfect peace all who trust in you, all whose thoughts are fixed on you!

ISAIAH 26:3

Focus is a powerful force. Once our minds really "lock in" on something, we can do things we never thought we could.

Think about it. What have you accomplished in life because you set your mind to it? A degree? A certain job? Eliminating a bad habit or acquiring a good one? Perhaps even finding a soul mate?

The mind is unstoppable when it is fixed on a task.

That's the kind of focus the Lord looks for in our relationship with him. He wants us to fix our thoughts on him and to trust him in all we do. If we can do this, he says we will experience a life-changing transformation. We will experience "perfect peace."

And no, this isn't always easy. Some of us are more distractible than others, and the turmoil in our lives shows it. But each time we choose to deliberately shift our focus back to God, to fix our minds on him once more, we'll come to the perfect peace we crave.

ASK YOURSELF

» How has focus helped you accomplish good things in the past? What motivated you to keep that focus?

» Is focus a challenge for you? What is the fallout of that distractibility in your life? What could you do to shift your focus back to God?

ASK GOD

Dear Lord, I am so easily distracted by the things that life brings my way, and I don't want to be. Teach me how to lock my thoughts in on you, and help me to trust you fully. I want to experience the perfect peace you have offered me.

Shelter from the Storm

The LORD is good, a strong refuge when trouble comes.
He is close to those who trust in him.

NAHUM 1:7

In many communities across the United States, storm shelters are common. People have learned that by securing themselves in an underground fortress before a tornado strikes, they can remove themselves from the risk of danger. But in order for the shelter to work, people need to be near it when the storm hits.

God is your shelter in this life. He is able to protect you from any trouble that comes your way, provided you stay close to him. So how do you stay close to God? How can you make sure that you have access to his "strong refuge" when difficulties strike?

God's Word says that "he is close to those who trust in him." That's the key. Trust in God completely and know that he will be there to protect you when the need arises. In him you have a portable shelter that surrounds you wherever you go.

The more you trust in God, the closer he is. Abide in him every minute of every day, and he will keep you safe.

ASK YOURSELF

» Do you have difficulty trusting God to take care of you in all situations? Why?

» What are some strategies that help you stay close to God?

ASK GOD

Dear God, it is such a comfort to know that you are always there to protect me when I stay close to you. You make it so easy to do that, and yet I sometimes complicate it. Help me to simply trust in you and know that is enough.

After a Little While

*In his kindness God called you to share in his eternal glory by means of
Christ Jesus. So after you have suffered a little while, he will restore, support,
and strengthen you, and he will place you on a firm foundation.*

1 PETER 5:10

Have you ever broken a bone? It's a frightening, painful, and debilitating experience, but it's not permanent. The healing process isn't pleasant, however. There will be some suffering, some discomfort, and a great deal of frustration before the bone mends. But with the proper correction and support, eventually the bone will be stronger than before.

Life on earth is a lot like this. The Bible says plainly that in this life we *will* experience suffering—ouch!—but that the suffering we experience is temporary. We will spend eternity with the Father "*after* [we] have suffered a little while." In the meantime, like the casts, braces, and other tools that support the healing of a broken bone, God is correcting you, shaping you, and strengthening you. In the process you will have some discomfort, but ultimately you will be on a firm foundation for eternity.

ASK YOURSELF

» Do you have any brokenness in your life that seems like it will never be fixed? What are the circumstances?

» Does the understanding that you are being perfected for eternity help you bear the suffering you are going through? Why or why not?

ASK GOD

Dear Lord, thank you for caring enough about me to take the time to correct me, shape me, and heal me. Help me not to grumble when the process hurts. I am grateful that you love me enough to prepare me for perfection in eternity.

The Pit

I waited patiently for the LORD to help me, and he turned to me and heard
my cry. He lifted me out of the pit of despair, out of the mud and the mire.
He set my feet on solid ground and steadied me as I walked along.

PSALM 40:1-2

If you aren't in the pit of despair right now, there has most likely been a season of your life when you were. Or—spoiler alert—there will be one in the future. The proverbial "pit" is deep. It's dark. It's lonely. And when we're down there, it's easy to wonder whether anyone, especially God, cares at all.

Having been rescued from the pit, the psalmist testifies to what is most true about that desperate experience of feeling swallowed up by despair. The truth is that no matter how it feels at the time, God does hear our cries in such times. Our tears and prayers aren't absorbed by the muddy walls. They reach God's ears. And he's going to rescue us.

We may have to wait for it. (God's timing isn't always the same as ours.) But eventually God will tip his face toward ours, reach down to lift us to safety, set us on solid ground, and steady us as we begin to walk again.

ASK YOURSELF

> » Have you ever experienced the pit of despair? What was it like for you? How did you get out?

> » Why do you think you often have to wait for rescue? What can you learn while you're down there in the pit?

ASK GOD

God, you have made yourself known as one who rescues your people. You led your people through the mighty sea, and you delivered your Son from death. Lord, I'm waiting. Please be my Helper today.

The Unexpected Response

See that no one pays back evil for evil, but always try
to do good to each other and to all people.

1 THESSALONIANS 5:15

The world thinks it very normal to pay back in kind. If someone hits us, we hit them back. If someone yells at us, we yell louder. If someone snubs us, we do the same. But what does all this payback get us? Loneliness, anger, emptiness, stress, and in some cases bruises.

God's Word contains instruction on every aspect of life, including how we should treat other people and how we should respond to the way others treat us. The Lord knows that we will be happier and healthier if we are kind to all and repay good for evil. But more important, he knows that if we follow these guidelines, other people will see the love of Christ in us. There is nothing more meaningful that you can contribute to this world than to let others see Jesus through you.

ASK YOURSELF

» How do you typically react when you have been wronged by someone?

» What would it take for you to return good for evil as the Bible tells you to?

ASK GOD

Dear Jesus, I need for you to walk beside me and show me how to love others as you do. I sometimes react much too quickly when I feel that I have been wronged. Help me to step back and really look at a situation before I give any kind of response. And when I do respond, let others see the love of Jesus in my actions.

Providing for Ourselves and Others

Make it your goal to live a quiet life, minding your own business and
working with your hands, just as we instructed you before.

1 THESSALONIANS 4:11

In his letter to the church in Thessalonica, Paul exhorts the body of believers to live holy lives. He warns the church to avoid sexual sin and to love one another. Paul also writes that living a quiet life and working with one's hands will be a witness to those who are not believers.

As we take our lives back, we do our best to be responsible and to provide for ourselves and others by working to earn money. That way, instead of needing so much from everyone else, we're able to provide for ourselves, help others, and even give back to the source of all goodness. But we don't work to the point of exhaustion, and we don't let our sense of self-worth depend on what work is available to us or how much we can earn. Instead, we trust God for provision and do what we can to keep our bodies and souls safe, protected, and healthy—even if that means working a little less. And when we give, we do it with grateful hearts, acknowledging that God has been present in every moment of our suffering and our surviving.

ASK YOURSELF

> » Are you able to provide for yourself today? If so, give thanks. If not, take this to the Lord and thank him for his provision.

> » In what ways are you equipped to give back to God and others?

ASK GOD

God, you have been a faithful Provider, and I long to reflect your generosity in my own living. Equip me to support myself and to be able to be generous to you and others from your bountiful gifts.

Perfectly Pampered

I have given rest to the weary and joy to the sorrowing.

JEREMIAH 31:25

Have you ever had one of those days where you feel so emotionally battered that you just want someone to take care of you? You wish that you could let go of everything and let someone else watch over you, perhaps even spoil you a bit. But how likely is that to happen?

If you are a child of God, it is very likely. The Lord longs to give you rest when you are overburdened and joy when you are downhearted. He wants to take away your stresses and replace them with joy, to take your weariness and turn it to exhilaration. But you have to let him. You have to recognize that you're at the end of your rope. And then, instead of wallowing in self-pity or lashing out in frustration, you need to turn to God for rest.

Be honest with God about how you are feeling—he knows anyway! He is just waiting for you to come to him so that he can care for you.

ASK YOURSELF

» Do you typically recognize when you have reached the limits of your human ability to cope? What do you do then?

» In practical terms, what does allowing God to care for you look like? How do you experience his comfort and rest?

ASK GOD

Dear Lord, help me to recognize when I am at the end of myself and to call out to you for comfort. Thank you for always being there for me in my time of need. I know I can always rest in you.

Direct Access

You haven't done this before. Ask, using my name, and you
will receive, and you will have abundant joy.

JOHN 16:24

Having direct access to a bank account, a computer system, or perhaps to private records indicates that we have some degree of status and recognition. It also simplifies life considerably because eliminating the middleman improves communication and saves resources. Direct access is a privilege to be treasured and used wisely, especially when it comes to our relationship with God.

For centuries, when God's people needed forgiveness for sin, they couldn't make a direct appeal. They had to go through an intermediary, a priest. Confession and forgiveness were filtered through these middlemen because human sin made it impossible for ordinary people to be in the presence of a holy God.

But the coming of Jesus changed all that. His life on earth, his death for our sake on the cross, and his resurrection cleansed us of our sin and gave us direct access to the Father. Anything we need from God, we can now ask for directly, and God will acknowledge us and answer.

What a privilege. And what a gift!

ASK YOURSELF

» How could you take better advantage of your direct access to the throne of God?

» Are you hesitant to approach God when you need something? What can you do to overcome this hesitancy?

ASK GOD

Heavenly Father, I know what a privilege it is to be able to speak to you directly and make my requests known to you. Help me to appreciate the relationship I now have with you and never to take it for granted nor let it go to waste.

Ask

Seek his will in all you do, and he will show you which path to take.

PROVERBS 3:6

Imagine that you walk into a restaurant and are seated. But instead of giving you a menu or asking what you want, the waiter just disappears into the kitchen and returns with a plate of food. It's fish. You hate fish. So the waiter runs back to the kitchen and brings out another dish. And he repeats the process again and again until he finally hits on something you like—or until you walk out. But he never once asks you what you want.

Ridiculous, right? Why would a waiter do that? But we do something similar to God all the time. We venture off without asking God what he wants us to do, and then we become frustrated when things go wrong.

God wants us to seek his will in everything we do. That means talking to him about our lives, asking questions, and listening to his answers. He promises to direct every step in our journey to take our lives back—but only if we *ask*. Why would we decline such an attractive offer—especially when the alternative is just to blunder about, hoping to get it right?

ASK YOURSELF

» Why do you think so many of us fail to ask for God's guidance?

» What are some things you've tried to figure out for yourself without asking for God's help? How did that work out for you?

ASK GOD

Dear God, without you I know I don't have a chance of getting my life right. You've promised to direct me if I ask, so I'm asking now. Help me to listen and obey.

Our Job Description

Go into all the world and preach the Good News to everyone.

MARK 16:15

Who doesn't appreciate a good job description, one that makes clear what is expected of us? Wise employers outline their expectations while still allowing employees the freedom to fulfill those expectations in their own way. The job description clarifies the overall responsibilities and objectives; the employee decides how to go about fulfilling them. And because we are all unique individuals, every person will go about accomplishing the same tasks in a different manner. How we reach the destination isn't so important. What matters is that we get there.

If we are Christians, our job description is clear. Jesus summed it up: "Go into all the world and preach the Good News to everyone." How's that for allowing creative freedom? We have the whole world as our workplace, and every person in it is our potential audience.

God has made each of us unique. He wants us to use our own special gifts and talents to spread his Word. It doesn't matter how we choose to do this. What matters is that we do.

ASK YOURSELF

> » If God were to review your "job performance" at this point in time, how would you fare?

> » What are some of the ways you have chosen to share the Good News? What are some other strategies you could try?

ASK GOD

Dear God, I know that sharing the Good News of salvation with others is my responsibility as a follower of Christ, but I don't do it often enough. Open my eyes to the opportunities that are all around me, and give me the courage to speak up. Please keep me from being complacent in this endeavor.

Relearning Trust?

Blessed are those who trust in the LORD and have made the LORD their hope and confidence. They are like trees planted along a riverbank, with roots that reach deep into the water. . . . Their leaves stay green, and they never stop producing fruit.

JEREMIAH 17:7-8

"No, no—don't do it!" Have you ever wanted to yell that at the screen when a TV character trusts the wrong person? You *know* the villain is bad news, but the victim doesn't have a clue. Tension builds as you wait for something bad to happen and—hopefully—for good to prevail.

For some of us, that tension is painfully familiar. When we were young, we naturally trusted our caregivers, but then we discovered they weren't entirely reliable. So in our subsequent relationships, we became more wary of trusting others.

But here's something interesting: Learning to trust God actually makes it easier to trust others. As we take our lives back and practice depending on the Lord instead of on other people, we become less needy and more secure. Then we can actually choose to trust others again, knowing they're not the ones responsible for our safety and well-being.

ASK YOURSELF

» Was there a person early in your life who wasn't entirely worthy of your trust? How has that affected your subsequent relationships?

» In what ways has God shown you that he can be trusted? Are you able and willing to trust him more as you learn to relate to others in healthier ways?

ASK GOD

Lord, I am so grateful that you can be trusted. Thank you for helping me grow as I choose to rely on you and for teaching me how and when to trust others so that my relationships can flourish.

A Purpose with Purpose

I replied, "But my work seems so useless! I have spent my strength for nothing and to no purpose. Yet I leave it all in the LORD's hand; I will trust God for my reward."

ISAIAH 49:4

Have you ever failed at something when you really wanted to succeed? Have you ever invested time and energy in a project that turned out to be unfulfilling? We've all been there at one time or another, and it feels awful.

But nothing in this life is without purpose if we put our trust in God. He can use every experience to build our relationship with him and help us take our lives back.

Perhaps he will teach us something through the experience that will help us succeed in the future. Perhaps he'll use the disappointment to move us in a different direction and give us a new, better purpose. Perhaps he'll just give us a new way of thinking that puts all our worldly failures in perspective. Whatever our failures, our disappointments, or our frustrations, we can put them all into his capable hands and trust him to work everything out.

ASK YOURSELF

» Do you tend to judge yourself too harshly when it comes to what you have accomplished—or not accomplished? Why do you think you have this tendency?

» What are some ways God has used your past failures to build your relationship with him?

ASK GOD

Dear Lord, I am quick to judge my performance in this life by human standards, but I know that your standards are the ones that really count. Help me to look at every experience in my life the way you look at it—as a chance for me to learn more and grow closer to you.

The Winner

Every child of God defeats this evil world, and we achieve this victory through our faith.

1 JOHN 5:4

Imagine the winner of a race refusing to accept her award because she just cannot believe she is good enough. The announcer calls her name and invites her to the stand. The presenter has the medal there with her name engraved on it. Everyone is watching and waiting . . . but the winner never moves from her place in the crowd.

Sounds ridiculous, doesn't it? What good does it do to run a race if you never claim your prize or acknowledge your winning position?

As a Christian, God has given you the ability to defeat the evil of this world. You are in the race. You have what it takes to win. In fact, God has promised that you *will* win. But do you have the faith to claim your victory?

Don't doubt your ability to make a difference in the life for which God has so masterfully equipped you. Step up and accept your position as the winner that God says you are as one of his children.

ASK YOURSELF

> » Have you ever missed out on what God has for you because you lacked faith? Are there things you could be doing in your life right now if you believed in yourself more?

> » How can accepting your winning position as a child of God help you take your life back?

ASK GOD

Dear God, I want to be a winner in this life. Show me how to grow my faith so I can experience the victory you have promised. Give me courage to step out boldly and take hold of everything you have given me through Jesus.

Eyes on the Prize

Foolishness brings joy to those with no sense; a sensible person stays on the right path.

PROVERBS 15:21

Have you ever seen a TV show—maybe like *Gilligan's Island*—where the character is just about to reach a milestone, but then is distracted by something silly and misses out on an opportunity that could have changed his or her life for the better? We certainly don't want to live it out in real life. And yet many of us find ourselves doing just that.

Any worthwhile achievement begins as a goal. And whether it's a spiritual goal, a professional goal, or a personal one, we're wise to have a plan for reaching it and we're sensible to stick with the plan. There will always be other interests and pursuits that seem to call to us along the way, but if they distract us from our goal, they're not worth pursuing. In the long run, that moment of frivolous fun will be forgotten, but the goals we accomplish will be with us forever.

If you want to be successful at taking your life back, keep your eyes on the prize.

ASK YOURSELF

» What are some of your spiritual, professional, and personal goals? Do you have plans in place for accomplishing them?

» Do you ever find yourself distracted or sidetracked on your journey of taking your life back? How can you keep your focus more successfully?

ASK GOD

Dear Lord, I want to accomplish so much, and I want to be wise in how I go about it. Please help me not to fall for the foolish distractions in this world. Teach me to keep my eyes on the target and my feet on the path.

Stress Relief

As pressure and stress bear down on me, I find joy in your commands.

PSALM 119:143

There's no way to avoid stress completely. And some stress can even be a good thing—improving motivation and creativity, boosting the immune system, and keeping us sharp and alert. But *too much* stress, especially when it's chronic, can damage our bodies, minds, and spirits. An important part of taking our lives back is learning to respond in healthy ways to the inevitable pressures we encounter.

One way to do this is to plan ahead. When we know what to expect and are well prepared to meet coming challenges, we can respond effectively and with less anxiety. Knowing we have support and guidance for making hard choices also cuts down on pressure and reduces stress damage. And learning to find comfort and rest in the midst of stressful situations is vital to reducing stress levels.

All these stress busters are available to us through God's Word and his presence in our lives. Because we know God is guiding us and because we know we can rest in him, we can remain confident and even joyful as the pressure mounts.

ASK YOURSELF

» What kinds of circumstances in your life tend to stress you out?

» How can the promises in God's Word prepare you to handle life events with less stress?

ASK GOD

Lord Jesus, I want to live a joyful life, not a frantic, stressed-out one. Help me remember to rely on you and your Word rather than trying to tough life out by myself. Teach me to face each day with a confidence that comes from trusting in you.

Heart of the Matter

Each heart knows its own bitterness, and no one else can fully share its joy.

PROVERBS 14:10

There is one place that each of us can go to truly be alone—our hearts. The Bible says no one else can fully feel the joy or pain that each of us carries inside us. And each of us is responsible for the condition of our hearts.

Whatever we take into our hearts affects the way we live and experience life. And whatever we choose to hold on to will tend to intensify—both the good and the bad. If you allow yourself to hold on to hurt or anger, for instance, it will grow into bitterness—a bitterness that you alone will bear. If you hold on to trust in God's love, you'll grow more and more confident and loving. So the more you can let go of the negative in your heart and hold on to the positive, the bigger steps you'll make in the journey of taking your life back.

ASK YOURSELF

» How do you respond to the idea that each of us is completely alone in our hearts? Does this feel like a good thing or a bad thing to you? Why?

» How would you go about taking inventory of what resides in your heart and letting go of the negative?

ASK GOD

Dear Lord, I am sometimes oblivious to what I am tucking away in my heart. I hold on to something and forget to give it to you. Then, before I know it, it has grown into something ugly. Help me to keep close track of what I am carrying in my heart—and only hold on to what is beautiful and good.

Be Prepared

A prudent person foresees danger and takes precautions. The
simpleton goes blindly on and suffers the consequences.

PROVERBS 27:12

Would you sail on a cruise ship whose captain did not review weather reports prior to sailing? Would you undergo surgery at the hands of a doctor who had no interest in your medical history or your current physical condition? How about investing your hard-earned money with a broker who made investments based on hunches and feelings rather than studied facts? Of course not.

Being prepared for what is likely to come our way—including potential problems—is a sign of wisdom. If we suspect that something less than ideal is likely to enter our lives, we should face the possibility, devise a plan for dealing with it, and move forward. Being prepared for the punches life can throw at us can be a source of immeasurable comfort.

Preparation is very different from worry, however. Wallowing in anxiety about what might happen is just as foolish as hiding our heads in the sand and refusing to plan. Instead, God wants us to look ahead, do what we can to get ready for what might come, and then trust him for the outcome.

ASK YOURSELF

> » Are you more likely to bury your head in the sand or to worry inces-santly about potential problems? What problems accompany each approach?

> » How can you plan responsibly yet trust completely?

ASK GOD

Dear Lord, I know that at times I either ignore potential problems in my life or worry too much about them. Show me the power that comes from preparing wisely and then trusting you for whatever comes.

The Best Defense

He will rescue the poor when they cry to him; he will help
the oppressed, who have no one to defend them.

PSALM 72:12

Has anyone ever stood up for you at a time when you could not stand up for yourself? Do you remember the relief you felt when you realized that you were safe because someone cared enough to help you? That's exactly what God does for his children.

How nice would it be to have your own personal bodyguard, someone who was looking out for your well-being 24-7? Surely that would change how you approached each situation in your life. You could take on any circumstance with confidence, knowing that someone had your back.

Around-the-clock protection is exactly what God has promised you. He is your Defender. You need only to cry out to him in your time of need, and he has promised to come to your rescue. His help might come in a form you weren't expecting, and you might not even realize what happened at the time, but his promise is dependable. You can count on him. What could be more comforting?

ASK YOURSELF

 » When you are in a defenseless position, are you more likely to immediately call on the Lord for help or to try to handle the situation yourself first?

 » What are some unexpected forms God's protection might take? Have you ever looked back and realized God was protecting you and you never even knew it?

ASK GOD

Dear God, I am so grateful that you are always there to protect me from harm. Help me to remember to ask for your assistance as soon as I have a problem and not after I have tried unsuccessfully to handle it myself.

Which Wisdom?

God has made the wisdom of this world look foolish.

1 CORINTHIANS 1:20

We need wisdom to make good choices. But not all wisdom is equal. More to the point, not all "wisdom" is godly.

Godly wisdom is taught in God's Word and grows in us as we live in relationship with him. And it can often seem foolish to the world at large, which has a different perspective and a different wisdom entirely.

Worldly wisdom isn't always wicked. Sometimes it's just limited. It advises saving for a rainy day, for instance, but has nothing to say about laying up treasures in heaven (see Matthew 6:20). But worldly wisdom can also actively contradict God's truth. It insists that might makes right, that we should always look out for number one, that whatever gets us through the night or keeps the wolf from the door is justified. From God's perspective, this cynical faux wisdom is utter folly and leads to destruction.

Every day of our lives calls us to make wise choices. But which wisdom will you choose—God's wisdom, which seems foolish to the world, or worldly wisdom, which isn't wise at all?

ASK YOURSELF

» How can you tell the difference between God's wisdom and worldly wisdom? If something *seems* right, does that mean it really *is* right?

» What are some examples of godly wisdom that might sound strange or foolish to the world?

ASK GOD

Heavenly Father, I want to look at life from your perspective, not the world's. Teach me your wisdom so that I can live my life to the fullest.

Get Your Thrills

You thrill me, LORD, with all you have done for me!
I sing for joy because of what you have done.

PSALM 92:4

Are you a thrill seeker? Do you love the rush of adrenaline that comes from risk or challenge—or the world's biggest roller coaster? Such thrill seeking isn't necessarily wrong, but it can become a problem if it leads to dangerous behavior—or if you become so focused on getting your excitement "fix" that you miss the deeper thrill of communion with God.

God knows that the excitement we find in this world will never satisfy us. It will always leave us wanting more—more risk, more challenge, more adrenaline, more danger. So in place of this world's "cheap thrills," God invites us to experience the real thing.

The thrill of being in God's presence may be quieter than a roller-coaster ride or a bungee jump, but it's infinitely more satisfying. It provides exhilaration with no regret or remorse. Experiencing God's energy in a personal way completes every aspect of your life.

Where are you seeking your thrills these days? Don't fall for the cheap imitations that this world has to offer. Go to the Source!

ASK YOURSELF

» Is thrill seeking a motivator in your life? Where do you go for your excitement "fix"?

» Are you skeptical that spending time with the Lord can bring the excitement that you crave? If so, what does that tell you about yourself?

ASK GOD

Dear Lord, I want to find my pleasure in you and to know the fullness of what you have made available to me when I get close to you. Let the biggest thrill in my life come through spending time in your presence. You are the only one who can satisfy.

Peace in Jesus

I have told you all this so that you may have peace in me. Here on earth you will
have many trials and sorrows. But take heart, because I have overcome the world.

JOHN 16:33

Jesus speaks these words to his disciples as he is about to be arrested and crucified. He has just finished explaining many things to them, including why he
has to die and who he will send to help them (the Holy Spirit). But even with
this preparation, he knew they were headed for tough times—times when they
would find it hard to remember what he had said and hard to believe in him.

We face times like that in our lives today. When we do, we can hold on to
two things in this verse.

First, peace is found *in* Jesus. That's why he tells us to abide in him. We
can rest in the security of our relationship with him, no matter what the
circumstances.

Second, he has overcome all the trials and sorrows of this world. He has
even overcome sin and its consequences. This is not something he will do
someday. It's already been accomplished. So when difficulties strike, we are to
keep our eyes on Jesus and trust him for strength and courage, knowing everything is working out the way it should.

ASK YOURSELF

» What differences can you describe between Jesus being in us and our
being in Jesus?

» How would you explain Jesus' words, "I have overcome the world"?

ASK GOD

Dear Jesus, this world seems so out of control. Help me to understand better
what you meant by overcoming it. Help me to see your hand in the mess and
to trust and rest more in you.

You Already Have the Answer

I take joy in doing your will, my God, for your instructions are written on my heart.

PSALM 40:8

Have you ever noticed how your spirit reacts to the choices you make in life? Maybe you choose to bend the truth a little with your spouse and feel a heaviness in your heart. Or you choose to give your lunch to someone who is not able to feed himself, and you feel a burst of joy and fulfillment.

The Bible says that God has written his instructions on our hearts, so it's no wonder we react this way. In fact, that little inner tug we feel is a good sign that we are actually paying attention to the presence of God in our lives. The key to living in God's will is learning to hear—and to heed—the "still, small voice" of the Holy Spirit inside of us.

When you are in doubt about how to proceed with any situation in your life, make it a point to stop and listen. You already have the answer deep inside. But you must choose to pay attention.

ASK YOURSELF

» Have there ever been times in your life when you consciously chose to ignore the "still, small voice" inside you? What happened as a result?

» How can you tell that an inner prompting is actually from God and not just a random thought? How can you recognize his voice more clearly?

ASK GOD

Dear Lord, I know your Spirit lives within me and communicates with me, even if I sometimes fail to hear or heed your voice. Give me ears to hear you, Lord, and a heart that is willing to obey.

Master Plan

Christ, as the Son, is in charge of God's entire house. And we are God's house,
if we keep our courage and remain confident in our hope in Christ.

HEBREWS 3:6

When a builder designs a house, he has a plan that will ensure the successful completion of the project. He knows the importance of a strong foundation and quality materials. He understands where support is necessary. He establishes the schedule and works with the finished house in mind. No one involved is more competent to call the shots than the builder.

God's Word says that you (as a believer in Christ) are his house and that Jesus "is in charge of God's entire house." God the Builder has a master plan for your life that you are not privy to. It is important that you trust him enough to listen to his instruction and to confidently move forward when he asks you to do something. Ignoring your builder's directions will lead to trouble. No one is better qualified to guide your construction than the one who designed you in the first place.

ASK YOURSELF

> » In what ways do you tend to fall into the trap of trying to design and construct your own life instead of letting God direct you?

> » Do you consciously listen for God's instruction in your daily life? How do you usually "hear" it?

ASK GOD

Dear Lord God, I want to develop into the person that you designed me to be. Help me to hear your voice and respond promptly to your direction. Remind me that I am the creation, not the Creator, and keep me from thinking that I know what is best for my life.

Changing Your Perspective

*My heart is confident in you, O God; my heart is
confident. No wonder I can sing your praises!*

PSALM 57:7

This world places a lot of value on being strong, confident, and self-reliant. And that's a good thing—to a point. It's smart to acknowledge our strengths and our talents, develop them to the best of our ability, and trust them. What is not smart is to place our confidence in ourselves alone.

The stresses and pressures of life are more than we humans can bear on our own. God wants us to be confident in ourselves and to recognize our abilities. He also wants us to share life with others and help each other appropriately. But he wants our ultimate confidence to be in him. If we learn to look to him first for guidance, protection, and sustenance, we'll be freed from the need to lean too much on others or rely on ourselves alone, and our joy and confidence will soar.

Trust in God. Praise him. Thank him for your abilities and make the most of them. Then rest in him and be joyful.

ASK YOURSELF

» Are you more likely to lean too much on others or to place too much trust in your own strength?

» What are some of the abilities, gifts, and talents God has given you? Are you making the most of these abilities?

ASK GOD

Dear God, thank you for all that you have enabled me to do and to be. Without you I am able to accomplish nothing of lasting value. Keep me mindful of the fact that my confidence should always be in you, not in other people or in myself alone.

What God Wants

It is impossible to please God without faith. Anyone who wants to come to him must believe that God exists and that he rewards those who sincerely seek him.

HEBREWS 11:6

When we set out to purchase gifts, we naturally want to make the recipients happy. And because everyone is different, we need to give careful thought to what each person likes. Books? Fragrance? Sporting goods? A gift card? This can be a challenging process, and we may despair of finding that perfect gift. We may even get to the point where we wish the recipients would just tell us what they want.

We don't have that problem when it comes to God. In his Word he tells us exactly what pleases him, so we don't have to guess.

God is pleased when we believe in him.

He is pleased when we trust him.

He is pleased when we want to be near him and when we obey him.

If we make seeking God a priority in our lives, we can be sure we're giving him exactly what he wants.

ASK YOURSELF

» What kind of reward do you think God gives us when we believe in him and "sincerely seek him"?

» Do you believe God is pleased with your life right now? Why or why not?

ASK GOD

Dear God, thank you for giving me your Word, which allows me to know you more intimately and tells me how I can please you. Help me to seek you in all that I do and to grow in faith every day.

How to Fear God

Show your fear of God by not taking advantage of each other. I am the LORD your God.

LEVITICUS 25:17

"Fearing God" as used in the Bible is not the same as being afraid of him. *Merriam-Webster's 11th Collegiate Dictionary* defines this kind of fear as having "a reverential awe." To fear God, in other words, is to understand just how powerful and holy he is. It's to take his bigness and his majesty seriously. It's to be so in awe of him that we wouldn't think of disobeying him or taking him for granted.

And how do we show this appropriate fear of the Lord? The book of Leviticus gives a practical example ("by not taking advantage of each other") that suggests a much larger theme. We show our healthy fear of God by listening to him, obeying his commandments, and doing our best to live his way—which means treating other people with respect as well.

We cannot truly fear the Lord and hurt or dishonor the people he loves.

ASK YOURSELF

» What might hold you back from showing God the respect and the reverence he deserves?

» What are some practical things you can do today to show your healthy fear of the Lord?

ASK GOD

Dear God, you are so loving and kind that I can easily put myself on your level, as though you were one of my earthly friends. Teach me to exalt you above all others, to fear you appropriately, and to live the way you want me to live.

Change When Hope Is Lost

Just then a woman who had suffered for twelve years with constant bleeding came up behind him. She touched the fringe of his robe, for she thought, "If I can just touch his robe, I will be healed." Jesus turned around, and when he saw her he said, "Daughter, . . . your faith has made you well." And the woman was healed at that moment.

MATTHEW 9:20-22

A woman who had been bleeding for twelve years really shouldn't have had any hope for getting her life back. Most likely her long search for relief had left her financially bankrupt, physically exhausted, emotionally spent, and spiritually weary. But if anything was ever going to change for her, she had to believe that healing was possible. The fact that she reached for the fringe of Jesus' robe proves that she did.

Maybe you're feeling exhausted, spent, and weary from your own journey. You may have all but given up on the possibility of change. But can you summon the merest smidgen of faith? Enough to lift your hand or your heart toward Jesus with trust that change might be possible? If you can do that, no matter what your circumstance, that hope won't be disappointed.

ASK YOURSELF

» Are you at a point in your journey when you're feeling exhausted? What specifically has worn you out?

» What are some ways that you can "touch the robe" of Jesus?

ASK GOD

Jesus, I confess that I feel beat up and weary. And yet as I fix my eyes on you, as I reach out to touch you, I believe you are the source of new life even for me. I'm putting my trust in you. Please don't let me go.

Sin Is Sin

Haughty eyes, a proud heart, and evil actions are all sin.

PROVERBS 21:4

"Nathan did it first!"

Children often try to extricate themselves from trouble or earn a lighter consequence by implicating a sibling in something worse.

This is how we, as immature Christians, sometimes react to sin in our own lives. We try to make ourselves look better by holding our sins up against someone else's and claiming ours are not as bad as theirs. But in God's eyes all sins are equally abhorrent.

Do you tend to categorize sin—identifying which sins outrank others, usually to justify the existence of sin in your own life? This is more common than you might think, but that doesn't make it any less foolish.

The Bible tells us that sin of any kind will separate us from God and that we're all equally in need of his remedy for sin: Jesus. Don't fool yourself into thinking one sin is worse than another. Sin is sin—period.

ASK YOURSELF

> » What are some of the "comfortable" sins in your life—the ones you tell yourself "aren't that bad"? What are the "biggies" that bother you most? Why?

> » If you were to develop zero tolerance for *any* sin in your life or the lives of others, what would have to happen?

ASK GOD

Dear God, I do not want to justify sin in my life. Show me how to see all sin for what it is—separation from you. Cause me to be just as incensed by one sin as I am by another, and help me strive to live a life that does not categorize any sin as minor.

Facing the Truth

Make them holy by your truth; teach them your word, which is truth. Just
as you sent me into the world, I am sending them into the world. And I give
myself as a holy sacrifice for them so they can be made holy by your truth.

JOHN 17:17-19

"Forgive and forget." "Let bygones be bygones." "Keep the past in the past."
"Don't poke a hornet's nest." Much of the popular wisdom in our culture
dissuades us from acknowledging the hurtful things that have shaped—or
misshaped—our hearts and minds today, especially the painful experiences
of our young years. The problem is that these catchy sayings—which support
our natural aversion to facing what may be difficult—keep us bound. They
keep us from healing our old relationships and repairing our current ones.

Healing always begins with acknowledging truth, and God strengthens us
to face it. Just as the truth of God's Word sanctifies us and makes us holy, facing
the truth of our experience and allowing God's truth to liberate us from the
past is how we heal today.

ASK YOURSELF

» Are you more likely to avoid looking at your past or to overanalyze it?
What are the pitfalls of either approach?

» Once you acknowledge the truth of your past, how can you move past it
toward healing?

ASK GOD

Faithful Father, I confess that it's often easier to avoid what happened in my
past. But because I trust you, I am willing to acknowledge the reality of my past
and release it into your care. Lord, teach me to face truth instead of hiding from
it—and then to forgive as you forgive.

Broken Hearts Healed

The LORD is rebuilding Jerusalem and bringing the exiles back to
Israel. He heals the brokenhearted and bandages their wounds.

PSALM 147:2-3

After the people of Israel sinned against God repeatedly, they were scattered from their homeland and suffered greatly in exile and captivity. But even though their exile was their own fault, God never gave up on them. In fact, he eventually brought them back to their lands and to himself. Then he began the process of bandaging their emotional wounds and healing their hearts.

All of us feel like exiles at times. We all know what it's like to be broken-hearted. And the pain isn't any less when we know we brought it on ourselves.

Whatever the cause of our heartbreak, God wants us to bring it to him. When we run to our heavenly Father with our pain, he responds the way any good parent does even with naughty children. He scoops us up, bandages our wounds, and cradles us in his arms of love as we recover. Yes, he will deal with our transgressions, but in the context of healing, not punishment. His dearest wish is for his children to be in his arms.

ASK YOURSELF

» Is there a hurt in your heart that's been slow to heal? Why do you think it has resisted healing?

» Do you find it harder to come to God with pain you brought on yourself? Why or why not?

ASK GOD

God who heals, I'm tired of carrying around the wounds of the past, and I long to be free. Today I commit to you my broken places—the pain from both the things I have done and the things that have been done to me. I put my faith in you as the Great Physician.

Jesus Gives Us Sight

The man they call Jesus made mud and spread it over my eyes and told me, "Go to the pool of Siloam and wash yourself." So I went and washed, and now I can see!

JOHN 9:11

In the ninth chapter of his Gospel, the apostle John spends some time describing an encounter between Jesus and a man who had been born blind. The disciples were curious about *why* the man was blind (see John 9:2). In the context of a culture that attributed misfortune to sin, they assumed someone must be at fault. Jesus' answer must have stunned them: "It was not because of his sins or his parents' sins. . . . This happened so the power of God could be seen in him" (John 9:3). Then, having set the disciples straight, he got down to the business of healing.

What Jesus did for that man he can do for us, both spiritually and emotionally. He takes the blinders off our eyes at last so that we can see those who wanted to control us and those who actually did. He reveals their manipulations, distortions, and denials—and our own as well. If we trust him and obey him, Jesus opens our eyes and shows us how to be healed.

ASK YOURSELF

» Describe a situation from your past when you were "blinded" for a period of time and just couldn't see the truth.

» How has God helped you to see what actually happened?

ASK GOD

Jesus, Son of God, you are the Light of the World! I thank you that you are in the business of giving sight. Remove the blinders from my eyes so that, with you at my side, I'll be able to see the truth of my experience at last.

Grown-Ups Being Grown Up

Then we will no longer be immature like children. We won't be tossed and blown about by every wind of new teaching. We will not be influenced when people try to trick us with lies so clever they sound like the truth. Instead, we will speak the truth in love, growing in every way more and more like Christ, who is the head of his body, the church.

EPHESIANS 4:14-15

If you've lived in a home with an adolescent, you know the teen years can be turbulent. These young people are buffeted by dramatic physical, emotional, and mental changes, and it can take them a while to adjust. In a variety of ways—from arguments to distancing behaviors, right down to choices about their appearance—they're prone to resist, justify, fight, and rebel. And while parents usually expect this bumpy passage, they also hope (and pray) it will pass quickly. They're as eager for their teens to grow up as the kids themselves are.

In his letter to the young church in Ephesus, the apostle Paul encourages believers to act like grown-ups. He expects us to make good choices and grow to look more and more like our Brother, Jesus. That was possible for the Ephesians, and it's possible for us as we surrender our lives to a God who is really there and who loves us.

ASK YOURSELF

» Do you know adults whose behavior resembles that of adolescents? Do you ever see such behavior in yourself? Give an example or two.

» What are you doing to grow into the likeness of Christ?

ASK GOD

Father of Jesus, I long to grow in maturity. Feed me with your Word and your wisdom so every day I will become more like Christ.

Embracing the New

We died and were buried with Christ by baptism. And just as Christ was raised from the dead by the glorious power of the Father, now we also may live new lives.

ROMANS 6:4

A baby in the womb has never known another life. That contained space is comfortable and familiar, if a little confined. And the process of birth might be frightening. But a baby who remained in the womb would never experience the potential she is destined to live out in the wider world.

When you received Christ as your Savior, you were "born again" into the Kingdom of God. You departed from the world you knew and entered a new life. But are you still hanging on to your old, familiar life as well? If so, you are like a baby who tries to return to the womb. Unless you let go of your past, you will never live fully in your new life.

That principle applies to recovery, too. Your old life might have been painful, but it was familiar. Your new, healthy life can be exhilarating but also challenging. You'll need courage and grace to take your life back and to embrace your new one. But the results are worth it. New life always is.

ASK YOURSELF

» Why do you think it's so tempting to hang on to an old life when a better one beckons?

» What could help you leave the past behind and thrive in new, unfamiliar territory?

ASK GOD

Dear Lord, I know that I have a new life, but I am not sure I have completely let go of my old ways. Grant me the grace to venture fully into the new life you have for me. Keep me from limiting myself by holding on to the past.

Forgiveness and Freedom

Get rid of all bitterness, rage, anger, harsh words, and slander.
. . . Instead, be kind to each other, tenderhearted, forgiving one
another, just as God through Christ has forgiven you.

EPHESIANS 4:31-32

In 1994, the Republic of South Africa ended the brutal system of racial segregation known as apartheid. But the bitterness caused by years of discrimination could not be wiped out with simple legislation. So the Truth and Reconciliation Commission was established. Chaired by Anglican Archbishop Desmond Tutu, the TRC focused on "restorative justice"—allowing victims to name what they had suffered but also offering amnesty to many who confessed and repented of their oppressive actions. Years later, Tutu and his daughter Mpho wrote *The Book of Forgiving* to articulate the counterintuitive reality Tutu observed in the TRC hearings—that forgiving the oppressor sets the oppressed free.

As we embrace our new lives, it's crucial that we not only face the pain of what has happened to us but also work toward releasing any bitterness that holds us captive. We do that through choosing to release our resentment to God and allow his grace to remove it from our lives. Such forgiveness is rarely easy, and it's almost never a onetime act. It's a process we must work on daily. But as we commit ourselves to ongoing forgiveness, we will also find increasing freedom.

ASK YOURSELF

» Is there a difference between forgiveness and reconciliation? Can you have one without the other?

» What would it take for you to find freedom by releasing your bitterness toward someone who has wronged you?

ASK GOD

God of grace, I recognize that when I harbor resentment, I am the one who stays bound. Help me find freedom by releasing those who have harmed me into your care.

The Healthy Art of Self-Comfort

Remember your promise to me; it is my only hope. Your
promise revives me; it comforts me in all my troubles.

PSALM 119:49-50

As we take our lives back, we discover we can find comfort for our pain in strategies that restore us rather than tear us down further. Some of us—like the psalmist, who puts his hope in God's promise—find comfort as we pray, meditate, journal, and spend time alone with God. Others of us find comfort in the company of trusted friends who are walking with us on this journey. Still others find comfort in creative expression as we write, draw, make music, or create in other ways. And many of us take advantage of all these means of healthy self-comfort.

It's not really *self*-comfort, of course. God is the ultimate source of all comfort, and all these strategies are simply means of opening ourselves to ways God touches us in this world. But by choosing to do something instead of wallowing in our pain and hoping someone will reach out to us, we take yet another step toward taking our lives back.

ASK YOURSELF

» What are some of the strategies you've discovered to comfort yourself? Which have helped you the most?

» Are there new healthy ways in which God might be inviting you to comfort yourself?

ASK GOD

God of all comfort, your promise revives me. Thank you that as you heal my heart you are also equipping me to find comfort in healthy ways. Guide me as I seek to find my life in you.

Saying a Good No

Just say a simple, "Yes, I will," or "No, I won't." Anything beyond this is from the evil one.

MATTHEW 5:37

Some of us were raised saying too many *yeses* and too few *noes*. We learned early what to say to please people and intuited quickly what *not* to say in order to keep the peace.

But today, in order to honor God, honor ourselves, and honor others, we're learning how and when to say a good *no*. We say it when a controlling or manipulative person jeopardizes our health, our welfare, or our recovery. We offer it when we're tempted to say *yes* out of fear or laziness—to avoid conflict or having to exert more energy than we want to give. We bravely say *no* when a *yes* would rob us of something amazing that God would have us do instead. And, gathering all of our courage, we say *no* when we're tempted to do something we've done over and over again that has held us back from healing.

Our good *noes* are a gift to ourselves, to God, and to others.

ASK YOURSELF

» What kinds of situations tempt you most to say yes for the wrong reasons? How long have you been doing this?

» What are some recent noes about which you feel most proud?

ASK GOD

God, I long to honor you, myself, and others with all that I say and do. Embolden me to say yes and no appropriately as you lead.

The Middle Is Just Fine

Give me neither poverty nor riches! . . . For if I grow rich, I may deny you and say,
"Who is the LORD?" And if I am too poor, I may steal and thus insult God's holy name.

PROVERBS 30:8-9

Most of us have financial goals and concerns. Sometimes those concerns are valid, and sometimes they derive from our desire to "measure up" to others. We must be very careful *not* to judge our life progress by this fraction of our lives.

The Lord will always meet our needs, but *how* he meets them is up to him. Sometimes he may meet them with lavish amounts, and other times he may meet them on a day-by-day, moment-by-moment basis.

What the writer of this proverb is saying here is that, financially speaking, the middle is just fine. In fact, sometimes it's the best place to be. But no matter our income bracket, we must learn to be content with where we are.

If you're well-off, be mindful of using God's financial blessing for his glory. If you're struggling, trust him to provide—and watch him work.

The most important thing to remember is that in God's eyes, your growth and your worth have *nothing* to do with money.

ASK YOURSELF

» Does your financial situation tend to determine the amount of peace and joy in your life?

» What would be a better way to measure your life progress?

ASK GOD

Dear Lord, help me not to measure my success, my life progress, or my personal value in numbers. Help me to be content with your provision and to know that what you have provided is exactly what I need at this time.

A Turtle No More

*I am giving you a new commandment: Love each other. Just
as I have loved you, you should love each other.*

JOHN 13:34

When turtles are threatened, they pull all their soft parts into their shells, retreating to the safety of their protective armor. Sound familiar? Before you decided to take your life back, you may have chosen isolation and detachment as a way to avoid getting hurt. Perhaps you lived in your own head and heart. You may have felt unworthy of connection and feared rejection. Perhaps it just felt safer to armor up.

If you've ever done that (or still do), you're not alone. But you don't have to live in isolation any longer. You can choose instead to connect with God and with others. You can poke your head out of your shell and come alive to Jesus' charge that we love one another the way he has loved us. As you do that, you'll discover the joy of knowing others, truly caring for them, and being known and cared for in return. With God's love as your protection, you don't have to armor up. Instead, you can enjoy mutual relationships and embrace authentic adulthood.

ASK YOURSELF

> » Do you tend to be a "turtle"? What does (or did) isolating and detaching yourself from others look like?

> » In what ways do you see your relationships improving as you continue on this journey of taking your life back?

ASK GOD

God, I believe that you created me to be in relationship with you and others. Thank you for the ways I'm coming out of my shell and beginning to embrace this gift. Teach me this day to love others the way you have loved me.

Not the Peace Police

*Work at living in peace with everyone, and work at living a holy
life, for those who are not holy will not see the Lord.*

HEBREWS 12:14

Though some of us might like to believe that the early church was perfect, it was still a community of sinners, just like our churches today. Squabbles and disagreements among those early believers were not uncommon. When one such conflict arose, the writer of Hebrews addressed it by exhorting believers to live in peace with everyone and work at living a holy life. Their job was the twofold task that's before us all: Be reconciled to others and be responsible for yourself.

But living in peace is different from keeping the peace. If we're only trying to keep the peace, we'll be tempted to enable unacceptable behavior, cover up problems, placate people, and comply with inappropriate demands. But when we purpose to *live in peace*, we gather the courage to own our own "stuff" by noticing our hurt places and confessing our sins. We also allow others to own their own stuff.

Living in peace, in other words, means that we have healthy boundaries.

ASK YOURSELF

» What kind of disagreements typically "disturb the peace" in your home or church? What is your instinctive reaction to those disagreements?

» How can you establish healthy boundaries in such instances and yet follow Jesus' command to "love one another"?

ASK GOD

God of peace, you have called your church to be a holy community with you as our head. Teach me to live the holy life to which you've called me and to also live at peace with my brothers and sisters. Train me in the holy art of loving deeply and yet maintaining healthy boundaries.

Light at Your Fingertips

I pray that your hearts will be flooded with light so that you can
understand the confident hope he has given to those he called.

EPHESIANS 1:18

A power failure at night can be frustrating or even frightening. You're sitting there doing what you always do when suddenly everything goes dark. No TV. No computer. No lights. Everything is black, even the ambient light outside.

Fumbling, you reach for your phone to access the flashlight app. And suddenly you can see again. That bright little LED is just what you need to make your way across the room to find the matches and candles. It's almost like magic.

It is important to keep God's light in your heart—as close by as your phone. The world's darkness is constantly trying to cast its shadow of confusion on your thoughts and on your life. Satan would love nothing more than to keep you in the dark so you cannot recover and reach the potential that God built into you.

But you have the power to prevent this. Keep your light source "charged" by communicating with God throughout your day, hiding his Word in your heart, and asking his Spirit to illuminate your every step. With God's light shining brightly, you will have a clear vision to see where you need to go next as you take your life back.

ASK YOURSELF

» Have you allowed any shadow of darkness to impede your walk with the Lord? What happened?

» What practices help you the most in keeping your light "charged" and ready for dark times?

ASK GOD

Lord, I want to experience a life so full of your light that no darkness can stop me. Help me to stay close to you so that my heart is always illuminated.

Is Anyone Faithful?

You, O Lord, are a God of compassion and mercy, . . .
filled with unfailing love and faithfulness.

PSALM 86:15

The more time some of us spend upon this earth, the less we expect from others. Why? This is a fallen world, and we humans are self-centered beings by nature. Even those we trust and admire the most will let us down on some level because they are human. This isn't as cynical as it may sound. It's just realistic!

Have you ever been disappointed by the actions of people in your life? Have they failed to meet your expectations, shown you a lack of respect, broken vows, or neglected you? Then you are absolutely normal.

This doesn't mean you can never have a relationship. It just means you cannot hold other people wholly responsible for your happiness. They don't have what it takes. Neither do you.

Human relationships can bring us a lot of joy. They can help us grow and be living conduits of God's love and grace. But they will always be imperfect. Only God is eternally faithful, flawlessly compassionate, and merciful. He's the only one who will never let us down.

ASK YOURSELF

» In what ways has God shown himself faithful to you in the past?

» How can trusting in a faithful God help you maintain loving but realistic relationships? What can make your relationships conduits of his love and grace?

ASK GOD

Dear Jesus, thank you for your faithfulness. Thank you that I can place my trust in you and never be disappointed.

It Takes Action

Turn away from evil and do good. Search for peace, and work to maintain it.

1 PETER 3:11

A veterinarian has access to many techniques and medications that can save an animal that has fallen ill. However, the best treatment will be of little or no use if the animal is being poisoned on an ongoing basis—say, through contaminants in its food. Until the harmful influence has been removed, the animal will not thrive.

Are there elements in your life you know should not be there? An attitude? An influence? A habit of thinking? What you are doing to take your life back and make a difference for God's Kingdom will bear little fruit if you are still holding on to mental, emotional, and spiritual poisons. They may feel familiar and almost comfortable, but they still hinder your spiritual health.

It is not enough to do the right things, in other words. You must also choose to "turn away" from the wrong ones and take action to discard them from your life.

ASK YOURSELF

» Identify one thing in your life that is not adding to the blessings God has for you.

» How can you go about discarding this "poison" from your life?

ASK GOD

Dear Jesus, the familiar sometimes feels like it belongs simply because it *is* familiar. Help me to discern the familiar but harmful things in my life that I should turn from. Make it clear to me what needs to go, and give me the courage I need to toss it out of my life for good.

Use the Tools God Gives You

*Whatever is good and perfect is a gift coming down to us from
God our Father, who created all the lights in the heavens.*

JAMES 1:17

Imagine a man digging a hole in the ground without a useful tool. He might find a stick to loosen the dirt. Maybe he will kick at that loose dirt with his shoe. He might even get down on his knees and claw at the ground with his hands. We might admire him for his tenacity—but not if we saw a shovel on the ground behind him.

Some of us find it difficult to ask for help from other people or make use of resources that are available to us. We persist in feeling that we have to do it all in our own strength and knowledge—or that simply praying about our problems will be enough. Praying is certainly important! But God's healing and his strength come to us in many different forms. He wants us to recognize and access the many good gifts he provides to help us heal: his Word, other helpful literature, supportive friends and fellow strugglers, wise counsel. As we avail ourselves of these helpful gifts, we start to make progress in taking our lives back.

ASK YOURSELF

» What forms of available help do you tend to resist using? Why do you resist?

» What are some of the resources God is offering you right now? Name one you have never taken advantage of. How could you make use of it in the coming month?

ASK GOD

Father God, Creator of the lights in the heavens, you are the Giver of every good and perfect gift. Thank you that you provide me with what I need to live the healthy life you intend for me.

Spoon-Fed Gospel

Love means doing what God has commanded us, and he has commanded
us to love one another, just as you heard from the beginning.

2 JOHN 1:6

In a world whose values are radically different from the values Jesus espouses in the Gospels, it can be hard to determine and then to live out what we value most. Should we pour our energy into working toward a six-figure salary? Should we push our children to attend the finest schools? How do we navigate the struggles that we and those we love are facing? Daily we're pulled in many directions.

Jesus recognized that we can be pulled not only by worldly concerns but also by our spiritual commitments. So at the end of his ministry, he compressed all he had taught into one simple commandment and spoon-fed it to his disciples: "Just as I have loved you, you should love each other" (John 13:34).

Today may not be the day you reach the dream salary or suddenly live without challenges, but you can do the one thing that matters most: Love others the way Jesus has loved you.

ASK YOURSELF

> » What are some of the commitments (including spiritual or religious) that compete for your time and attention? How can Jesus' simplified commandment help sort these out?

> » Who is it that Jesus is calling you to love today? How can you love that person most effectively?

ASK GOD

Jesus, I thank you for all the ways you've loved me and led me. Today I ask that you would open my eyes to those you would have me love in your name. Show me how to love the way you love.

Faith through Hearing

Not everyone welcomes the Good News, for Isaiah the prophet
said, "LORD, who has believed our message?" So faith comes from
hearing, that is, hearing the Good News about Christ.

ROMANS 10:16-17

Do you remember the first time you heard the Good News of the gospel of Jesus Christ? Maybe a stranger shared it with you. Perhaps a Christian built a friendship with you and offered you the chance to believe. Or maybe you were raised in a household of faith, and one day the lightbulb of God's love at last lit up your own heart. However it happened, you heard the Good News of Christ and came alive to a life of faith.

If that bulb has grown dim, if the Good News has become so-so news for you, God longs to breathe new life into your faith. Read the Gospels. Listen with fresh ears. Engage with Jesus as a child would. And don't forget to ask God specifically for a fresh infusion of faith.

Know that the Good News is still *very good* and that your faith can be enlivened by God's Spirit.

ASK YOURSELF

» Describe some of the ups and down of your faith over the years. How would you describe the state of your faith right now?

» What are some things you can try to access the "good" of the gospel once again (if you need to)?

ASK GOD

Jesus, Savior and Redeemer, thank you for coming to me and transforming my life. Enliven my spirit again with your Good News. Give me the eyes and ears of a child to receive you and your Word afresh today, for your glory.

Through the Deluge

No eye has seen, no ear has heard, and no mind has imagined
what God has prepared for those who love him.

1 CORINTHIANS 2:9

Driving through the night in a pounding rainstorm, you hunch over the steering wheel, straining to see more than twenty feet in front of the vehicle. You creep along, foot resting lightly on the gas, anxious because you can't see what's ahead. Your entire existence seems reduced to the swipe of a windshield wiper, a nearby crash of lightning, a dim taillight.

When the storms of life hit, we can have trouble seeing past our own noses. Imagining a bright future—in this life or the next—can feel next to impossible in the thick of the storm. But that's when we have to get a firm grip on God's promises and just keep creeping along.

Paul's first letter to the Christians in Corinth assures them that, despite their challenges, God has a wonderful future prepared for them. The fact that we can't imagine it has nothing to do with whether it's true. It is! You can hold on to God's promises of sunshine even when you're creeping along in the dark and white-knuckling the road to recovery.

ASK YOURSELF

> » Have you gone through seasons when you just couldn't see where you were going? What was the outcome?

> » How can you hold on to God's promises during those dark, stormy times?

ASK GOD

God of heaven and earth, you are all-knowing and all-seeing. I confess that my vision is limited. I struggle to believe that you have generously prepared a good future for me. Forgive my unbelief and help me to trust you even in the dark.

Life Is Bigger than You

The humble will see their God at work and be glad. Let
all who seek God's help be encouraged.

PSALM 69:32

It is hard to see anything else when we are focused on ourselves. It's only when we look outside of ourselves that we are able to see the bigger picture and know what joy and encouragement are really all about.

The world would like for us to believe that joy comes from what we can get for ourselves and what we can get others to do for us. The world couldn't be more wrong. If we look around, we can see a multitude of unsatisfied people grasping for more, more, more and never being fulfilled. The secret to finding true happiness is becoming part of what God is doing in the world around us.

We're not taking our lives back just for our own sakes, in other words. We're learning to be stronger, healthier, more trusting, and more confident in God's love so that we can then reach out to share that love with others. As we serve God and others with humble hearts, we will find that gladness becomes a part of who we are.

ASK YOURSELF

» Do you agree that we only find true joy when we look outside ourselves? Has this been your experience?

» So far, has the process of taking your life back helped you reach out to others? Why or why not?

ASK GOD

Dear Lord, teach me how to look at the bigger picture and see the needs of those around me as well as my own. I want to learn to love others the way you do and be part of your work in the world. Please show me how.

True Treasure

Store your treasures in heaven, where moths and rust cannot
destroy, and thieves do not break in and steal. Wherever your
treasure is, there the desires of your heart will also be.

MATTHEW 6:20-21

People spend thousands of dollars on elaborate security systems to protect their valuables—everything from intricate wiring on doors and windows to security cameras to tracking devices on vehicles, computers, and phones. We spend our limited time working to make money, happily spend that money on possessions, and then spend even more time and money protecting those possessions.

Ironic, isn't it? But it also illustrates the truth of Jesus' words about treasure. What we value most, he said, will eventually take ownership of us. We'll always focus the bulk of our limited time and energy on our true "treasure." So we should make sure our treasure is really worth what we pay to own and maintain it.

Investing too much in worldly possessions and pursuits is ultimately an exercise in futility because nothing we acquire on this planet will follow us into eternity. It makes so much more sense to invest our precious resources into what has lasting value.

ASK YOURSELF

» What possessions or pursuits tempt you to spend your time, money, and energy? What does this tell you about your values?

» What are some better investments or "treasures"?

ASK GOD

Dear Lord, I want to spend my limited time on earth wisely. Help me to keep a healthy balance between the temporal and the eternal and to hold my worldly possessions lightly. Please give me the wisdom to determine which things are worthy of my precious time and to focus on them.

Just Lucky, I Guess

Lazy people are soon poor; hard workers get rich.

PROVERBS 10:4

Have you ever looked at someone who has done really well in life and thought, *Boy, is that person lucky!* All of us have probably done that. But the funny thing about life is that the harder you work, the luckier you get.

God is not surprised that hard work brings rewards. That's the way he made the world—and us. We're designed to get satisfaction from working hard for the things we need. It's not necessarily about material gain. It's about using our gifts and talents effectively and enjoying the intrinsic reward of a job well done.

The mentality of the world today tends toward laziness. We play electronic games rather than getting physical exercise. We pop a frozen meal into the microwave rather than preparing dinner. We look for shortcuts and quick fixes rather sticking with a project to the end. But in the process, we miss a lot of the satisfaction life has to offer.

It is easy to be lazy—we simply exist. But if we want to move ahead in life, we need to evaluate our God-given attributes and opportunities, develop a plan to use them, and start working.

ASK YOURSELF

> » What are some of the talents and abilities God has given you? Think again. Is there something you've missed?

> » Have you taken the time to draw up a plan for your future? If not, how could you begin working on this?

ASK GOD
Dear Jesus, help me recognize the value in who you've made me to be and what you've given me to do. Remind me that "luck" comes from hard work, and show me where to start.

Give God Your Worries

"God opposes the proud but gives grace to the humble." So humble yourselves
under the mighty power of God, and at the right time he will lift you up in
honor. Give all your worries and cares to God, for he cares about you.

1 PETER 5:5-7

Taking our lives back is a stressful process. We're working—with God's help—
to create something new on the inside so that our external behaviors change
as a result. But when we get frustrated with our progress, our pride can begin
to awaken. It's easy then to attempt to take back the initiative and try to make
things happen on our own instead of letting God do the work in us.

But Peter reminds us that changing on the inside is accomplished through
an attitude of humility, which releases the mighty power of God in our lives.
That is the only way true change will be accomplished.

Peter also reassures us that we can trust God to take care of our worries,
our cares, and our anxieties. He draws from Psalm 55:22, where David shares
his hard-won wisdom in the exhortation, "Give your burdens to the LORD, and
he will take care of you."

This was true for David throughout the twenty years he ran for his life from
Saul. It was true for Peter. And it's true for us today.

ASK YOURSELF

» What do you worry about most? What makes it hard to trust God with
that part of your life?

» How can you humble yourself before the Lord?

ASK GOD

Dear God, forgive me for the times I think I know better and I step in to retake
control of my healing process. Help me to humble myself under your mighty
power.

Counterintuitive Kindness

You have heard the law that says, "Love your neighbor" and hate your
enemy. But I say, love your enemies! Pray for those who persecute you!

MATTHEW 5:43-44

It's clear from Jesus' Sermon on the Mount that he understands how we're made. He knows that if someone hurts us, our impulse is to hurt them back. If they cheat us or steal from us, we demand to be made whole.

But Jesus, who understands what's best for us, wants so much more for us than what comes naturally. He wants us to be better than that. So he gives us instructions that fly in the face of every natural instinct.

Love our enemies? Pray for them? When the hurt is still raw, we don't even want to be in the same room with them! But Jesus' instruction to love those who've hurt us is for our good. It's one of the keys to finding true peace. Best of all, we don't have to do it on our own. In fact, we can't. We must depend on the Holy Spirit's help to help God's Kingdom come in every counterintuitive moment of our lives.

ASK YOURSELF

» Who in your life would you count as enemies? To what degree have you been able to love these people and to pray for them?

» What is God asking you to do *now*? How is he challenging you to live differently in relation to your enemies?

ASK GOD

Faithful Father, you know the places where my heart stings with the pain of old hurts. In my flesh I'd rather nurse those hurts than offer them to you. But today I give you my pain and ask you to teach me how to love my enemies. Show me how to pray for each one.

Just Making Noise

Spouting off before listening to the facts is both shameful and foolish.

PROVERBS 18:13

Have you ever heard the saying that people are "talking just to hear their heads rattle"? That accusation isn't very flattering to those who are doing the talking, but they probably won't notice because, well . . . they're talking.

No one wants to hear someone who talks and talks without making a point, without having any facts to back up what he or she is saying, or without giving anyone else a chance to speak.

You might think this is a twenty-first-century problem, but it has been going on for as long as there have been humans on this planet. The Bible says that such spouting off "is both shameful and foolish." And whether it stems from nervousness, arrogance, or just bad habits, such overtalking is far from harmless. It can spread misinformation, damage relationships, and actually hinder communication, because those who can't reasonably escape the conversation are likely to just tune out. The real tragedy in talking too much is that when the talker finally has something important to say, no one may be listening.

ASK YOURSELF

> » Do you tend to talk too much or to speak before you think? Why do you think you do this?

> » Who in your life could use your prayers in this area?

ASK GOD

Dear Lord, I want to contribute something of value when I speak. Keep me mindful of what I say and also of my reasons for speaking. Help me to think before I open my mouth, and help me to refrain from talking just to make some noise.

Enjoy the Journey

The LORD directs our steps, so why try to understand everything along the way?

PROVERBS 20:24

Have you ever traveled by train? There is something relaxing about sitting back and watching the scenery go by while someone else worries about getting you to where you're going. You have no worries and no responsibilities for staying on schedule or operating the vehicle. Someone else is in charge of this journey, so you can enjoy the ride and arrive at the destination refreshed and ready to go.

In life, God is the engineer of your train, and he wants you to sit back and enjoy the ride. Don't worry about whether or not you are traveling at the right speed, headed in the right direction, or staying on schedule. Trust God to get you to the right place in life at the right time. He has everything under control, including how to take your life back. (He'll direct you when you need to be somewhere or do something.)

When you worry about the details, you take away from the peace and joy that God wants you to experience. Micromanaging the journey will rob you of the blessings he wants you to encounter along the way.

ASK YOURSELF

» What internal or external circumstances keep you from relaxing and enjoying your own life?

» Which of these could you release to God in order to experience more peace and joy?

ASK GOD

Dear Lord, too often I attempt to take the controls and run my own life. Why do I feel compelled to "help" you get me from point A to point B? Please teach me how to let go. Help me to follow where you lead without worrying too much about where you're taking me. Show me how to relax and enjoy the ride.

Your Real Life

*Think about the things of heaven, not the things of earth. For you died
to this life, and your real life is hidden with Christ in God.*

COLOSSIANS 3:2-3

What is the sense of investing all our time and energy in this temporal world? Nothing in this life is going to last, and nothing we gather here can be taken with us when we go. Investing too heavily in the temporal is like building a house on someone else's property. We can't stay there, and we can't take it with us, so what is the point?

If we believe that our "real life is hidden with Christ in God," then we should act like it. We should live with an eternal focus. This doesn't mean we refuse to participate in this life. It simply means we will be more concerned about building our eternal future than we are about accumulating power and possessions on earth.

The "real life" application of an eternal focus begins in the heart. It begins with setting our hearts on furthering God's Kingdom—which is, after all, our future home.

ASK YOURSELF

» How does keeping an eternal focus change the way you live on earth?

» What are some things you could do to invest in the eternal while here on earth?

ASK GOD

Dear Jesus, sometimes I forget that my life on this earth is short and temporary. I get so busy working out the details of my earthly life that I lose focus on my eternal home. Help me to keep this temporal life in perspective, and prevent me from investing so heavily in it that I have no time to invest in my eternal future.

God Wants Your Garbage

*Then Jesus said, "Come to me, all of you who are weary and
carry heavy burdens, and I will give you rest."*

MATTHEW 11:28

"Jewelry and electronics stolen in home invasion." If you were a victim of a theft like that, you'd probably be angry, sad, and worried.

But imagine the headline read, "Thief steals broken vacuum cleaner, rusty bike, two bags of rotted vegetables." If someone did that to you, you'd just be confused. Who could possibly want your garbage?

God does. He wants the bad stuff in your life—your troubles, your worries, your sins and failures. But why would he want that?

Is there someone in your life whom you love so dearly, someone whose burdens you would gladly carry if you could? Well, that is how God feels about you. He loves you so much that he wants to take on everything that's cluttering your life and weighing you down. If you have been hesitant to hand these things over to the Lord, don't wait any longer. He is ready to take your trash so that you can have peace and joy in your life.

ASK YOURSELF

» Name some of the "trash" in your life that has been tripping you up, weighing you down, and getting in your way.

» Are you hesitant to heap your bad stuff on Jesus? Why or why not?

ASK GOD

Dear Lord, sometimes I feel I am drowning in the garbage of my life. Please help me remember to give it all to you so that I can be freed to do other things. I want to experience the peace and joy that come from giving my worries and cares to you.

Who You See Is Who You Get

Jesus grew in wisdom and in stature and in favor with God and all the people.

LUKE 2:52

Little children love to try on different personas. In the morning a toddler might wear a cape and be a superhero. In the afternoon she might don a bear mask and become a wilderness beast. At bedtime, in her cuddly, soft pajamas, she might be willing to be a vulnerable child once again.

That's fine and appropriate for children. Unfortunately, some of us live that same way as adults—and for less innocent reasons. Because we feel shame or discomfort over aspects of our lives but don't want to give them up, we end up splitting off parts of ourselves that don't mesh. We may dress up the spiritual part of ourselves for church but fail to integrate our Sunday morning selves into the rest of our week. We may have a self who plays around sexually, who binges on food, or who loves to hang out in bars. We may even have trouble knowing which one is the real us.

But taking our lives back means letting God heal those splits as we grow into the likeness of Jesus, who also matured mentally, physically, spiritually, and socially. It means learning daily to integrate all of who we are, to jettison shame, and to live with consistency and congruity.

ASK YOURSELF

» Is there a part (or parts) of yourself that you have split off to avoid discovery or judgment?

» What would your life look like if you functioned as an integrated person?

ASK GOD

God, I thank you that as I mature in you, you are integrating my mind, body, spirit, and heart. Give me the courage to live an integrated life.

The Right Standard

Better to be patient than powerful; better to have self-control than to conquer a city.

PROVERBS 16:32

The world's standards and God's standards are almost always at odds. For instance, it is common for the world to see patience and self-control as signs of weakness. But the Bible says it is "better to be patient than powerful" and "better to have self-control than to conquer a city."

The contrast between the world's view and God's view leaves each of us with a choice. Do we want to measure ourselves by the world's criteria or by God's? Aligning ourselves with biblical standards might make it hard for us to fit in at times, but it will also develop us into persons of strength and character—persons who can be used by God.

In the long run, the world's opinion of us is meaningless. It is God's assessment that will count for eternity. So before we try to evaluate our progress in life, it's good to make certain that we are using the correct standard of measurement.

ASK YOURSELF

» What are some other ways God's standards differ from the world's standards? Are you comfortable with not fitting into the world's mold, or is this something you need to work on with God's help?

» Do you consider yourself patient and self-controlled? If not, what can you do to develop these qualities in your life?

ASK GOD

Dear Jesus, I do not want to be someone who looks good to the world but disappoints you. Help me to be patient and kind and self-controlled, and show me how to live in a way that pleases you, not the world.

Under the Surface

People may be pure in their own eyes, but the LORD examines their motives.

PROVERBS 16:2

Have you ever come across a little sprout in the ground and wondered what kind of plant it would grow to be? It's very difficult to tell in the early stages just what a sprout will grow into, but with time, it will become evident. Even though you can't easily identify a plant by looking at a sprout, its species has already been determined by the seed from which it came. No amount of watering, sunshine, or care will be able to change what it is destined to be. If a flower is planted, a flower will grow, and if a weed is planted, a weed it will be. The fact is, it's all about what happened underground.

Sometimes we do things that look good on the outside, and the world may be impressed. God, however, looks much deeper—below the surface, to the "seed" of our motives. He isn't nearly as concerned with what we have done as he is with why we have done it.

ASK YOURSELF

> » Do you think it's possible to have impure motives and still do things that are good and worthwhile—or act from pure motives and still do something harmful or unwise? Why or why not?

> » What "weeds" have you allowed to grow in your life that need to be pulled before they cause trouble?

ASK GOD

Dear Jesus, thank you for looking below the surface and into the heart of my actions. Teach me to do everything with pure motives. Show me how to identify any "weeds" that have sprouted in my life, and help me to extract them.

In Our Darkest Moments

[The LORD said to Joshua,] "No one will be able to stand against you as long as you live. For I will be with you as I was with Moses. I will not fail you or abandon you."

JOSHUA 1:5

In his powerful memoir, *Night*, Holocaust survivor Elie Wiesel recounts an event that was horrific even by Auschwitz standards—the brutal hanging of a child. Too light to die immediately, the boy dangled, slowly suffocating, and his fellow prisoners were forced to watch. A man standing behind Wiesel cried out, "For God's sake, where is God?" And from within himself, Wiesel reports hearing a voice: "This is where—hanging here from this gallows."

In the midst of suffering, it's only human to wonder where God is. We ask why God doesn't prevent such horrors—why God doesn't fix our situation.

God's ways are not easy to understand. He does not always act the way we expect or perform as we would prefer. But God is never absent. He never abandons us in our suffering. That truth should be becoming clearer to you as your recovery progresses. You may be awakening to the startling reality that even when you thought you were most alone, God was there with you. A living faith is being formed in you to guide you each day—faith in a God who may be inscrutable but who does not fail us.

ASK YOURSELF

» Describe a moment (or moments) in your history when you suspected God had abandoned you.

» What would change if you allowed yourself to see God in that moment?

ASK GOD

God, just as you were with Joshua, and just as you have been with all who suffer, I believe that you are with me. Thank you.

Obedience Is Number One

Listen! Obedience is better than sacrifice, and submission
is better than offering the fat of rams.

1 SAMUEL 15:22

King Saul had blatantly disregarded God's instructions. He'd been told to destroy everything associated with Israel's enemy, but instead he and his army had kept the best of the enemy's sheep, goats, and cattle for themselves. When confronted by the prophet Samuel about this, Saul claimed he had kept the animals to make a sacrifice to God. But Samuel was having none of Saul's excuses and kept on pressing Saul. Finally the king admitted that he had disobeyed because he "was afraid of the people and did what they demanded" (1 Samuel 15:24).

We know how easy that is to do. Just as we are making progress in taking our lives back, someone "demands" that we do something that calls a halt to our progress. Because we fear their opinion, we fail to obey what we know God wants us to do. Even worse, we rationalize our disobedience by telling ourselves we did it because we cared or because someone needed us. We'll only get back on course when we stop making excuses and dare to do what we know is right.

ASK YOURSELF

> » What situations make it hard for you to stay the course in your recovery? What is it about these situations that makes them difficult for you?

> » What's the best way to get back on track if you've found yourself disobeying God and making excuses for it?

ASK GOD

Lord Jesus, obedience can be scary and difficult, and it's so tempting to rationalize my failures to obey. Please give me the courage to face my failures honestly and to keep moving forward in obedience to you.

Be Happy to Change

*Consider the joy of those corrected by God! Do not despise
the discipline of the Almighty when you sin.*

JOB 5:17

Have you ever watched professional athletes who, when called out by a referee, stand and argue the point, even though they know the decision is not going to change? How childish is that? And yet it happens all the time.

It is important that we as Christians respect God's authority, especially when he is correcting us. He takes the time to do that because we matter to him, and that should make us happy.

The next time God "calls you out" on a sin in your life, take notice of how you respond. Do you argue or throw a tantrum, hoping that God will change his mind? Do you try to justify yourself or rationalize? Do you just ignore the correction and keep doing what you were doing? Or do you thank God for caring enough to correct your path and then make the necessary changes in your behavior to get on the right track? If you want to live the joyful and productive life that God has designed for you, the best response is gratitude . . . and change.

ASK YOURSELF

» What are some of the ways you know that God is correcting or disciplining you?

» How do you usually respond to such correction? How could you do better?

ASK GOD

Dear God, I do not want to act like a spoiled child when you correct me. Teach me to listen to your direction and to be thankful that you care. Help me not to be stubborn or argumentative, but make me ready and willing to change.

Who Can You Trust?

Trust in the LORD with all your heart; do not depend on your own understanding.

PROVERBS 3:5

Over the past decades, a multitude of financial scams have bilked innocent people out of their life savings. These people weren't stupid, and they didn't just throw their hard-earned money to the wind. Most of them made the wisest investments they could through what seemed to be solid, well-placed brokerages. But their worldly wisdom let them down, and they were left penniless.

How often do we give more credence to our own understanding than we do to the Word and the leading of God? We "trust our gut," but we don't trust the Lord of the universe. And the trouble is, our gut and our judgment are fallible. We just don't have the capacity to see the big picture that God sees.

Only fools ignore the limits of their wisdom. Only fools fail to understand that in this world we can't depend completely on anyone or anything, including ourselves—only God is dependable.

Take all your decisions before the Lord in prayer. Trust him to give you direction, then follow his lead. Let his Word and the whispering of his Spirit—not your gut—be your ultimate guide.

ASK YOURSELF

> » Are you in the habit of seeking the Lord's counsel before making big and little decisions in your life? What could help you adapt this habit?

> » How can you distinguish between your "own understanding" and the inner promptings of God's Spirit?

ASK GOD

Dear Lord, forgive me for the times when I trust in my own wisdom and do not involve you in my decisions. Help me recognize that even when I feel my judgment is adequate, I still need your input. Help me place my ultimate trust in you.

Who Do You Think You're Talking To?

We are confident that he hears us whenever we ask for anything that pleases him.

1 JOHN 5:14

It would be easy to take this verse the wrong way—as a picture of a petty God who requires us to figure out exactly what will please him to have any hope of being heard. Or a childish God sticking his fingers in his ears and humming to avoid hearing something he doesn't want to hear.

But this verse isn't saying we must second-guess our prayers or worry that God won't listen unless we word things just right. It's just reminding us that real communication involves knowing who we're talking to. If we want God to hear us, we must pray to him as he really is, not who we think he should be.

Can we come to God just as we are, with our pain and troubles and even our temptations? Of course. The Bible says God wants us to do that. But can we ask God to help us cheat an elderly neighbor? That would be a waste of time because God never sides with wrongdoers. If we really knew him, we wouldn't bother to ask.

That's an extreme example, but the principle holds. If we actually want to communicate with God, we must remember who we're talking to.

ASK YOURSELF

» How can you *know* what pleases God?

» What are some ways you could improve the way you communicate with God?

ASK GOD

Dear Lord, I know that you care about me, and I do want to please you. Help me to know your heart and to pray in accordance with who you are.

It Takes a Little Work

Turn away from evil and do good. Search for peace, and work to maintain it.

PSALM 34:14

You're invited to a birthday party for a friend. Gift in hand, you make your way to the venue. Then you do a double take. The room is decorated with balloons. But instead of cheerful, colorful bubbles of latex, all you see are limp, lifeless tubes dangling from strings all around the room. An interesting effect, perhaps, but surely not what was intended. Did nobody bother to blow up the balloons? Or were they blown up but not tied off? Either way, the party feels as deflated as the decorations.

The good things in life are a lot like balloons. Every day you can choose whether to accept them as they are or to put forth an effort to make them better. Rather than just avoiding evil, you can actively work to do good.

If you choose to improve upon what life hands you, be sure to keep working to maintain what you have worked for. After all, what good is blowing up the balloons if you don't tie them off so they will hold the air?

ASK YOURSELF

> » Do you tend to just take circumstances as they come, or do you try to make them better? Which do you think is preferable? Why?

> » What areas of your life could use a little extra effort?

ASK GOD

Dear Lord, I don't want to merely avoid evil. I want to do good. And I don't want to just cruise through life, taking things as they come. Help me to face every aspect of my life with an eye to making it better. I want everything in my life to lead me to you.

Speak Up for Peace

People who wink at wrong cause trouble, but a bold reproof promotes peace.

PROVERBS 10:10

Have you ever met any pot stirrers? They're the folks who can't seem to abide peace and harmony within a group. Instead, they get a kick out of shaking things up. They may act innocent, but they're always on the lookout for opportunities to toss a little fuel on the fire just to enjoy the combustion. An insinuating comment here, a "devil's advocate" remark there, and soon people are at each other's throats.

God calls us all to be peacemakers, but that's not the same as just smoothing things over or avoiding conflict. In the case of pot stirrers (and other circumstances as well), peacemaking may call for confrontation—calling attention to what's going on and demanding that it stop.

That might offend some people, who might even accuse *you* of making trouble. Don't let it stop you. Make sure God is really calling you to get involved. Then focus on doing what he says and let him handle the fallout. Do your best to present the truth in love so that peace will be the outcome.

ASK YOURSELF

> » Why do you think pot stirrers do what they do? Do you ever have the urge to stir things up in this way?

> » How would you know when God is calling you to this active kind of peacemaking? Has it ever happened to you?

ASK GOD

Dear Lord, please help me never to be guilty of encouraging bad behavior in others. Give me the wisdom to discern right from wrong and the courage to obey when you call me to speak up for peace.

You Are Who You Follow

Deceit fills hearts that are plotting evil; joy fills hearts that are planning peace!
PROVERBS 12:20

Think about the people who have had the greatest impact on your early life—your parents, probably, and perhaps a teacher or friend. Children pick up mannerisms, speech patterns, thought processes, and even belief systems from such role models. To a great extent, what you see—and who you follow—determines what you become.

The Bible says that "deceit fills hearts that are plotting evil." If we allow the father of lies (Satan) to influence us, we shouldn't be surprised when our hearts fill with deceit.

On the flip side, God's Word tells us that "joy fills hearts that are planning peace." Model yourself after the Prince of Peace, follow him closely, and watch as the joy level in your life rises.

ASK YOURSELF

» Who are your most important role models? What impact—positive or negative—have they had in your life?

» What changes would you make if you deliberately chose the Prince of Peace as a role model?

ASK GOD

Dear Jesus, I want to be more like you. Make me aware of the times when I follow the wrong models and draw me back quickly so that I do not get lost. Let me be a positive role model for others—a bearer of peace and joy to all I come in contact with.

Hope for Times of Doubt

When doubts filled my mind, your comfort gave me renewed hope and cheer.

PSALM 94:19

Taking our lives back isn't easy. It can be slow, discouraging work. After all, we're trying to change deeply imbedded habits and attitudes. So there will inevitably be times when we're full of doubt about the whole process. Is recovery even possible? Is it worth the effort? How can we know for certain that we're doing the right thing?

The truth is, most of the time we *don't* know for certain. But certainty isn't really what we need to counter our doubts. What we really need is hope. Hope to keep trying. Hope to pick ourselves up when we fail. Hope to maneuver through awkward relationships and miscommunications. Hope that our pain won't have the last word.

That hope is what God offers us if we turn to him. He doesn't promise to remove all doubts from our minds. But he does give us the encouragement we need to keep trying in spite of our doubts. He opens our minds to new possibilities and our hearts to fresh energy. That's hope—and it's exactly what we need most in times of doubt.

ASK YOURSELF

» What doubts have you had about the process of taking your life back?

» Where have you found hope in the process?

ASK GOD

Father in heaven, I admit there are times when I doubt that I'll really be able to lead a saner, healthier life, but I don't want to wallow in that doubt. Help me to lean on you when I am uncertain and discouraged so you can renew my hope.

Defending Yourself

Come with great power, O God, and rescue me! Defend me with your might.

PSALM 54:1

One aspect of taking your life back is learning to defend yourself. This doesn't mean getting defensive when someone points out a flaw that needs your attention. It certainly doesn't mean resorting to violence. It simply means standing up for yourself in healthy and appropriate ways. It means refusing to be used or abused by others and asserting your right to be who God has created you to be.

You are not the helpless victim you may have once thought you were. You can say *no*. You can refuse to go along with manipulative or abusive behavior. You can leave the room, ask the other person to leave, or at least devise an exit strategy. You can call a friend for support or schedule a counseling session.

But before you can do any of this, you must open your heart to the fact that you have a right to be yourself. You have a right not to be controlled. You have a right to tell the truth as you see it, without recrimination. These rights were given to you by the Lord of the universe—your true Defender. It is he who gives you the strength and the wisdom to stand up for yourself as you move toward healing.

ASK YOURSELF

> » In what circumstances or with what people do you find it difficult to stand up for yourself?

> » What are the differences between defending yourself and getting defensive?

ASK GOD

Father God, thank you for being my Defender—and for giving me the strength and courage to stand up for myself. Please help me do this with wisdom and compassion.

The Sting of Betrayal

The traitor, Judas, had given them a prearranged signal: "You will know which one to arrest when I greet him with a kiss. Then you can take him away under guard."

MARK 14:44

Sooner or later in this life, someone will betray us and let us down. That's just the reality of living in a fallen world. But taking our lives back means we don't allow these people to change who we are.

Even Jesus had close companions who failed him miserably. Some, like Simon Peter, failed him unintentionally because of their human weakness. Others, like Judas, failed him on purpose. If Jesus had allowed the actions of those who betrayed him to affect how he lived and treated others, where would any of us be today?

If you have experienced betrayal, do you find it harder to trust the next person you encounter? Letting another person's past weakness or ill will affect our future choices is classic reactive behavior. Instead, if we let him, Jesus can help us learn to use the hurts in our lives to become stronger and more like him.

ASK YOURSELF

» How do you tend to project your past hurts and betrayals on your current relationships?

» What can you do to make sure you give everyone in your life a fair chance?

ASK GOD

Dear Lord, I don't want to let past hurts affect my future relationships. Please remove this fear of betrayal. Help me to judge all people on their own merits and to give them a chance to prove themselves. Please do not let me become bitter and distrusting, but rather let me grow more like Jesus through every trial in my life.

The Gift That Keeps on Giving

I am leaving you with a gift—peace of mind and heart. And the peace
I give is a gift the world cannot give. So don't be troubled or afraid.

JOHN 14:27

Can you remember the excitement you felt as a child on the night before Christmas, wondering what presents you would receive? There is nothing like that feeling of anticipation. But can you remember what you received for Christmas when you were seven years old? How about when you were nine or eleven? Chances are, you can't.

Contrast the material gifts that so excited you as a child with the gift that Jesus talks about in this passage. He left you the gift of peace—peace of mind and peace of heart. The gift that God has given to you through Jesus will last forever and will never lose its significance. Your life has been eternally changed by God's gift, and because of it, you can have the ability to overcome trouble and fear. Have you thanked God lately for the peace he has placed in your heart and mind?

ASK YOURSELF

> » If God has given you the gift of lasting peace in your mind and heart (he has!), why don't you always *feel* peaceful?

> » What will help you claim the gift of peace Jesus has left for you?

ASK GOD

Dear Jesus, thank you for the peace you have placed in my heart. I am so grateful that you gave me something that those in the world only wish they could have. Cause me to recognize the incredible blessing I have in my life because of what you did for me.

Character-Building Trials

*Endurance develops strength of character, and character
strengthens our confident hope of salvation.*

ROMANS 5:4

Believe it or not, our problems are not a source of entertainment for God. He doesn't afflict us with difficulty just to watch us jump. He wants to use everything that happens to us for his Kingdom—and for our ultimate benefit.

God knows how we benefit from seeing a problem through to the end. He knows that it causes growth in the knowledge of who we really are, thus defining our character. And building character is crucial to our growth. It calibrates our moral compass and builds our faith as well as increasing stamina and strength.

When you are going through a prolonged trial and think that you cannot endure one more moment, hang tough and remind yourself what is really happening. You will grow closer to God during these times of testing than at any other time in your life, and your trust in him will grow exponentially. When you truly believe that suffering shapes your character, strengthens your faith, and builds your trust in God, you can find joy in anything you face on this earth.

ASK YOURSELF

» Do you think trials and problems automatically build character? Why or why not?

» What choices can we make in the midst of trials to cooperate with what God is doing?

ASK GOD

Dear Lord, give me patience and help me to be strong when I encounter problems in my life. Remind me that through these trials I will be made stronger and more like you. Give me a new perspective when I face a difficult situation. Help me look past the problem and see the benefit to come.

Follow the Leader

Household gods give worthless advice, fortune-tellers predict only lies, and interpreters of dreams pronounce falsehoods that give no comfort. So my people are wandering like lost sheep; they are attacked because they have no shepherd.

ZECHARIAH 10:2

Have you ever made the mistake of following the person in your group with no sense of direction? You know, the guy who motions to you out the car window, indicating that you can follow him to your destination, and then proceeds to make every wrong turn possible. Nothing is more frustrating and unproductive than following the wrong leader.

In life, we can choose to follow the wrong leader too. God's Word likens this to "wandering like lost sheep"—and it's a very dangerous situation to be in.

As you seek to take your life back, if you choose to follow the lead of anyone but Christ, you can expect to find yourself going in circles or stuck on dead-end streets, with very little to show for your efforts. You'll be more open to attacks of fear, confusion, and self-doubt.

No one can lead you to the right place but God. If you are wise, you will follow him closely!

ASK YOURSELF

» What kinds of unreliable leadership are you most tempted to follow? What "attacks" are you most vulnerable to when you fail to follow Christ closely?

» Do you think God ever directs you through the counsel, advice, and leadership of other people? How can you take advantage of such help without being led astray?

ASK GOD

Dear Jesus, you know everything about me—my past, my present, my future, and what is best for me. I don't want to waste precious time following anyone other than you. Direct me in the way I should go and help me to listen carefully.

Not Coming Back

Those who belong to Christ Jesus have nailed the passions and desires
of their sinful nature to his cross and crucified them there.

GALATIANS 5:24

Imagine a fly buzzing around your plate at the dinner table. You swat it with a newspaper and kill it. Then you sit back down at the table and enjoy your dinner with no concern that the fly will ever return. Why? Because that fly is dead. If you kill something, it is not coming back.

When you accepted Jesus as your Savior, your sinful nature was nailed to the cross and crucified with him. That means it's a thing of the past. It died with Jesus and it's never coming back.

Does that mean you will never have to struggle with sin again? Sadly, no. Although your essential nature—the part that makes you *you*—is now a new creation in Christ, you're still living in a body that is part of the fallen world. Your flesh—your body, your brain, your emotions—is still subject to temptation and sin. But all that is temporary. The part of you that lives forever can never again be touched by sin.

ASK YOURSELF

» Do you have difficulty believing that your sinful nature died with Christ? Why or why not?

» How can this understanding of what happened to your sinful nature on the cross help you confront the vestiges of sin in your life?

ASK GOD

Dear Jesus, thank you for dying for me at Calvary. I am grateful that when I received you as my Savior, you nailed my sinful nature to the cross and killed it. Help me live into the reality of my new nature so that the whole world can see you through me.

The One Who Is Right beside You

I know the LORD is always with me. I will not be shaken, for he is right beside me.

PSALM 16:8

Are you familiar with Martin Handford's perennially popular picture book *Where's Waldo*? It's essentially a puzzle book. Readers search intricate illustrations to locate the book's hero, Waldo, wearing his signature red-and-white striped shirt and hat. It's not always easy. But if you trust the author that Waldo is really there somewhere, you'll find him. With enough squinting and scouring, you'll finally spy Waldo amid the chaos of a circus, a parade, or a football game.

The psalmist had that kind of faith in God. He believed his Lord's promise to be with him even in the most chaotic circumstances. With the eyes of his heart, the psalmist could recognize God standing right beside him. Can you? In the midst of your most difficult days, can you share the psalmist's confidence that God is present with you?

ASK YOURSELF

- » What circumstance in your life today makes it difficult for you to sense God's nearness?

- » When have you recognized God's presence during a painful or difficult season?

ASK GOD

Lord, I need you. I long to sense your palpable presence with me in the midst of my chaotic days. Father, I claim the confidence of the psalmist in believing that I cannot be shaken because you are at my side.

The Ultimate Hiding Place

You are my hiding place; you protect me from trouble.
You surround me with songs of victory.

PSALM 32:7

Do you ever get so frustrated, tired, or fearful that you just want run away and hide? Most of us know that feeling.

Some people hide in plain sight, staying so busy that they have no time to think. Others actually separate themselves from other people and avoid interaction with the world. Still others hide by using mind-altering substances or shutting down emotionally. But all of these hiding places have a significant drawback. They can't hide us from the major source of our problems—ourselves.

God, however, offers us the perfect hiding place—himself. When we turn to him for refuge, we have no need to hide from ourselves because God actually changes us. He fills us with the power of the Holy Spirit and builds us back up so we can face the world again and even experience joy.

When things in this world become too great a burden . . . are you hiding in the right place?

ASK YOURSELF

» What kind of circumstances in your life make you want to hide? What is your earthly hiding place (or places) of choice?

» Describe some practices that could help you find refuge in God. Was there ever a time in your life when you were aware of hiding yourself in him?

ASK GOD

Dear Lord, I know you are always there to shelter and protect me. Show me the foolishness of trying to hide anywhere other than in your presence.

Inside Out

Let your good deeds shine out for all to see, so that
everyone will praise your heavenly Father.

MATTHEW 5:16

If you make significant changes on the inside, there will be evidence of these changes on the outside. If you cut back on calories, for instance, you will eventually lose weight. Even those who have no idea that you modified your diet should be able to see the results of your actions. And if there are no outward signs of change, that could be a sign that something is wrong.

What about taking your life back? That involves some big internal changes. Perhaps you've found healing for old wounds. Perhaps you've learned to focus on reality rather than appearances. Hopefully you're leaning more on God for validation instead of expecting it from other people, and you're responding out of love rather than reacting in fear.

But how do you measure what progress you've made? If the outside isn't changing to match the inside, it might be time to pay attention. Ask yourself: *Am I more settled, more confident, more independent—more faithful and less fearful? Am I taking better care of myself? Am I comfortable saying no (kindly) and yes (wholeheartedly)?* These are good indications that you are really healing. It will show.

ASK YOURSELF

» What changes have you made so far in the process of taking your life back?

» What do you think these changes look like to those who know you? How could you find out?

ASK GOD

Father in heaven, thank you so much for your dependable love, which makes it possible for me to make all these changes. I want my entire life to shine so that the whole world will see you in me.

The God Who Sees You

*Thereafter, Hagar used another name to refer to the LORD, who had
spoken to her. She said, "You are the God who sees me."*

GENESIS 16:13

Have you ever attended a costume party or masquerade? No one is who he or
she appears to be, and this can be a liberating experience—for one night. The
problem with an ongoing masquerade is that it does not allow for any depth in
relationships. Hiding behind a mask may seem to simplify life, but all it really
does is create an empty existence.

In a world where so many fear to be genuine, failure to connect with others
is common. Some put on the mask of "everything's fine" when they're really in
pain. Some pretend to be what others want them to be and lose track of who
they really are. Still others put on a facade of successful self-importance, making sure that nobody sees their vulnerability.

Such masquerades are not only unhealthy; they're also futile. We may be
able to fool other people, but we will never fool the God who created us, who
sees us for exactly who we are—and loves the real us.

ASK YOURSELF

> » What kind of mask are you most likely to hide behind? What has been
> the result of your masquerade?

> » What would it take for you to be vulnerable enough to allow others to
> see the real you?

ASK GOD

Dear Lord, so often I find myself hiding behind the facade that I have created
for myself. Help me be comfortable with the person you see when you look at
me, the person you created me to be.

Look at Me!

The wise don't make a show of their knowledge, but fools broadcast their foolishness.

PROVERBS 12:23

How can you spot the fools in a crowd? They're the ones who won't stop talking about themselves. The foolish will always try to draw attention to themselves one way or the other, oblivious to the fact that they are really drawing attention to their mindlessness.

Wise people, on the other hand, tend to go about their business quietly and let their accomplishments speak for themselves. There is no reason to avoid a wise person, but we have all gone out of our way to avoid interaction with a fool.

When you are tempted to "toot your own horn," be careful that you don't become that mindless fool droning on and on. Evaluate your motives, test your heart, check your reasoning, and be certain you are not broadcasting the wrong message. If you are simply saying, "Look at me," save your breath.

As you work toward taking your life back, try to stay humble, seeking God's direction and exercising wisdom in your choices. You can trust the Lord to bring your actions to light. He will see that you get the recognition you deserve when the time is right.

ASK YOURSELF

» What is the difference between "tooting your own horn" and following Jesus' instructions to "let your light shine" (Matthew 5:16, NIV)?

» What is the appropriate way (if any) to talk about yourself and your accomplishments?

ASK GOD

Dear Lord, help me to be humble and wise in the way I present myself to the world. I know you are aware of all that I do each day. Please let me be satisfied with the recognition you give.

Knowing and Doing

You are so proud of knowing the law, but you dishonor God by breaking it.

ROMANS 2:23

Do you remember how proud you were when you finally got your first driver's license? You'd worked so hard to get it—memorizing all of the relevant traffic laws, pestering your parents into letting you practice, and white-knuckling it through your written exam and driver's test. Then you were the proud possessor of a card that authorized you to drive on a public street. Your license was proof that you knew what was expected of you. You would never have earned it if you hadn't known the laws and shown you could follow them.

Does having a license guarantee that you will obey the traffic laws? No. There are consequences if you ignore the law, but you can still choose to do it—just as you can ignore God's laws.

God is not just concerned with your head knowledge. He is also concerned with your obedience to what you know. Knowledge without obedience is contemptuous and disrespectful. And just as knowing the laws of the land and choosing not to obey them has consequences, so does knowing the will of God and choosing to disobey it.

ASK YOURSELF

» Have there been times when you knew exactly what you should do but didn't do it? What were the consequences?

» Are there areas of your life where you're not quite certain what God expects? What is the best way to find clarity?

ASK GOD

Dear Jesus, I don't just want to listen to you. I want to obey you too. I don't want to disrespect you by knowing something and then failing to act on it. Walk with me, Lord, and show me how to please you.

Step Back

*Can all your worries add a single moment to your life? And if worry can't
accomplish a little thing like that, what's the use of worrying over bigger things?*

LUKE 12:25-26

So many things in life come down to perspective. Just stepping back and looking at our lives from a different position can make it much easier to see what
isn't working. That's exactly the perspective Jesus gives us in the famous verse
from his Sermon on the Mount where he points out just how futile it is to
worry.

What would you think of someone who couldn't walk one mile, yet registered to run a marathon? Clearly, that person would be deluding himself and
wasting his time. If we cannot do something on a small scale, why in the world
would we magnify the task and think the outcome will be any better?

You can apply the same logic to your worry. When was the last time that
worrying about something made it any better? Whether the problem is big or
small, worry has the same effect on its outcome—zero.

Doesn't it make more sense to take your concerns to the Lord and let him
handle them?

ASK YOURSELF

» Does realizing that worry is futile help you not to worry? If not, what
can help?

» What are some of the ways you can step back from your life and gain
a fresh perspective?

ASK GOD

Dear Lord, there are times when I allow worry to occupy my mind. Logically,
I know that it fixes nothing, but it sneaks into my thoughts anyway. Give me
the perspective to recognize worry for what it is and to hand my concerns over
to you as soon as I am aware of them.

Unopened Gifts

Live in harmony with each other. Don't be too proud to enjoy the
company of ordinary people. And don't think you know it all!

ROMANS 12:16

We've all done it at one time or another. We meet people and make a knee-jerk
assessment as to whether they are people we want to spend time with.

Maybe it's the clothes they wear or the car they drive.

Maybe it's the music they listen to or what they eat.

Or maybe a casual comment makes us suspect they might differ from us
politically or subscribe to a different "flavor" of Christianity.

They might even represent a culture or nationality that makes us
uncomfortable.

Our competitive and status-conscious society often makes us inclined to
size each other up and judge each other by the most superficial of standards,
and social media just makes the problem worse. But these kinds of snap judg-
ments are just the opposite of what God wants for us. His desire is that we give
each other the benefit of the doubt. That we actually listen to people and get
to know them instead of assuming we know what they're like.

Excluding people before getting to know them is like throwing away a present before we open it.

ASK YOURSELF

» What kinds of attributes tend to make you uncomfortable when meeting someone new?

» Are we ever justified in excluding or avoiding someone *after* we get to
know them? Why or why not?

ASK GOD

Dear Lord, so often I close myself off from others and don't give them a chance.
Help me to look past outward appearances to the heart of everyone I meet. Let
me see in every individual what you see when you look at them.

Treasure Hunt

Keep on asking, and you will receive what you ask for. Keep on seeking, and you will find. Keep on knocking, and the door will be opened to you.

MATTHEW 7:7

Did you ever participate in an Easter egg hunt as a child? Do you remember how much trouble your parents (or whoever sponsored the hunt) took to prepare and hide all those eggs? They did it because of the joy and excitement the hunt brought to you and other children. There were always one or two eggs that had been especially well hidden, but you would never think of quitting until you had found them all. In fact, it was the best-hidden eggs that brought the most excitement.

God has hidden a depth of treasure in the Bible, and nothing makes him happier than watching you seek it out. You can open your Bible with as much excitement as a young child getting ready for an Easter egg hunt. The Lord has so much waiting for you to discover, and he is eager for you to find the treasure he has so carefully hidden away for you in his Word.

ASK YOURSELF

» What is your usual approach to Scripture reading? Do you read and study with the anticipation of finding the treasure God has hidden for you there, or do you usually just go through the motions?

» Have you ever experienced that little thrill that comes from discovering something new in a passage you've read again and again? What actions on your part might make such discoveries more likely?

ASK GOD

Dear Lord, cause me to see your Word for what it is—hidden treasure, put there just for me. Give me the heart and the wisdom to "dig" for it every day. I thank you for loving me enough to provide me with insight into who you are through your inspired Word.

Seeking Favor

Many seek the ruler's favor, but justice comes from the LORD.

PROVERBS 29:26

In the workplace, people will often do anything to stay on the good side of the boss. They'll spare no time or expense in cultivating relationships they hope will further their careers. And that might work if they could be certain that the boss would always be the boss—but they can't. They will always be a firing, a promotion, or a bad decision away from having to start all over with a new higher-up.

There's nothing wrong with trying to do a good job, with doing your best to fulfill an employer's expectations (within reason). But focusing on finding favor with someone whose power will always be temporary is a waste of time and energy. Instead, we should be seeking the favor of the only one who can make a real difference in our lives. God alone has the power and the desire to help us become the people we were meant to be. And because God is just, we can be sure his interaction in our lives will bring about the fulfillment we seek.

ASK YOURSELF

» Have you ever spent too much time or energy trying to stay in the good graces of someone you thought could help you? What was the result?

» Do you think it's possible to trust in God completely and still seek the help of others who are in power positions over you? Why or why not?

ASK GOD

Dear Lord, it is so easy to fall into the trap of trying to please others, especially those who are in positions of power in my life. Help me instead to place my security and my future in your hands.

No Fear of Bad News

How joyful are those who fear the LORD and delight in obeying his commands. . . .
They do not fear bad news; they confidently trust the LORD to care for them.

PSALM 112:1, 7

Do you ever find yourself anticipating bad news, waiting for the other shoe to drop, tensing in the expectation of unpleasant surprises? Do you sometimes avoid the mailbox, turn off the news on the radio, or wince when a car appears in the driveway? Whether you have reason to expect bad news or just dread what *might* happen, that's a miserable way to live.

What's the alternative? The psalmist suggests that our confident trust in the Lord is our antidote to fear of bad news. Bad news is always a possibility. So is good news. But whatever happens can be faced with confidence when we trust the Lord to care for us.

Note that the psalmist isn't advocating a generic "trust the Lord" here. He reminds us to trust specifically that the Lord will care for us. We know God is always with us. But what gives us confidence to face our problems is the reassurance that no matter what happens, the Lord will be actively looking out for our welfare.

ASK YOURSELF

» What possibilities tend to stir up fear in you instead of confidence? What bad news do you dread?

» Do you find it difficult to believe that God will actively care for you if you receive the bad news you most dread? Why or why not?

ASK GOD

Lord God, I need more confidence in facing both what is happening in my life and what I fear *might* happen. Help me learn how to trust not only in your presence but also in your care.

Shining on a Hilltop

You are the light of the world—like a city on a hilltop that cannot be hidden.
No one lights a lamp and then puts it under a basket. Instead, a lamp is
placed on a stand, where it gives light to everyone in the house.

MATTHEW 5:14-15

There is nothing quite as mesmerizing as city lights, whether viewed from the air or from the ground. The lights seem to take on a life of their own when the sun goes down. And there is no hiding the lights of a city. They can be seen for miles. Each individual light has a specific function, but together they create something truly breathtaking.

God's Word says that we who follow Jesus are "the light of the world." The question is, are we allowing that light to shine on those around us, or are we trying to hide it? There are many reasons why Christians do not make their beliefs known to others, but none of them will hold up in God's eyes.

Besides, if we are depending on God, people will see our light anyway. What's the point of trying to cover it up? Instead, why not let them know who is powering the shine—so they can light up too.

ASK YOURSELF

» When are you most tempted to hide your true self?

» What people have you encountered recently who could have benefited from seeing God's light in you?

ASK GOD

Lord Jesus, what you have done in my life is amazing, and I want to let it shine out into the lives of those around me. Show me how to do that effectively so that I reveal your beauty in the world.

Let It Go

Give to anyone who asks; and when things are taken
away from you, don't try to get them back.

LUKE 6:30

Have you ever lost an object that was important to you—something you thought you just couldn't live without? What happened? Chances are that you got along just fine once you came to terms with your loss.

God wants us to enjoy the provisions he has given us. What he doesn't want is for us to be tied to our possessions or controlled by them. Our things are just that—things. No one will leave this planet with any of them. But while we are here, they can be valuable tools for sharing God's love. And because the world places such value on stuff, we can make an important statement by *not* hanging on to ours too tightly.

Do you really want the world to see Jesus through you? Then hand over your good suit to someone who needs to apply for a job. Buy a tank of gas for someone at the pump who is putting in the bare minimum. Share your lunch with someone who could use a meal or a friendly conversation. When you have the chance, explain your motivations—and watch people's eyes open to the possibilities of the gospel.

ASK YOURSELF

» Do you think you are too attached to the things in your life? Why or why not?

» What do you have that could be put to better use by giving it away?

ASK GOD

Dear heavenly Father, thank you for everything you have provided for me. Show me how to use my material possessions to bless others. I want to be sensitive to those in need and compassionate enough to share what I have with them.

Listen to Your Conscience

They demonstrate that God's law is written in their hearts, for their own
conscience and thoughts either accuse them or tell them they are doing right.

ROMANS 2:15

Have you ever disobeyed your GPS device, intentionally or otherwise? It's funny, isn't it? The GPS voice will immediately tell you to make a U-turn— attempting to correct your path as quickly as possible so that you don't get too far off course. If you do not comply, the GPS will continue to shout corrective directions until you either follow them or turn it off.

The conscience works a lot like this. God has given each of us a conscience to keep us on track. Its purpose is to make us aware when we are drifting off course and to correct our movement so we don't end up in the wrong place. The conscience, like a GPS device, can be ignored or turned off, but neither is advisable.

If you recognize your conscience as a guidance tool that God has given you for your own well-being and protection, then listen to it. Ignoring the pull of your conscience will always have negative consequences. Why would you want to be lost?

ASK YOURSELF

> » Do you listen to your conscience and follow it? How can you become more in tune with the leading of your conscience?

> » Do you think a person's conscience can ever become unreliable? If so, how does that happen? How can you keep it from happening to you?

ASK GOD

Dear heavenly Father, thank you for giving me a conscience to guide me through this life. When I feel the tug of conscience, teach me to call upon you for the strength and courage that I need to follow the right path.

Wait Patiently

Wait patiently for the LORD. Be brave and courageous. Yes, wait patiently for the LORD.
PSALM 27:14

The writer who penned Psalm 27 had clearly seen his share of trouble. He wrote of enemies accusing him and armies ready to attack. Yet the psalm is saturated with confidence in God's power and ultimate victory. And the last three lines, with great calmness, advise us to "wait patiently for the LORD."

That's the last thing most us want to do when we're surrounded by trouble. We want to be rescued—now!

But don't you recognize that voice—the one that offers peace in the midst of chaos and patience when circumstances seem most desperate? It's the voice of God's Spirit. When our eyes are fixed on the hardships we're facing, the Spirit gently and graciously whispers to our hearts, "Be brave and courageous. Yes, wait patiently for the LORD."

When circumstances overwhelm us, this is the voice we need to listen for. It's the one that assures our hearts that God is in control after all.

ASK YOURSELF

» In what kinds of circumstances do you find it hardest to wait on the Lord? When are you most tempted to take things into your own hands?

» What helps you find patience when your troubles are mounting?

ASK GOD

Lord, I confess that when I'm facing mighty enemies it is really hard to wait on you. I don't want to be patient. My flesh shouts out for your deliverance. But grant me the courage this day to wait on you anyway. I choose to trust that you are in control.

Honest Self-Evaluation

Because of the privilege and authority God has given me, I give each of you
this warning: Don't think you are better than you really are. Be honest in your
evaluation of yourselves, measuring yourselves by the faith God has given us.

ROMANS 12:3

The fourth step of twelve-step programs invites participants to conduct a "fearless moral inventory" of their lives, with a particular eye to noticing how they have sinned against others. It urges them to be brave and honest and unflinching in examining their hearts and actions. It's an impressively effective strategy, but it's not really original. The apostle Paul gave the same instruction to believers in his day.

In his letter to the young church in Rome, Paul warns followers of Jesus to be honest in how we see ourselves and to avoid the temptation to believe we are a little better than we actually are. The more honest we can be about who we are, the more effective we can be in taking our lives back.

ASK YOURSELF

» Is there an area of sin in your life that you're usually tempted to overlook? Why do you often gloss over it?

» Where would you find the courage to take an unflinching look at your life? Why do you think this is so important to the process of healing?

ASK GOD

God of grace, nothing is hidden from you. Give me the courage to look at the areas of my heart I'd rather hide. Equip me to be honest about who I've been and who I am. I trust you to be my Helper and to forgive my sins in Jesus' name.

Look in the Mirror

How can you think of saying to your friend, "Let me help you get rid of that
speck in your eye," when you can't see past the log in your own eye?
MATTHEW 7:4

Would you take financial advice from someone with an overdrawn checking account? Would you seek legal advice from someone who is incarcerated? Would it seem off-balance to accept weight-loss counseling from someone who is morbidly obese? Wouldn't you think it necessary for these people to correct their own failures before they try to correct what is lacking in others?

The answer seems obvious. But if it is, why are most of us so quick to criticize others? What is it about pointing out others' faults that brings such satisfaction? What allows an imperfect, flawed person to feel justified in pointing out the flaws in another? This all-too-human tendency may have complex roots—jealousy, denial, insecurity, guilt, pride, even fear—but in the end it boils down to pure, blind foolishness.

Don't be a fool. Focus your criticism on what you can actually change—yourself.

ASK YOURSELF

» Do you tend to nurture a critical spirit? Do you have any sense of why? What do you fear about letting God take care of the shortcomings of others?

» What can you do to safeguard yourself from being critical of others?

ASK GOD
Dear Jesus, I know I'm guilty of being critical toward those around me. I'm not sure why I do this, but I know it is wrong. I want to spend my time correcting my own faults rather than pointing out the faults of others. Please quicken my spirit whenever I begin to criticize, and help me change my heart.

Remedial Mothering

Can a mother forget her nursing child? Can she feel no love for the child
she has borne? . . . Even if that were possible, I would not forget you!

ISAIAH 49:15

Babies are designed to attract the attention of their mothers. Their skin is
soft to the touch. Their eyes are wide and curious. They have that delicious
new-baby smell (most of the time). And if all else fails, they can scream like
nobody's business. Little ones need their mother's presence to survive physically and emotionally, and these God-given attributes are usually successful in
getting them the care they need.

Usually, but not always.

Sometimes a mother is absent due to alcohol or drugs. Sometimes she's
unable to care for her children and relinquishes them to foster care or adoption.
Sometimes mental or physical ailments or events beyond her control—even
death—prevent her from giving her children the care and presence they need.

If your mother was unable or unwilling to care for you effectively, you have
some healing to do. But while you're working to take your life back, you can
still turn to God for "mothering." God is always there for you. God loves you
as tenderly as any mother loves her infant. And no matter what happens, God
will never forget you.

ASK YOURSELF

» Was your mother able and willing to be available to you in your earliest
days? What is the fallout of your early experience on your life?

» How can God's "mothering" care help you heal?

ASK GOD

Gracious God, I thank you for your steadfast, available presence. You are completely reliable. You never fail me. I trust you to meet the deep needs of my
heart. Please receive me into your loving arms.

Protector of Those Who Suffer

He gives prosperity to the poor and protects those who suffer.

JOB 5:11

Have you ever seen a foal being born on a nature program (or in person)? Within an hour the baby horse can stand on its spindly new legs, and within two hours it is able to take its first walking and running steps. Compared to newborn humans, most newborn animals are remarkably *able*. In fact, a human would need to gestate at least eighteen months to match the cognitive development of a chimpanzee at birth.

When you were born, you were entirely dependent on your caregivers to nurture, protect, and provide for you. And ideally those caregivers were able and willing to give you what you needed. But perhaps they did not, and you suffered as a result. This may be the main reason you need to take your life back today. You may still be recovering from emotional issues created by that suffering.

If that's true for you (or for someone you love), you need to take today's verse to heart. God cares for the vulnerable and protects those who suffer. No matter how it felt at the time, God was attentive to your pain and is alert to it today. You can count on his provision and protection.

ASK YOURSELF

» Looking back, can you point to times when God protected you even in the midst of your suffering?

» What would help you trust more completely in God's provision and protection?

ASK GOD

Mighty God, you have shown yourself to be a defender of those who are vulnerable and suffering. I trust that you are with me and for me. Deliver me in the strong name of your Son, Jesus.

Continually

Search for the LORD and for his strength; continually seek him.

1 CHRONICLES 16:11

When do you need to look for God? How often should you seek his guidance? When should you draw strength from him? Once a day? Once a week? Once a month? If you want to live the life that God has designed for you, the answer to all of those "how often" questions is "continually."

Continually is defined as "without interruption," and that is how often God wants us to look for him—every minute of every day. You don't have to put your life on hold to do it. In fact, you seek him best by involving him in your life moment by moment. Praise him, acknowledge him, and learn about him by reading his Word. Seek him in every situation and talk to him the way you would talk to anyone else who is an integral part of your life. He wants you to know he is with you. He is ready and willing to help with whatever you need.

ASK YOURSELF

> » How can you break the habit of seeking out God only when you have a problem to solve?

> » What circumstances tend to distract you from seeking God on a moment-by-moment basis? How can you prompt yourself to turn to him more often?

ASK GOD

Dear God, your Word commands me to seek you out continually. I want to do this, but sometimes I get distracted and go about my life as if you're not even there. Please forgive me for not making you a part of everything I do. Remind me that you are always with me, and teach me to seek you and your strength moment by moment.

Humble Enough to Learn

Take my yoke upon you. Let me teach you, because I am humble and gentle at heart.

MATTHEW 11:29

There's more to being humble than not being conceited or full of ourselves. Humility also involves being teachable—being willing to learn from God and from our own experiences. And such teachability is essential because the journey of healing is basically a learning experience.

What and how do we learn as we take our lives back? We learn new ways of living, interacting, and relating. We learn from our defective choices and from those great moments when we choose the next right thing and reap the rewards of living beyond our own immediate urges or impulses. We learn to be grateful for the simplest pleasures and the most complex difficulties. We learn to set boundaries and prevent others from crossing them—but also, eventually to give to others out of the abundance of God's love for us. And most of all, we learn from Christ, who teaches us his ways as we choose to follow him.

Every day can be a learning and growing experience if we're humble enough to realize we don't know it all.

ASK YOURSELF

> » What are some of the most surprising things you have learned so far in your journey to take your life back?

> » What attitudes besides pride can hold you back from learning?

ASK GOD

Dear Jesus, I want to learn from you, but my stubbornness and pride sometimes get in the way. Please forgive me. Teach me your ways as I continue my journey toward health.

The Good We Choose

By fearing the LORD, people avoid evil. When people's lives please
the LORD, even their enemies are at peace with them.

PROVERBS 16:6-7

Some of us feel overwhelmed by the lives we're living. We're stressed at work. We're overwhelmed at home. We're burdened with family concerns. We struggle to pay the bills. And much of what we face is outside of our control: the unreasonable boss, the unexpected bill, the spouse who drinks too much, or the child who makes bad choices. When we face such circumstances, God invites us to release each one to him. But he does hold us responsible for what we *can* control—such as whether we will avoid evil or embrace it. We've been charged to live lives that are pleasing to the Lord, and when we do that we experience the fruitfulness that comes from faithfulness. By fearing the Lord and avoiding evil, we can experience God's peace even in the face of difficulty.

ASK YOURSELF

> » What difficult circumstances in your life right now are beyond your control? Is it easy for you to relinquish these to the Lord? Why or why not?

> » What situations in your life right now call for decisions or action on your part? What choices do you think will be most pleasing to the Lord?

ASK GOD

God of grace, help me to distinguish between what I can't change and what I can—and to faithfully choose your way whenever I can. Lord, I release to you those circumstances in my life that are out of my control, and I ask for wisdom and courage to make right choices about the rest. Please grant me strength as I purpose to live a life that is pleasing to you.

Touched to Touch, Saved to Save

Encourage each other and build each other up, just as you are already doing.

1 THESSALONIANS 5:11

A woman who experienced abuse now volunteers at a shelter for women and children fleeing domestic violence. A man who was caught in the grip of alcoholism now serves others as an AA volunteer. A teen who tried to take her life now offers hope and encouragement over a suicide hotline. Once we make some progress in taking our lives back, God will often call us to reach those whose stories match the ones we've lived.

God can use you and me to reach fellow strugglers as we pass along the hope that has made such a difference in our lives. Sharing our stories with others brings value to them and value to what we've endured. Though once we may have waited for others to reach out to us and felt resentful that it didn't happen, today we take the initiative to reach out to others in need.

Our suffering and pain were not without meaning. We can find new life and further growth by helping others.

ASK YOURSELF

» How do you articulate the hope you've received? Is there someone whose journey has been similar to your own whom you can encourage this week?

» Do you think we need to be fully healed—or at least well along on the journey—before we can help others? Why or why not?

ASK GOD

Lord, thank you for your faithfulness in redeeming my life from the pit. I believe that no part of my journey has been wasted. Lord, use me and my story to reach those you long to touch and to heal.

Which Way?

Letting your sinful nature control your mind leads to death. But letting the Spirit control your mind leads to life and peace.

ROMANS 8:6

Imagine that you are standing at a crossroads with two road signs pointing in opposite directions. One sign says, "This Way to Certain Death," and the other sign says, "This Way to Life and Peace." Which do you choose? The answer seems obvious. Unless you are in a comedy skit or you have some reason to distrust the signs, you are going to take the path that leads to life and peace.

If we're really talking about road signs, the whole scenario seems unlikely. But if we're talking about life, it's absolutely real. In fact, we all make this same choice every day. The Bible says we must make a conscious choice between letting our sinful nature lead us toward spiritual death or following God's Spirit in the direction of life and peace.

So what are you choosing? In what direction are your decisions leading you? If you look at your life honestly, you'll get a clear indication of where you are heading—and who is leading you there.

ASK YOURSELF

» What does the state of your life right now tell you about the decisions you are making every day?

» Are there specific situations where you tend to let your sinful nature run your life?

ASK GOD

Dear Lord, sometimes I seem to stumble blindly through this life. Open my eyes to the choices I make each and every day, and teach me to choose the path that leads to life and peace. You are so patient with me—thank you, Lord!

The Right Companions

A friend is always loyal, and a brother is born to help in time of need.

PROVERBS 17:17

Do you remember how Dorothy's journey to the Emerald City unfolded in the 1939 film classic *The Wizard of Oz?* First she met a friendly, weak-kneed scarecrow, then a man made of tin, and finally an anxious lion. One by one, they joined her on the road to the city. And though they didn't recognize it at the time, each of these companions possessed a unique gift or ability that would enable the group to reach its destination. The scarecrow offered wisdom, the tin man exemplified a loving heart, and (in a pinch) the lion displayed great courage.

On your healing journey, ask God to provide the traveling companions you need. They might be friends, relatives, or professionals. The best partners on your journey are those who can be there for you in the ways you need most. (You'll be there for them, too.) But don't worry too much about seeking out those companions. Make it a matter of prayer instead. You can trust the Lord to connect you with the right people at the right time.

ASK YOURSELF

» Can you look back on your life and recognize some of the faithful people who have already journeyed with you?

» Who are some of the folks you think would be dependable companions during this season? Are you open to the possibility that God might provide someone you don't expect?

ASK GOD

God, I trust that you are the one who is leading me during this season of growth. Thank you for faithful human companions who support me on this journey. I am grateful for the ways they reflect your steadfast presence and your unfailing love.

When You Think No One Is Listening

I love the LORD because he hears my voice and my prayer for mercy.

PSALM 116:1

Do you ever feel that no one understands your pain? Have you grown tired of looking for comfort and support from others because they seem incapable of providing it or unwilling to do so? Don't be disheartened. You've simply been looking for help in the wrong place. You are a child of God, and he wants to meet your needs.

Living in this earthly realm, it is natural to look to your fellow humans when you need help. And often you get it, especially when those others are tuned in to God's calling. Unfortunately, every one of those fellow humans will let you down in one way or another. Most people can barely keep their own lives on track and have little left over for others in need. So if you are feeling that no one is there for you, you are right in a sense. But you are also wrong, because God is always there for you. And unlike your fellow humans, he always listens.

ASK YOURSELF

» Who in your life has disappointed you or let you down in a major way? How has that disappointment affected your life?

» Is God your first source of comfort when you are feeling down? How do you reach out to him for comfort?

» Are you placing unrealistic expectations upon the people in your life? If so, what could you change?

ASK GOD

Dear Jesus, help me learn to come to you first with all of my needs and desires. In my times of trouble, let me learn to depend on you first. As I reach out to the people in my life, let me not expect more from them than they are humanly able to provide. Thank you for listening, Lord.

Getting Together with the Father

When you pray, go away by yourself, shut the door behind you, and pray to your
Father in private. Then your Father, who sees everything, will reward you.

MATTHEW 6:6

The alarm clock buzzes, and another crazy day begins. You hustle to get your household ready for the day, grab a quick coffee, and fight traffic to get to work or school. And the frantic pace doesn't let up until you fall into bed that night, exhausted.

Sound familiar? Details might differ, but your life is probably pretty full. If it's feeling a little *too* full, take heart. You can choose to build an island of sanity and peace in the middle of the most hectic day.

Simply identify a comfortable, quiet spot where you can pause to reflect on your life. Find a time that works for you—morning, afternoon, even late at night—then put it on your calendar. Make it a daily date with yourself and God—and try not to break it. This time you steal away from your crazy-busy life to be in your Father's presence will help keep you from living constantly in reaction mode. If you choose to write down your reflections, you can return to them later to learn from the wisdom you've received.

ASK YOURSELF

» Where is the best place and time for you to pause, pray, and reflect?

» What prevents you from carving out a time to be still in the midst of your full life? How could you get past these obstacles?

ASK GOD

Father, I hear your invitation to spend time with you and, when I'm honest, it's what I most hunger and thirst for. Please meet me in a quiet place and speak your wisdom to my heart.

Where You Belong

You belong to God, my dear children. You have already won a victory . . . , because
the Spirit who lives in you is greater than the spirit who lives in the world.

1 JOHN 4:4

Each one of us is born with a deep yearning to belong. And yet some of us grew up feeling like outsiders or outcasts. Others lived with the pain of belonging to something or someone that hurt us deeply. The whole idea of belonging became deeply problematic for us.

But that, by God's grace, was then—and this is now.

Now we know we belong to God. We belong to God's people. We belong to healthy families or can create healthy families that help us heal. Now we have a place at the table. We deserve to show up, and others deserve to have us there. We are official. We are included. We know the joy of being part of something far greater than ourselves.

And whenever that old sense of being an outsider raises its head—as it probably will—we can reject it for the lie that it is. In Christ we can claim our victory over alienation and isolation because "the Spirit who lives in [us] is greater than the spirit who lives in the world."

ASK YOURSELF

» Do you relate to either the "then" or the "now" descriptions above? Why or why not?

» How can you help others feel the same sense of belonging you are learning to embrace?

ASK GOD

Father, thank you for calling me your own and making me part of your family. You are the one in whom I find my true identity and my true sense of belonging.

Exposing the Lies

When the Spirit of truth comes, he will guide you into all truth.
He will not speak on his own but will tell you what he has heard.

JOHN 16:13

If someone told you that apples were purple and grapes were turquoise, that would be a lie. If someone insisted that dogs could fly, that would also be a lie. But those are the kinds of lies that are easy to sniff out. The ones that are more treacherous—the ones that tap into our fear or shame or guilt—are lies about who we are and who God is.

The enemy of our souls told these lies as a sneaky serpent in the Garden of Eden and as a tempting devil in the wilderness. And he keeps spewing the same falsehoods today. He hisses that we're not worth loving and that God can't be trusted. But we don't have to fall for his whoppers because we know better. We know we can trust God's Spirit to expose the deceiver's twisted lies. Better still, we can trust Jesus to be our way, our truth, and our life (see John 14:6).

ASK YOURSELF

» What are some of the lies you've believed about yourself and your belovedness? What are the lies you've believed about God and his unfailing love?

» What are the truths that expose the enemy's lies? Repeat them to yourself out loud.

ASK GOD

Gracious God, I confess that I've believed the enemy's wily lies. Forgive me and, by the truth of your Spirit, set me free. Expose the twisted fallacies I've swallowed whole and reveal your truth to my heart and mind. Today I choose to believe you.

Never Stop Growing

You must grow in the grace and knowledge of our Lord and Savior
Jesus Christ. All glory to him, both now and forever!

2 PETER 3:18

It is amazing to watch the growth of a human being from infancy through young adulthood. The physical changes are a marvel, and they seem to happen overnight. Typically females keep growing until they are about sixteen and males usually reach their full growth by eighteen. By young adulthood, physical growth is usually complete.

The same is not true of our spiritual and emotional growth, which continues—and should continue—through our whole lives. If we're not growing, in fact, in some ways we are dying.

Ongoing growth enriches our lives and expands our perspectives. It also increases the possibilities for new dimensions in our lives to emerge. Those of us who are taking our lives back soon learn that continuing to grow is the only way to be satisfied with our lives—especially when we're growing in the grace and knowledge of Jesus Christ.

ASK YOURSELF

» Have some periods of your life been more stagnant in terms of growth than others? Why do you think this happened?

» What kinds of practices help you grow? What are some ways to work more of these into your life?

ASK GOD

Lord, I thank you that I am alive in you. I long to grow in my relationship with you, my relationships with others, and my relationship with myself. Feed me by your Word and increase my capacity to love and be loved, for the sake of your glory.

Don't Neglect to Meet

Let us not neglect our meeting together, as some people do, but encourage
one another, especially now that the day of his return is drawing near.

HEBREWS 10:25

Members of twelve-step groups have discovered that the support, encouragement, and kinship they find by attending meetings empower them to survive and thrive in ways they've not been able to manage on their own. Members share the same goals and inspire one another to be the people they were created to be. They glean strength and momentum from a community of like-minded folk.

The author of Hebrews encourages the early church with the wisdom that twelve-steppers would discover centuries later. Acknowledging that some Christians had stopped meeting together, the writer urges believers to meet regularly and to encourage one another.

The life of faith was never meant to be flown solo. You will find nurture and momentum for your own spirit as you gather with like-minded believers.

ASK YOURSELF

» Are you in the regular habit of meeting with other believers for encouragement? What opportunities has God provided for you to gather and be strengthened?

» Do you have any baggage from your past that makes you shy away from churches or other Christian groups? What are your fears and concerns? How can you handle them so you can obey God's Word in this regard?

ASK GOD

God of grace, I thank you that you have called me to yourself and have knit me into a body of believers for my sake, for their sake, and for yours. Strengthen me as I commit to meeting with others and offering them encouragement in your name.

The Upside

We also pray that you will be strengthened with all his glorious
power so you will have all the endurance and patience you need.
May you be filled with joy, always thanking the Father.

COLOSSIANS 1:11-12

Almost everyone is willing to sacrifice something they like in order to gain something they desire more. If you have ever been on a diet, you are living proof of this fact. You were willing to give up the "ooey, gooey" foods you love because you wanted to look better and feel better. You recognized that the pain of giving up your edible pleasures would be offset by the resulting weight loss. So your sacrifice had an upside: a slimmer you.

Believe it or not, the problems and trials we experience in this world have an upside as well—they build our endurance. When we allow God to guide us through a trying situation, we will come out stronger on the other side.

This is helpful to remember when trouble arises. If we can keep our focus on what we can gain from the situation rather than on what we're going through now, we'll be better equipped to make it through. And if we keep in mind that God will never allow us to go through difficulty alone, we'll find another upside: joy.

ASK YOURSELF

» What problems are you facing in your life right now? What good could eventually result from them—or in them?

» What are some things you can do to survive while you're waiting to see the upside of your suffering?

ASK GOD

Dear Jesus, sometimes it is hard for me to see my way out of life's troubling situations. Help me to remember that if I rely on you, there will always be an upside to my suffering.

What to Say No To

We are instructed to turn from godless living and sinful pleasures. We should
live in this evil world with wisdom, righteousness, and devotion to God.

TITUS 2:12

An important key to taking our lives back is knowing when to say a good, courageous *no*. Sometimes that's easier said than done. If we're saying no out of fear, defensiveness, or a desire to manipulate or get revenge—that's not a good no. We always need to be asking for God's wisdom to examine our current situation and reveal our true intentions to ourselves.

But Paul's brief letter to Titus reminds us that certain situations are actually pretty clear. Saying no to godless living—our own and others'—and to sinful pleasure are among those. If a yes will propel you into sinful choices or will enable someone else's, then a courageous, holy no is in order. And you can be confident that God's Spirit will equip you to live faithfully into that no.

ASK YOURSELF

> » Can you think of a time in your past when you were asked to say yes to something that could (or did) lead to sin? What was your answer? What was the result?

> » What kinds of needs or desires could tempt you today to give in to an easy yes? What could help you offer a firm, loving no?

ASK GOD

Lord, I confess that I need you to guide and strengthen me. I'm sorry for the times when I've chosen an easy yes instead of the hard no that would have honored you. Forgive me. Give me the courage to honor you and to love others with my words and my actions.

A Balanced Confidence

I pray that God, the source of hope, will fill you completely with
joy and peace because you trust in him. Then you will overflow
with confident hope through the power of the Holy Spirit.

ROMANS 15:13

God wants us to have confidence in who we are. But many of us have trouble striking a balance in this regard. Some are so confident in their attributes and abilities that they become conceited and vain. Others have little or no confidence in themselves and believe that they are "lesser than" everyone else. And many of us veer between the two positions, depending on what attributes we're thinking of.

All of these unbalanced attitudes can be a problem. When we're too confident, we end up taking credit for all that is good about us—as though we created ourselves. When we belittle ourselves, we're discrediting God's creation. And when we do both, things get really confused.

So how can we develop a healthy, balanced confidence? By accepting the truth that God made us with exactly the mix of attributes he wanted us to have. Our responsibility is to develop this God-given mix of gifts and talents and use them for his glory.

ASK YOURSELF

» Do you think your confidence in yourself is well-balanced? Why or why not?

» Make a list of the attributes and talents God gave you when he created you. Are you making the best use of these that you can?

ASK GOD

Dear heavenly Father, thank you for making me *me*. Help me to keep a balanced view of myself and to remember that the places in my life where I excel and those where I am lacking are by your design. Help me to follow your lead in becoming the person you made me to be.

What Do Your Actions Say?

I trust in God, so why should I be afraid? What can mere mortals do to me?

PSALM 56:11

We drive up to a valet attendant and hand him our car keys, trusting that he will park our vehicle safely and return it when we're ready to depart.

We deposit our paycheck in the bank, trusting the institution to guard our funds and make them available to us when we need them.

The point is, we place our trust in fallible human beings and entities every day without giving it a second thought. We go about our business and let them do their jobs. We don't second-guess every little detail unless we have good reason to expect problems. And yet many of us tend to mistrust and second-guess the only one in the universe who is entirely trustworthy.

How would we live if we really trusted God? We would move through this world freely, unburdened by fear. We would boldly expect that good things were going to happen no matter the circumstances. And we wouldn't waste time and energy trying to control every detail of our lives. We would let God take care of us, just as he has promised.

ASK YOURSELF

> » What do you think your actions show about how much you trust God?

> » When you fail to trust God, what are the negative effects on your life?

ASK GOD

Lord Jesus, I know you are able to handle every detail in my life if I will get out of the way. Forgive me for my mistrust and my attempts to tell you what to do. Help me to move forward with confidence because I trust you completely.

Uneven Exchange

I will turn their mourning into joy. I will comfort them
and exchange their sorrow for rejoicing.

JEREMIAH 31:13

When you go to the store to exchange an item, the store will usually allow you to trade it in for something of equal or lesser value. There is no additional cost to you for the exchange, and the store will happily assist you as a matter of goodwill. But should you wish to exchange your item for something better, something of greater value, then the store will require that you pay the difference.

That is just the way business works. Thankfully, it's not the way God works.

If you are experiencing pain and sorrow, the Lord is ready and willing to exchange it for comfort and supernatural joy. You can hand over the misery you are experiencing in exchange for comfort from the Holy Spirit. You can hand God your grief, your regret, and your sorrow and allow him to exchange them for something better.

The Lord is offering you a free upgrade. Why not take him up on it? You can take your life back!

ASK YOURSELF

> » Are you holding on to pain and misery rather than giving it to God? How does hanging on to negative things affect you on a daily basis?

> » Do you think the supernatural exchange of misery and joy happens instantly, or is there often a time lapse? If so, why might that happen?

ASK GOD

Dear God, you are so gracious and kind. I want to exchange all of the things that tear me down for your comfort and joy, which I know will lift me up.

Growing to Lead

Be an example to all believers in what you say, in the way
you live, in your love, your faith, and your purity.

1 TIMOTHY 4:12

God has always chosen some of the most unlikely folks to be leaders. He called Moses when he was an exile with a stutter living in the wilderness. He called Samuel when he was a child interning in the Tabernacle. He chose David to be anointed as king when he was just a shepherd boy, and he called Timothy to pastor a church when he was a young man with no experience. And as you make progress in taking back your life, he may well be calling you to be a leader as well. A growing capacity for leadership, in fact, is a sign that you're getting healthier.

By God's grace, you are no longer defined by the dependencies and confusion that once held you back. As you reclaim the life you were made for, you gain a newfound confidence that you have something valuable to offer to others. You lead as your life reflects the good news that God has something more for you and for others than suffering and surviving. Having found a way out of both, you now lead others to the source of this new way of living.

ASK YOURSELF

» What opportunities is God providing for you to shine as a leader today?

» Is leadership the only way you can give something valuable to others? What are some other ways?

ASK GOD

God, I thank you that I am no longer defined by my past. As one who has been set free from the will and whims of others, my life is now defined by you. Equip me to lead as your faithful servant.

No U-Turns

I listen carefully to what God the LORD is saying, for he speaks peace
to his faithful people. But let them not return to their foolish ways.

PSALM 85:8

What would you think of someone who started a journey with great excitement, carefully followed the directions given to them, and almost reached their destination—only to turn around and head back home? That just wouldn't make sense, would it?

In life, God provides us with a clear map to our destination, and following his directions can remove a lot of stress from our life journey. But human beings seem to have a hard time following directions. Some start on the path God has marked for them but take a wrong turn. Some stop in their tracks and refuse to go forward. And then there are the U-turn folks who end up back where they started.

The Lord calls all of this foolishness. He wants us to be faithful in our walk with him, to not only follow his directions but also persist until we reach our destination. A road map is great, after all, but if we don't actually finish the journey, what have we gained?

ASK YOURSELF

» Looking back at your life, what are some times when you have veered from the right path or even gone backward? What was the result?

» How can you find encouragement to keep going when you're tempted to give up or take another direction?

ASK GOD

Dear Lord, I know you are holding the road map for my life. Please keep me motivated on my journey. Forgive me for the times I have allowed myself to be sidetracked or discouraged. I want to follow you all the way.

Jesus Helps Us See

> *Go back to John and tell him what you have heard and seen—the blind*
> *see, the lame walk, those with leprosy are cured, the deaf hear, the dead*
> *are raised to life, and the Good News is being preached to the poor.*
>
> MATTHEW 11:4-5

For the first time in his life, John the Baptist was having doubts. He'd started his public life as a prophet in the wilderness, preparing folks for the coming of his cousin, Jesus, who he believed was the long-awaited Messiah. He had even baptized his cousin—and witnessed God's miraculous act of approval.

But now John had been thrown in prison, and he was beginning to wonder if he had been right about Jesus. Had all his work been in vain? So he sent emissaries to find out if Jesus was indeed the awaited Messiah. Jesus answered with a long list of wonderful things that were happening as a result of his ministry. One of them was that "the blind see."

What Jesus did in the first century for those who were physically blind, he does today for those of us who suffer from blindness of heart or mind. As we reclaim our lives, we'll find that we are finally able to see ourselves, other people, and the circumstances of our lives as they really are. We're aware of our vulnerabilities, but we're also able to see our ability to choose life and health.

ASK YOURSELF

> » What are some of the internal and external circumstances that make it hard for you to see yourself or others accurately?

> » How do you see your life differently as a result of your healing journey?

ASK GOD

Lord, open my eyes that I might see you, myself, and others as we truly are.

Burdens Shared, Burdens Lifted

Share each other's burdens, and in this way obey the law of Christ.

GALATIANS 6:2

Sharing our hopes, fears, and struggles with another person sounds like a good thing—and it is. For some of us, though, it takes some getting used to.

When we were young, we longed for someone to talk to, someone who would listen and reflect our reality back to us. We longed for a sympathetic friend who would weep over our hurts and flash with anger when we were mistreated. But in the absence of that person, we came to faulty conclusions—that we were unworthy, that we deserved what we got, that we would never have anyone to share our burdens.

If that was your experience, hopefully you know better now. Now you understand how opening up to someone else—sharing what you have done and what has been done to you—can bring God's healing grace into your life. As you have gained experience sharing your stories with safe people, you've discovered what you didn't think was possible—that you are still loved and accepted. But you could never have learned that without taking the brave step of sharing your burden with someone who cares.

ASK YOURSELF

> » When you were growing up, did you have anyone to share your burdens or reflect your experience? If not, how did your early circumstances influence your life today?

> » Who are the ones you can trust today to receive and honor your experience?

ASK GOD

God, I confess that I once believed I could not share the most painful parts of my journey with someone else. But today I believe you have provided faithful companions to join me on the journey. Thank you for the gift they are.

Make Peace a Priority

Better a dry crust eaten in peace than a house filled with feasting—and conflict.

PROVERBS 17:1

The irony of this life is that we can have everything money can buy and still have nothing.

Think about it. How many times have you wanted something so badly that you couldn't focus on anything else until you got it? Now fast-forward a week or a month or a year (the time frame is irrelevant) and remember when that thing just didn't do it for you any longer. You were on to the next "want" and the next one. Why? Because things never satisfy for very long!

You would do much better to seek after what is lasting and eternal—especially God's peace, which is life changing. Nothing you can accumulate on this earth is worth having if you do not have his peace. So the next time you are pining away, thinking about your next acquisition, take a moment to check the level of peace in your life. Without it, you won't be able to enjoy anything you have acquired. Make peace a priority!

ASK YOURSELF

> » Do you tend to seek fulfillment through material things? What other sources of fulfillment have you tried? What was the result?

> » What would your life be like if you desired God's peace above everything else? How can you find that peace?

ASK GOD

Dear God, I know that focusing on temporal things is a waste of time. Thank you for showing me the way to true happiness. Help me to value a life filled with your peace above all else.

What Do You Love?

Those who love your instructions have great peace and do not stumble.

PSALM 119:165

In life, there are things you detest, things you avoid, things you tolerate, things you can take or leave. Then there are the things you never want to be without. Those are the things that you love. When you truly love something, you want as much of it as you can get. You just can't get enough of it.

God's Word says that those who love his instructions will have "great peace" and will "not stumble." Notice that it does not say, "those who *tolerate* [his] instructions" or "those who *sometimes follow* [his] instructions." It says, "those who *love* [his] instructions."

The Lord has prepared instructions to get you through this life and to bring you into eternity with him. Those instructions are found in his Word. If you look at the Lord's direction as a cumbersome set of rules imposed on you against your will, you will tolerate it at best. But if you see it for the gift that it is, you will love it—and you'll be rewarded with peace and sure-footed confidence.

ASK YOURSELF

» What is your attitude toward the instructions God has given to you in his Word? Do you seek out God's direction and look forward to following where he leads you? Why or why not?

» What would help you love God's instructions more?

ASK GOD

Dear Lord, you have gone to such lengths to provide me with the perfect set of instructions for life. Please give me a love for your Word and a desire to apply your instruction so that my life can be filled with your peace and I will not stumble.

Reconciled

Since God chose you to be the holy people he loves, you must clothe yourselves
with tenderhearted mercy, kindness, humility, gentleness, and patience.
Make allowance for each other's faults, and forgive anyone who offends
you. Remember, the Lord forgave you, so you must forgive others.

COLOSSIANS 3:12-13

Have you ever known people who are in the habit of being reconciled to others? When they mess up, they ask forgiveness. When they are offended, they seek to clarify and forgive. Even when it is easier to let a conflict fester, they do the hard work of resolving the issue and healing the relationship.

That's who we're learning to be as we walk the road of recovery.

Though we may have avoided conflict or confrontation in the past, God is growing us into people who are free and confident in addressing issues we have with others and seeking resolution. We make peace when we can and clarify whenever possible. We seek the understanding we need to make right what has gone wrong.

And we do it all in the name of one who called us to be his holy people.

ASK YOURSELF

» Was there a time when you avoided conflict, even to the detriment of your relationships? Is this still a challenge for you?

» How have you grown in your ability to resolve disagreements with other people?

ASK GOD

God, you have charged your children to be reconciled with one another, and you have equipped me to do just that. Help me to bring peace, clarity, and understanding where there is chaos, darkness, and misunderstanding—so that you are glorified through my relationships.

Set Free to Reach Higher

Work hard so you can present yourself to God and receive
his approval. Be a good worker, one who does not need to
be ashamed and who correctly explains the word of truth.

2 TIMOTHY 2:15

In 1943 psychologist Abraham Maslow presented a theory of human motivation based on a "hierarchy of needs." He suggested that certain basic needs must be met before we'll be strongly motivated to pursue high levels of fulfillment. For instance, if our physiological needs—for air, water, food—are not met, we'll be unlikely to worry about our self-esteem. And if we are unsure about our safety—because of war, family violence, or other trauma—we probably won't put a lot of energy into realizing our full potential. Having basic needs met, however, frees us to pursue loftier goals.

The experience of many on the road to recovery illustrates Maslow's ideas. Before we begin the journey of taking our lives back, our energies are poured into survival. But as our basic needs are met, we are enabled to pursue higher goals. Now we can search for truth, for the best, for God's will, and for what God would have us do with all that we are and all we've been through.

ASK YOURSELF

» In what ways did you have to fight for physical and emotional survival when you were growing up?

» How are you motivated today to pursue God's truth about yourself, about God, and about others?

ASK GOD

God, you call us to be stewards of what is true and good. Equip and inspire me to pursue your truth today and to make sense of what that means for me and for the world you love.

Not a Victim

*I have told you all this so that you may have peace in me. Here on earth you will
have many trials and sorrows. But take heart, because I have overcome the world.*

JOHN 16:33

Do you ever let your problems get you down? Most of us do at one time or
another. We fall into the "poor me" role when things don't go our way. But as
Christians we must resist this all-too-human tendency.

Jesus made it clear that "trials and sorrows" are just part of living in this
world. There will always be problems to be solved and pain to endure, and Jesus
wants us to be prepared for that. But he also wants us to know that because of
who he is, all these problems are temporary. They're just something we have to
get through (and learn from) on our way to eternity with him.

In Jesus, in other words, we are not victims, even if we sometimes act like
it. If we take his promise to heart, we should be able to find comfort and even
peace right in the midst of our chaotic, confusing reality.

ASK YOURSELF

» What promises of Jesus have been most meaningful for you when
problems arise?

» How can you take your problems seriously (so you can solve them if
possible) and still keep the perspective that they are temporary? How
can you be honest about your pain and still experience God's peace?

ASK GOD

Dear Jesus, I know that you have already claimed the victory for all of those
who love you. I do love you, Lord. Teach me how to claim what is already mine.
Remind me that I'm not a victim.

Self-Entrapment

An evil man is held captive by his own sins; they are ropes that catch and hold him.

PROVERBS 5:22

Would you put out a trap if you knew you'd be the one to get caught in it? That would be the height of foolishness. But that's exactly what we do when we allow sin in our lives.

Sin is sneaky. In the beginning it may even let us think we are in control. But before we know it, the sin is controlling us.

God understands this. (He's been dealing with sin for a long time.) That's why he warns against allowing even "minor" or "harmless" sin into our lives. He knows that once sin gets its foot in the door it will end up holding us captive. Why would we choose that?

One of Satan's favorite tricks is to make us think that God is depriving us of something we deserve to have. He used that ploy in the Garden of Eden. But he was a liar then and he's still a liar today.

If we look at God's instructions from the right perspective, it's easy to see that they are given to protect us, not spoil our fun.

ASK YOURSELF

» When (if ever) have you been deceived into seeing sin as something attractive God is withholding from you?

» How can you use your past mistakes to help you recognize the trap of sin before you fall into it?

ASK GOD

Dear Lord, please give me eyes to see sin for exactly what it is. Thank you for loving me enough to write a book of instructions to keep me from harm. Make me wise enough to heed them.

Three Key Ingredients

Look at those who are honest and good, for a wonderful
future awaits those who love peace.

PSALM 37:37

Have you ever followed a recipe to make a cake from scratch? Every ingredient listed serves a purpose. Some enhance the flavor, some insure the proper texture, and still others cause the cake to rise. Can you add other good ingredients to the mix? Probably. Just don't leave out anything that is called for in the recipe because the finished product may not be desirable if you do.

God has given you a recipe for a wonderful future. It starts with being honest, being good, and being a lover of peace. Can you add other good things to your life? Of course you can. Can you leave out any of these ingredients? Not without compromising the results. Each one plays an important role in making you the person God intends you to be. So strive for a life that is honest and filled with goodness; seek peace in every situation and celebrate when it prevails. This is a recipe for a blessed future.

ASK YOURSELF

> » Which of the three ingredients—honesty, goodness, and peace—are most evident in your life right now? Are there any you need more of?

> » What other good things would you like to add to the mix? What matters most to you in addition to honesty, goodness, and peace?

ASK GOD

Dear God, I want to live in accordance with your Word—to be honest, do good to others, and actively promote peace. Teach me to recognize those times when my life does not meet the standards you desire. Set me on the path to a wonderful future.

Don't Hang On

*If you try to hang on to your life, you will lose it. But if you
give up your life for my sake, you will save it.*

LUKE 9:24

How effective would a fisherman be if he was so worried about losing his bait that he refused to put it in the water? Not very. Fishermen know they must put their bait out there to attract what they are really seeking—fish. They must let go of one to gain the other.

Our minds are so finite when compared to God's that we often fail to see the bigger picture. We persist in focusing on the narrow scope of our own needs and wants when we are actually only a very, very small piece of what God is doing in this world.

That doesn't mean we're not worthy or important. But it does mean we're not the center of the universe. Coming to terms with that truth means letting go of our limited viewpoints. It means loosening our grip on our personal needs, wants, and goals so that we can be part of God's greater agenda. If we can't bring ourselves to do that, we will never get what we are seeking, and we will miss out on the eternal prize.

ASK YOURSELF

> » What specific desires and goals mean the most to you? Are they in sync with God's wider agenda?

> » How do you focus on your own recovery while still keeping an eye on the bigger picture?

ASK GOD

Dear Lord, I need help letting go of my shortsighted focus on me. Help me to look at my life through your eyes and to become a part of your plan instead of expecting you to be a part of mine.

The Language of Love

Love is patient and kind. Love is not jealous or boastful or proud.

1 CORINTHIANS 13:4

Have you ever watched a TV program in a foreign language? You can get a general idea of what is going on by watching the actions of the people involved, but you have no way of knowing what is really being said. Your interpretation of the show could be spot-on, or you could be way off base because you do not speak the language.

That is what love is like without Jesus. It means something different to everyone, and all of the definitions are lacking.

The world's definition of love will vary from person to person, but it will always be flawed because humans are flawed. God's love, on the other hand, is perfect. The Word tells us that it is "patient and kind," that it is "not jealous or boastful or proud." It is satisfying to all because it is pure and selfless.

To those who do not know God personally, this kind of love is a foreign language. But to those of us who follow Jesus, it should be our native tongue. We should speak it fluently and often.

ASK YOURSELF

» Does your life exemplify the kind of patient, kind, generous, and humble love that the Bible talks about? Where do you typically fall short?

» What is the best way to "brush up" on God's love language?

ASK GOD

Dear Jesus, I want to share your love with everyone I meet, but sometimes I'm a poor ambassador of godly love. Teach me to share your love with the world. Let your love be my first language.

Tough Love

My child, don't reject the LORD's discipline, and don't be upset when he corrects you. For the LORD corrects those he loves, just as a father corrects a child in whom he delights.

PROVERBS 3:11-12

A mother is walking down a busy street with her toddler. One moment they are laughing and playing games, and the next she is jerking the child up by one arm and screaming at him.

Has the mother lost her mind? Has she stopped loving her child? Did she never love him at all? The answer to all of these questions is a resounding no. The mother is simply reacting to her child's quick movement from the sidewalk into the busy street. She acted immediately to protect her child from harm.

God may respond this way when we are about to put ourselves in harm's way. He may "jerk" us or apply some other type of unpleasant correction in order to protect us. Or he may let us go ahead and then teach us through the natural consequences of our actions. Either way, he disciplines us because he loves us with all his being and wants to keep us safe.

ASK YOURSELF

» What are some ways you have experienced God's correction? How have you tended to respond?

» Do you sometimes misinterpret God's correction in your life as something other than love? What can you do to change this tendency?

ASK GOD

Dear Jesus, thank you for always being there to protect me and for loving me enough to be tough when it is necessary. Show me how to recognize your correction for what it is and respond to it quickly.

Think on What Is Good

Now, dear brothers and sisters, one final thing. Fix your thoughts on what
is true, and honorable, and right, and pure, and lovely, and admirable.
Think about things that are excellent and worthy of praise.

PHILIPPIANS 4:8

There are a lot of things in this world that we can't control. We can't control whether the sun shines or whether it's eclipsed by thundering rain clouds. We can't control whether someone we love gets sick. We definitely can't control other people's behavior and choices. There's a lot that's simply out of our hands.

What we do have control over is *ourselves*. We may not be able to choose whether a family member treats us poorly, whether we get the flu, or whether our car gets a flat tire, but we can choose how we respond to each of those situations. In the daily grind of life, we can choose to welcome God into our thoughts and thus transform the way we experience our circumstances. And that's one of the most powerful ways we can take our lives back.

ASK YOURSELF

» What painful life circumstances are out of your control right now? How would bringing God into the situation change your thinking about these situations?

» Have you chosen today to meditate on what is true and honorable and right and pure and lovely and admirable? If not, what is holding you back?

ASK GOD

Holy God, I admit to sometimes letting my thoughts run wild with lies and corruption and loveless musings. But today I offer you my mind as well as my heart and ask you to change me. Help me choose to fix my thoughts on what is true this day.

What We Can Give God

The time is coming—indeed it's here now—when true worshipers
will worship the Father in spirit and in truth. The Father is
looking for those who will worship him that way.

JOHN 4:23

Have you ever had a friendship where the other person did all the talking or all the taking? Maybe she monopolized every conversation, not allowing you to get a word in edgewise. Or maybe he was always asking something of you but seemed unable or unwilling to reciprocate. Such a relationship can be profoundly unsatisfying—even to God.

Though many of us are quick to thank God for being our good Provider, we might be slower to recognize that we have something to contribute to him—our praise and worship. When we lift our hands, bow our heads, bend our knees, and raise our voices to worship the one true God who brought us on a journey to freedom and gave us the strength we needed to take our lives back, we're only giving him his due. It doesn't come close to matching what God has given us, but it's a way of making our relationship with God a little more mutual.

ASK YOURSELF

> » Have you ever thought of praise as a way of giving to God? How does thinking that way affect your approach to worship?

> » What other actions on your part can improve your relationship with God?

ASK GOD

Father, you have been a faithful Provider to me in so many ways. Thank you. Today I offer you the praise and worship that you so richly deserve. Receive the offering of my heart, in Jesus' name.

Watch Your Step

People with integrity walk safely, but those who follow crooked paths will be exposed.

PROVERBS 10:9

Integrity is defined as soundness, especially moral soundness, so it stands to reason that a lack of integrity would denote a fundamental *un*soundness. If something is unsound, it is unstable and not to be trusted.

When people are guided by integrity, they walk on a stable foundation, and that is why they walk safely. Those who lack integrity walk on crooked paths that are easy to wander from, and that is why their ways are likely to be exposed. Why do we fail to grasp this simple concept in our daily lives?

If you want to identify a person of integrity, look at the condition of his or her life. There will always be a direct correlation. There is no way to lead a stable life if we are not founding it on integrity.

The world will tempt us to stray from integrity in return for something we want, claiming that the benefit is worth the risk. But compromising integrity is not really a risk. It's a choice with a guaranteed consequence. God's Word tells us that. If we want to live stable, secure lives, we will pay attention to God's wisdom.

ASK YOURSELF

» Have you ever compromised your integrity for the hope of some added benefit? What was the result?

» What can you do to maintain your integrity in all areas of your life?

ASK GOD

Dear Jesus, you give me so much wisdom through your Word. Teach me to read it and act upon it. Make me a person of strong moral character, and keep me from trading my integrity for anything the world has to offer. Thank you for showing me the way to lead a stable life.

True Love

When we were utterly helpless, Christ came at just the right time and died for us
sinners. . . . For since our friendship with God was restored by the death of his Son
while we were still his enemies, we will certainly be saved through the life of his Son.

ROMANS 5:6, 10

Let's look again at how God loves us.

Paul tells us in the book of Romans that "when we were utterly *helpless*, Christ . . . died for us *sinners*" and that "our friendship with God was restored by the death of his Son while we were still his *enemies*" (emphasis added). Think of that. When we were helpless, sinners, and enemies of God, he still loved us so much that he chose to send his Son to die—just for us.

That's love.

Now if God loved us when we didn't in any way deserve it, what is going to stop him from continuing to love us? Absolutely nothing. Or, as Paul put it, "Neither death nor life, neither angels nor demons, neither our fears for today nor our worries about tomorrow—not even the power of hell can separate us from God's love" (Romans 8:38).

That's true love! And that is how God continues to love each of us.

ASK YOURSELF

» What makes it hard for you to believe you are truly loved by God, your Creator?

» What is your response to being loved that way?

ASK GOD

Loving heavenly Father, I don't even have a way to fully understand how much you love me. But I believe what Paul said, and I thank you for never giving up on me.

Fear versus Hope

The fears of the wicked will be fulfilled; the hopes of the godly will be granted.

PROVERBS 10:24

In life, we all have hopes and fears. Fear is experienced in anticipation of some specific pain or danger. Hope is tied to the feeling that a specific desire will be fulfilled. Both emotions involve anticipating something to come. Fear anticipates that something bad will happen, and hope anticipates something good.

Even though we all experience both of these emotions, neither has any real power over the future. It is our relationship with God that determines what will actually come to pass in our lives.

If we are children of God, we ultimately have nothing to fear. We have plenty to hope for, but even that emotion shouldn't occupy too much of our time or attention. It's enough to simply recognize our hopes, pray about them, do what we can to further them, and leave the rest up to the Lord, confident that "the hopes of the godly will be granted."

ASK YOURSELF

» Does the fact that we ultimately have nothing to fear mean we will never experience the emotion of fear? Why or why not? What is the best way to confront any fearful feelings that do arise?

» Is there a difference between what we wish for and what we hope for? What is it? Does the promise that our hopes will be granted mean our wishes will be fulfilled?

ASK GOD

Dear Jesus, help me give all my emotions over to you, trusting that you will calm my fears and bring my hopes to fruition in your perfect timing. Help me to rest in the knowledge that you have my future in your hands.

Good Ambassadors

We are Christ's ambassadors; God is making his appeal through us.
We speak for Christ when we plead, "Come back to God!"

2 CORINTHIANS 5:20

An ambassador is an official or unofficial representative of a nation, a company, or another kind of organization. He or she represents the organization's best interests and acts as its face and voice.

Ambassadors don't represent themselves, and they don't create the messages they carry. If they do their jobs right, whoever comes in contact with them receives an accurate and favorable picture of the entity they represent. But if they neglect their duties, their organizations won't receive the attention they deserve. For this reason, organizations choose their ambassadors very carefully.

With all this in mind, consider what it means to be ambassadors for Christ. We are his representatives, chosen to spread his love and his message of salvation to the world. This is both an honor and a huge responsibility. After all, some will never hear his message unless we speak it. Some may never know the love of Christ unless we share it. And some may never know him at all unless they see him first in us.

ASK YOURSELF

» How would you rate your performance as God's ambassador to the world? Would anyone who meets you get an accurate and favorable impression of who Christ is? Would they see Jesus in you?

» Do you think the process of taking your life back makes you a more effective ambassador for Christ? Why or why not?

ASK GOD

Dear Jesus, prepare my heart to share your Word. Give me the desire to reach those who do not know about you and to share the message of salvation with them. Keep me from being so busy with my own life and my own healing that I neglect to be the ambassador you have called me to be.

Boomerang

Give freely and become more wealthy; be stingy and lose everything.

PROVERBS 11:24

Do you ever feel that the more tightly you hold on to something, the more it slips away? This is actually a biblical principle, just as applicable today as when it was written down thousands of years ago. And the converse is biblical as well—the more freely you give, the more returns to you.

When we are willing to share what we have with others, God will give us more. But when we hoard everything, eventually we will lose it. What we share will come back to us many times over, and what we "pile up" for ourselves will waste away.

This principle makes no earthly sense. It goes against all logic. And yet it has proven to be true over and over again.

When we come to the place where we trust God's Word implicitly and act upon it, we will see principles like this proven in our own lives. And when we experience their truth firsthand, our lives will never be the same.

ASK YOURSELF

» Have you had a chance to live out this principle firsthand? What was your experience?

» What needs and emotions in your life tend to make you want to be stingy with what you have? How can you change this tendency and become more generous?

ASK GOD

Dear Jesus, help me to follow the instruction in your Word even when it goes against the world's logic. Thank you for all that you have given to me. Teach me how to bless others by sharing it.

Learning to Listen

Fools think their own way is right, but the wise listen to others.

PROVERBS 12:15

Isn't it frustrating to be in the company of people who think they are always right? We all know someone like this. Sometimes it's us!

It's easy to assume that our way of thinking is the right way. After all, it's familiar. It's part of us. But that doesn't mean we're correct—or that we can't benefit from another's perspective.

If we really want to grow and heal, we must learn to listen to others and consider their input. That doesn't mean we let ourselves be driven by their opinions, just that we pay attention and keep an open mind. If we are wise, we will hear what others have to say, consider it to see if it has any value, and form our own conclusions.

Imagine how lacking you would be if, since birth, you had chosen to decline any outside information. There are things you can learn from others that you might never have the opportunity to learn on your own. So be wise. Listen. Open your mind. Filter the information through God's Word, and grow. Then . . . repeat.

ASK YOURSELF

> » Are you more likely to be a know-it-all or to be overly dependent on other people's opinions? How can you find a more balanced approach?

> » What are some ways you can enhance your listening skills?

ASK GOD

Dear Lord, I don't want to be so foolish as to think that I know everything. Show me how to listen carefully and then make my own judgment according to the information that has been provided. Make me wise, Lord. Teach me how to be open-minded, and help me to open my ears when others speak.

Let God Guide

Trust in the LORD with all your heart; do not depend on your own understanding.
Seek his will in all you do, and he will show you which path to take.

PROVERBS 3:5-6

Have you ever set out on a journey—across town or across the state—and gotten lost, even though you were certain you knew the way? After missing a turn or passing the correct exit, you figured out that you were not where you wanted to be.

Long before GPS and even a few millennia before printed paper maps, human nature was the same as it is today. Whether we're driving across the city, choosing who we're going to marry, or even deciding whether or not to clean up the most recent mess of someone who's addicted, we naturally rely on our own understanding. But as we choose to live responsively rather than reactively, God will be faithful to guide us down new paths.

ASK YOURSELF

» When in the past have you gotten off track by relying on your own understanding and choosing your own way?

» What difficult decisions are you facing right now? Do you have a sense of how God might be directing you? If not, what steps can you take to avail yourself of his direction?

ASK GOD

God, I confess that I prefer to be in control of the choices I make and the paths I choose. But seeing where that has gotten me, I release command to you. Show me your ways and guide me in the paths you've prepared.

Giving Freely

Though he was God, he did not think of equality with God as something
to cling to. Instead, he gave up his divine privileges; he took the
humble position of a slave and was born as a human being.

PHILIPPIANS 2:6-7

We're taken by fairy tales in which a king or queen decides to relinquish his or her royal privilege for the sake of love. We're captured by the hero who's willing to sacrifice everything for another. That kind of forfeit is exactly what Jesus chose when he gave up his divine privilege and took on human flesh. In his life we discover what it means to lose our lives in the healthiest way possible.

That's a crucial part of the journey of taking our lives back—learning to give ourselves to others not out of our own need but from the strength God gives. Learning to care about others from an overflow of the love we have received, not because our care was demanded or we were shamed into it. Once we've taken our lives back, we can choose—out of love—to follow Christ's example and give ourselves away. In sacrificing our lives in this way, we find them.

ASK YOURSELF

> » Have there been times in your life when you gave because it was demanded of you? How did that experience compare to others in which you gave out of love?

> » How are you learning to give generously and freely today?

ASK GOD

Faithful Jesus, thank you for your humble sacrifice. Teach me this day to give generously because I have been given everything. Help me to live as I was designed to live by imitating you.

Your Safe Place

God is our refuge and strength, always ready to help in times of trouble. So we
will not fear when earthquakes come and the mountains crumble into the sea.
Let the oceans roar and foam. Let the mountains tremble as the waters surge!

PSALM 46:1-3

Your local community probably has a plan in place for what to do when natural disasters strike—and no doubt that includes establishing emergency shelters. At the first report of an oncoming flood, blizzard, hurricane, or earthquake, disaster teams will transform schools, stadiums, and other sturdy public buildings into places of refuge for those who are displaced or in danger.

These locations are widely broadcast, so if you're in trouble, you'll know exactly where to go. But do you know what to do when spiritual and emotional trouble strikes your life?

The psalmist calls God a "refuge" and "strength" in times of trouble. God is the strong structure where we can find protection from the devastation going on around us. During our most chaotic seasons, God promises to protect and preserve us. Can you close your eyes and visualize God as that safe, solid place for you?

ASK YOURSELF

> » Is there a situation in your life right now that feels like a disaster? What is happening?

> » What does it look like for you to huddle under God's shelter during this season?

ASK GOD

Dear God, I read in your Word that you have been a strong shelter for your people, and I trust that you are a shelter for me during times of trouble in my life. Today I rest securely in the safety of your strength and protection.

Do It for God

Work with enthusiasm, as though you were working for the Lord rather than for people.

EPHESIANS 6:7

Do you sometimes find it hard to get motivated? Lack of motivation makes it hard to accomplish anything substantial—like slogging through mud.

There are many causes for a deficit of enthusiasm—boredom, low self-confidence, a belief that we are too good for the task. In some cases, it can even be a signal that we need to be doing something else. Whatever the reason, an unmotivated attitude can make everyone miserable if we don't address it.

Fortunately, there is a simple solution for your lack of motivation: Change your perspective. Consciously shift your focus from yourself and your feelings to God and what will please him. Once you start thinking that way, you'll find either the motivation you need to keep doing what you do or the motivation to try something different. Either way, you'll be working for the Lord.

It always helps to broaden the scope of your thinking. Look beyond yourself. Look beyond your boss. Look beyond this world. Live with a focus on the eternal, and watch your motivation grow. Nothing will motivate you more than pleasing the Lord.

ASK YOURSELF

» What are some necessary tasks in your life that you just don't like? How can changing your perspective help motivate you for these tasks?

» How can you discern when to stick with a task and change your attitude about it and when to seek a different task? How does keeping an eternal focus help in either case?

ASK GOD

Lord, there are times when I lack the enthusiasm I need for particular tasks. Show me how to find the right motivation by dedicating everything I do to you.

Running on Full

The faithful love of the LORD never ends! His mercies never cease.
Great is his faithfulness; his mercies begin afresh each morning.

LAMENTATIONS 3:22-23

Imagine you're running a marathon. You've hit mile twenty-three, and your resources are low. Your muscles are fatigued. You're not well hydrated. You're blistered and exhausted.

Then you spot what looks like an oasis in the desert. It's a rest station where you can drink some water, have a bite to eat, and relax. And the magic is that you can stay there as long as you like without putting time on the clock.

If you're like a lot of us who were once living on empty, this might not even sound wonderful to you. You're so conditioned to neglect your own needs, you might not even realize how desperately you long for the good gift God offers to you every day—the gift of rest and refreshment. It's available to you as you spend regular time in his presence.

The Bible tells us that God's mercies toward us are new every morning. We can't fill up for a month at a time. Instead, God longs to meet our needs every day.

ASK YOURSELF

> » How do you know you're running on empty? What are some of the familiar signs?

> » Have you developed a regular rhythm for receiving from God's bountiful presence? If not, what change do you need to make in your life?

ASK GOD

God whose mercies are new every morning, thank you for your gift of refreshment when I'm running on empty. Fill me with your gracious presence so that I might live as your beloved child this day.

Being Built Anew

Together, we are his house, built on the foundation of the apostles and
the prophets. And the cornerstone is Christ Jesus himself. We are carefully
joined together in him, becoming a holy temple for the Lord.

EPHESIANS 2:20-21

In the classic children's story "The Three Little Pigs," a triumvirate of barnyard swine build themselves houses—one made of straw, one made of sticks, and one made of bricks. The first two houses are blown away when the big bad wolf huffs and puffs. But the brick house withstands the assault and shelters all three pigs from harm.

The house where you were raised may have felt as unstable and unsubstantial as an edifice of straw or sticks. You may have felt that everything was falling apart around you, that the best you could do was to pick up the pieces and hold on to them as the wolf approached your door.

Today, though, you are standing on a solid foundation—of willingness, humility, truth, wisdom, faith, and intimacy. With God and with others, you are building something of meaning and worth from the broken pieces of your past. Building has become the business of recovering your life and taking it back.

ASK YOURSELF

» How would you describe your earliest home and how it affected you?

» What specifically have you seen God building in you as you work with him to take your life back? Who else has been involved in your building process?

ASK GOD

God, you promised that you are making my life part of a holy dwelling place with Jesus Christ as the cornerstone. May I and all your children find shelter in him.

Your Money and Your Message

Honor the LORD with your wealth and with the best part of everything you produce.
Then he will fill your barns with grain, and your vats will overflow with good wine.

PROVERBS 3:9-10

If a rich person handed you 90 percent of her wealth, you'd probably consider yourself pretty fortunate. It would be like winning the lottery, and I doubt you'd mind if your benefactor kept a mere 10 percent for herself.

So why do we tend to squirm whenever the topic of tithing comes up?

Everything we have comes from God. He is our Provider, and he asks that we give 10 percent back to him as a way of recognizing his provision.

Think about the practice of tipping for food service. The standard tip for acceptable service is 15 to 20 percent. We might acknowledge exceptional service with a larger amount and poor service with a lesser tip or even no tip at all. Our choice sends a message about how much we value the service we've received.

It's worth considering: What are you saying to God with your tithe?

ASK YOURSELF

» Do you tend to get uncomfortable when churches or Christian organizations start talking about money? Why do you think you feel this way?

» Have you chosen to tithe or to give back to God a percentage of your income? How did you make that choice?

ASK GOD

Dear Jesus, I know that everything I have comes from you. Thank you for taking care of my needs. Remind me that when I tithe, I am acknowledging that you are an awesome Provider and showing that I am grateful for all that you do for me.

A Clean Slate

Yes, what joy for those whose record the LORD has cleared
of guilt, whose lives are lived in complete honesty!

PSALM 32:2

If you've ever gotten a traffic ticket, you know it can stay on your record for years. Your car insurance rates can go up, and too many citations can even cost you your driving privileges. So if you are given the opportunity to have a citation removed—perhaps by attending traffic school or participating in an "infraction deferral program," you'll probably jump at the chance. You'll happily give up valuable time or pay a little extra for the chance to clear your record, and you'll probably be elated when the offense has been erased.

If clearing your driving record can make you feel so good, how much more joy should the clearing of all sin from your eternal record bring you? The sacrifice that Christ made, giving his life to give you a new start, is a *big* deal. Do you have an appropriate appreciation for what you have received?

ASK YOURSELF

> » Is there anything particular in your "record" that still haunts you? What will it take for you to fully accept that the record just isn't there anymore?

> » Since we all continue to sin even after we've accepted Christ, what do you think happens with our new "citations"? What must happen for us to keep our record clean?

ASK GOD

Thank you, Lord, for dying to cleanse my record of all my sin. I sometimes take this for granted, and I don't want to. Give me a new awareness of the magnitude of your sacrifice for me. Let my life be a living example of my gratitude for what you have done for me.

Trusting God When Hope Has Expired

There he met a man named Aeneas, who had been paralyzed and bedridden
for eight years. Peter said to him, "Aeneas, Jesus Christ heals you! Get
up, and roll up your sleeping mat!" And he was healed instantly.

ACTS 9:33-34

While it can be tempting for us to "spiritualize" some of the stories we read in the Bible, try to resist that temptation as you consider the story Luke recounts in Acts about a man named Aeneas.

This guy had been paralyzed for eight years when he met Peter. His condition was exactly like that of someone today who was paralyzed by a car accident or a stray bullet almost a decade ago. Even with excellent care and weeks or months or years of physical therapy, hope for recovery would not have lasted eight years.

And yet when Peter announced that Jesus had healed Aeneas, this man who had been bedridden for eight years stood up and walked.

This is the word for you today. Wherever hope has expired in your life— that is the place Jesus longs to touch.

ASK YOURSELF

> » Have you run out of hope for any situation in your life? Are you willing to believe that Jesus can redeem it? Why or why not?

> » What is the difference between accepting something you cannot change and giving up hope for that situation?

ASK GOD

God of healing and redemption, you have shown yourself to be full of grace and power. I confess that I've been slow to believe you can change the most difficult areas of my life. Today I offer you my stuck places, and I trust in your mercy.

Truth and Freedom

Jesus said to the people who believed in him, "You are truly my disciples if you remain faithful to my teachings. And you will know the truth, and the truth will set you free." "But we are descendants of Abraham," they said. "We have never been slaves to anyone. . . ." Jesus replied, "I tell you the truth, everyone who sins is a slave of sin."

JOHN 8:31-34

Freedom isn't always an easy concept to understand. It was certainly confusing for the followers of Jesus who first heard his famous statement, "The truth will set you free." They immediately protested, "But we're not slaves!" So Jesus explained that he was talking about freedom from sin—because "everyone who sins is a slave of sin."

God's truth, according to Jesus, is what sets us free from sin. And truth is also what sets us free from pain and dysfunction in our lives. Healing always begins with acknowledging the truth of where we've been and where we are now. The path to spiritual freedom that Jesus describes—being set free from sin and death—parallels the path to emotional freedom.

In both our spiritual lives and our emotional lives, it is *truth* that sets us free.

ASK YOURSELF

» What difficulties have you experienced in facing the truth about your past—both what you have done and what has been done to you?

» What is the truth about your life as you understand it right now?

ASK GOD

Dear Lord, thank you for setting me free from sin and death by the truth of your Word. I believe you can also set me free from what is holding me back emotionally. Give me the courage to face the truth of my life.

Created in God's Image

God created human beings in his own image. In the image of God
he created them; male and female he created them.

GENESIS 1:27

In the ancient Near East, the inherent value and dignity of every individual wasn't assumed. In fact, it's not assumed in many places in the world today. So when the author of Genesis affirmed that men and women and children were created in God's image, that was a radical claim. And it still is.

If every one of us has been crafted in the image of God, that means we have inestimable worth and value in God's sight. It also means that other people's opinions of us matter relatively little.

Whenever you catch yourself tipping your eyes toward somebody else to affirm your value, look in the mirror and choose to believe the truth instead: *I am worthy because I've been created in the image of God.* As you live into this transforming reality, you will not only move toward taking your life back. You'll also begin to treat others as the precious and valuable people they really are.

ASK YOURSELF

» What does it mean to you to be created in the image of God? How do you resemble him?

» How can you live day by day to reflect God's character to the world? How will you speak? How will you act? How will you treat people?

ASK GOD

Maker of heaven and earth, I believe you when you say you created me in your image. Today I choose to believe that I am precious in your sight and that you created me for a purpose. Help me to know you so I can represent you better to the world that you love.

Grieving Your Childhood

The LORD is close to the brokenhearted; he rescues those whose spirits are crushed.

PSALM 34:18

No one has a perfect childhood. All of us were raised by flawed human beings who made mistakes. But some of us experienced more than our share of pain when we were children, stemming from the way our parents or parental figures treated us.

If this is true of you, you probably take one of two approaches to your parents. You may refuse to entertain any negative thoughts about them because they "did the best they could." Or you may blame them for everything and live with unrelenting anger and bitterness. Unfortunately, neither attitude is helpful in taking your life back.

Instead, you need to remember and understand what happened, place and accept responsibility where it belongs, grieve what was lost in your childhood, protect yourself from repetitive hurtful behaviors, and ultimately find freedom by forgiving your parents.

This can be a difficult process, but you'll never be alone as you go through it. Remember that God your heavenly Father is with you as you grieve and is faithful to support and comfort you as you journey toward healing.

ASK YOURSELF

» What losses from your childhood or younger days do you need to spend time grieving?

» When thinking of your past, are you most likely to offer forgiveness too quickly or to reserve your forgiveness altogether?

ASK GOD

Dear heavenly Father, I thank you that you are close to me as my heart is healing from my childhood pain. When my spirit is crushed, you are near. Because you are with me on this journey, I have the courage to grieve what I've lost and the strength to eventually forgive.

Let God Handle It

Don't say, "I will get even for this wrong." Wait for the LORD to handle the matter.

PROVERBS 20:22

Vigilante "justice" is a scary thing. High emotions paired with a disregard for rules or regulations and a complete lack of impartiality is a recipe for disaster. The reason laws were created and the court system exists is to keep justice just. Unless the prosecution is impartial, justice cannot exist, and if justice doesn't exist, we are all in trouble.

If you have been wronged, the Lord will see that justice is done—but you need to stay out of the way. Human nature craves vengeance, but that just leads to an ongoing cycle of violence—never true justice, and never peace.

If you believe God's Word, you know that God is your Defender. He has promised to right every wrong in his perfect timing and to see every matter through to the end. He will deliver justice, and it will be truly just.

ASK YOURSELF

» Do you find it difficult to let God take care of administering justice on your behalf? Why or why not?

» What does your life look like when you know without a doubt that God has your back?

ASK GOD

Dear Jesus, sometimes I allow my temper to get the best of me and try to take justice into my own hands. Please teach me how to trust fully that you will take care of things for me. Show me how to step back and release my frustrations and my resentments so that you can step in, administer justice, and bring me peace.

One Day at a Time

Seek the Kingdom of God above all else, and live righteously, and he will
give you everything you need. So don't worry about tomorrow, for tomorrow
will bring its own worries. Today's trouble is enough for today.

MATTHEW 6:33-34

One nugget of wisdom often shared in the recovery community is the encouragement to take "one day at a time." When we dwell on the past, we can wallow in shame and regret. When we anticipate the future, we can waste energy on what may or may not come to pass. Focusing on how we'll live today is enough.

This wisdom comes straight from Jesus' own lips. In his Sermon on the Mount he addressed concerns that were common to his audience and are just as relevant today: *What will I eat and drink? What will I wear? Where will I live?* Jesus directed his listeners' gaze not to their pay stubs or mortgage statements but toward their heavenly Father. Jesus knew the Father to be a good provider, and he urged his listeners to trust God to meet their needs one day at a time.

The message is appropriate for us as we move toward taking our lives back. Whatever we face today, God can be trusted to care for us.

ASK YOURSELF

» What are the daily worries for provision that tend to plague your thoughts?

» How has God met your needs *this day*?

ASK GOD

God, you have always been my faithful Provider. Today I choose to trust you to meet my needs. Tomorrow I'll do the same.

God Is for Us

What shall we say about such wonderful things as these?
If God is for us, who can ever be against us?

ROMANS 8:31

A friend of mine went to a few different doctors for a chronic ailment and left each office feeling despondent because the doctors didn't seem to take her problem seriously. She knew she'd found the right physician when he assured her, "It may take some time, but we're going to get you some relief." She wasn't healed right away, but she found tremendous comfort knowing that her doctor was working with her.

In the struggles of our daily lives, God is not a magician who snaps his fingers to change things on demand or a quack doctor who offers simple prescriptions (or a pat on the head) for a complicated situation. What we can trust, though, is that, like the gracious doctor my friend found, God is *for* us. That's no small thing! Today you can trust that in your suffering, in your struggles, and in your healing, God is actively at work on your behalf.

ASK YOURSELF

» Has there been someone in your life who wasn't able to be there for you in the way you needed him or her to be? How has that affected you?

» Does God's being *for* us mean he supports everything we do and furthers all our agendas? What does it mean to you?

ASK GOD

God who is good, forgive me for doubting that you are, in every moment, with me and for me. Give me eyes to recognize your steadfast, loving presence in my life as one who is always for me. And grant me faith to believe that your love never fails.

Getting Up . . . Again

Jesus took the blind man by the hand and led him out of the village. Then, spitting on the man's eyes, he laid his hands on him and asked, "Can you see anything now?" The man looked around. "Yes," he said, "I see people, but I can't see them very clearly."

MARK 8:23-24

Sometimes when we pray for God's grace and healing in our lives, we imagine the desperate, hurting folks who were healed with a single touch from Jesus. We imagine that we'll straighten up like the woman who was bent over, or pick up our mats and walk like the paralyzed man who was healed. But more often, our healing is gradual. It's more like that of the blind man who received fuzzy sight at first and then, on round two, full sight.

Maybe you're now on round twenty-seven of your quest for healing. Maybe you're disheartened that your healing wasn't swift like it is for some. But if you manage to get back up each time you fall down, you are doing all God has asked you to do. As you muster the faith you need, you will persevere through the most difficult times to experience the blessings God has for you and those you love.

ASK YOURSELF

» What has disappointed you about your quest for healing? What doesn't seem to be working?

» Describe what has already changed for the better in your journey. What kind of "second touch" do you need right now?

ASK GOD

Father, you are the source of my life and my strength. Fill me with your power this day so that I have the endurance and patience to go on—and to get back up when I fall.

When Righteousness Rules

Justice will rule in the wilderness and righteousness in the fertile field. And this
righteousness will bring peace. Yes, it will bring quietness and confidence forever.

ISAIAH 32:16-17

The prophet Isaiah, speaking for the Lord, painted a beautiful word picture of what it would look like when Israel was finally delivered by the king God had promised. People would recognize truth, crops would spring up, and livestock would graze freely. One of the hallmarks of this blessed deliverance, said Isaiah, would be the comprehensive peace the Hebrew Scriptures call *shalom*. When righteousness reigned and justice ruled, he promised, so would peace.

God's promise to Israel is a promise for us as well. We also will experience peace in our lives when justice and righteousness rule. When we fail to pursue righteousness, our lives remain in chaos. When we fail to establish justice, bitterness and resentment grow. But as we release areas of sin in our lives to God, as we draw closer to living rightly and justly, we will experience more and more of the quietness and confidence God longs to give us. As we submit ourselves to him, he will be faithful to transform the areas of our lives that fall short of his righteousness.

ASK YOURSELF

> » What areas of sin in your life can you release to God today?

> » What habits can you pursue that produce justice and righteousness?

ASK GOD
Gracious God of peace, I know your will for all your people is righteousness, justice, and all-encompassing peace. I want those conditions to rule in my life as well, so I submit it all to you.

Eternal Workout

Physical training is good, but training for godliness is much better,
promising benefits in this life and in the life to come.

1 TIMOTHY 4:8

We do a lot of things in life because we know they're good for us. Brushing our teeth is one. Losing weight is another. And exercising is yet another. Most people work out not because they love to do it but because they appreciate its benefits. Regular exercise has been proven to strengthen our bodies and extend our lives. So we go to the gym or hit the track because we care about our physical health.

Yet the physical body is mortal. Even the healthiest person on earth will die someday. So if we are willing to invest our time improving a body we know will not last, doesn't it make sense to give at least equal time to building up our spirits, which are eternal?

That's what "training for godliness" means—finding ways to "exercise" your spirit. Do you spend quiet time with the Lord every day? Do you digest his Word to keep you healthy and strong? Is your prayer life vital and growing? Do you spend time with other believers and reach out in love to people Jesus loves? All of these things are essential to strong spiritual health.

ASK YOURSELF

» Would you say you are in fair spiritual shape right now? Why or why not?

» What changes could you make this week to train for godliness and build your spiritual fitness?

ASK GOD

Dear Lord, I want to spend more time with you than I do. I know that many of the things I allow to get in the way are just not as important as I allow them to be. Help me to get my priorities in the right place so that I grow closer to you every day. Teach me to invest more time in the eternal than I do in the temporal.

Don't Fool Yourself

If you think you are too important to help someone, you are
only fooling yourself. You are not that important.

GALATIANS 6:3

Sometimes we get so caught up in ourselves and what we are doing that we develop an overinflated sense of our own importance and start believing that certain people and tasks are unworthy of our time and energy. No one is so important or so busy that he or she cannot reach out and help someone in need.

Jesus was the Son of God in human form, and yet he spent time with little children, beggars, prostitutes, tax collectors—all the people that Hebrew society tended to look down on. He was even willing to die on the cross to pay for their sins—and yours, and mine. If anyone should consider himself too important to bother with the little guy, wouldn't it be the Lord of the universe? And yet he showed compassion and respect to everyone he encountered—except perhaps the self-important religious leaders of his day.

If Jesus, being God, was willing to give up his life to save ours, we must never be foolish enough to think we are too important to help someone else.

ASK YOURSELF

> » Do you tend to identify more with the busy person who doesn't have time to help or the "little guy" who needs help? Would someone who knows you well agree with your assessment?

> » What's the difference between learning to say a healthy no and refusing to help or care about others?

ASK GOD

Dear Jesus, teach me to see everyone through your eyes. Make me sensitive to the needs of those around me, and keep me from ever getting so caught up in my own issues that I fail to care.

The Foundation That Does Not Fail

The grass withers and the flowers fade beneath the breath of the LORD. And so it is with people. The grass withers and the flowers fade, but the word of our God stands forever.

ISAIAH 40:7-8

All around us, every day, we encounter people whose worlds have become shaky. A woman has been diagnosed with breast cancer. A man has been sent to prison for white-collar crime. An unmarried teenage girl has just taken a pregnancy test—and it's positive. A grad student has attempted to take his own life. Just as an earthquake rocks the foundation of a home and everything that rests on it, a sudden life event can quickly wreak havoc in our lives and the lives of those we love.

In the midst of these ruptures, however, one thing remains sure, solid, and sound: God's Word. Anchored in the character of God, available to all who seek wisdom, the Bible provides a steady grounding in the midst of life's quakes. It is the reliable source of life and hope in the darkest of times.

ASK YOURSELF

» Would you describe your life, in this moment, as being solid or shaky? Why?

» Have you experienced God's Word to be your solid place? If not, where do you typically turn for stability?

ASK GOD

God who made the heavens and the earth, I put my trust in you. Even when the earth under my feet feels shaky, when the grass withers and the flowers fade, I am confident that you cannot be moved and that your Word is true. Thank you that I can depend on that.

The Power of Connection

If we are faithful to the end, trusting God just as firmly as when we
first believed, we will share in all that belongs to Christ.

HEBREWS 3:14

It was late in the evening when a man drove past a church in a neighboring town. The windows were dark, and all meetings were clearly over, but a small group of people stood talking in the parking lot. Curious about why they lingered instead of dashing home, the man called the pastor of the church to ask. The pastor laughed. "Oh, they're always doing that." Apparently the people in the parking lot were part of a twelve-step group that met at the church.

It doesn't have to be a twelve-step group, of course. It could be a Bible study or just friends sharing coffee. But there's something about a caring community that transforms suffering. When we connect with others who understand our pain, that pain is somehow redeemed. Powerful and healing connections form as we listen to others' stories and tell our own. While connecting may once have felt dangerous to us, it now brings us life and peace.

ASK YOURSELF

> » Have you found fellow travelers with whom you've been able to connect and share support? If not, what are some places you could look?

> » How will you encourage someone who is walking the same path today?

ASK GOD

God, thank you for the people you have given me as companions for my journey. Help me to build others up so that they might remain faithful to the end, trusting you in all things.

Anyone There?

Listen! The LORD's arm is not too weak to save you, nor is his ear too deaf
to hear you call. It's your sins that have cut you off from God. Because
of your sins, he has turned away and will not listen anymore.

ISAIAH 59:1-2

Have you ever been given the silent treatment? Those who are closest to you
can be the best at this. At first you think they just didn't hear you. But after your
third or fourth attempt to communicate with them fails, you start to realize
that you might have angered or offended them. It's time to pay some serious
attention to the state of your relationship.

That's helpful advice when it comes to your relationship with God as well.
When it seems as if he isn't communicating with you, consider what is going
on in your life. Could your unconfessed sin be getting in the way?

God's Word makes it clear that he does not listen to those who are actively
involved in sin. So if you feel that God is not hearing you, take a good look at
the sin in your life. Confess it—he'll listen!—ask forgiveness, and turn from
your sin. Get on your knees and get the lines of communication open again.

ASK YOURSELF

> » How can you tell when communication has broken down between you
> and God? What does this feel like?

> » What else besides unconfessed sin hinders communication between
> you and God?

ASK GOD

Dear God, sometimes when I pray, I feel as though I'm not getting through. If
sin in my life has built a barrier between us, please show me what it is. I want
to always have a direct line to you, Lord.

How to Help

The generous will prosper; those who refresh others will themselves be refreshed.

PROVERBS 11:25

Anyone who has sat on a plane that was preparing to depart has heard the standard flight attendant spiel about what to do in emergencies. We know there are flotation cushions under our seats, and we understand that we're supposed to secure our own oxygen masks before assisting small children or those with special needs. It all makes perfect sense.

But such advice might have once felt completely counterintuitive to us. Because our lives were in chaos, we were clueless about how to help another person appropriately. We didn't even know how to get our own needs met!

All that has changed as we've made progress in taking our lives back. Now we nurture our friends and family with time and attention so they can grow. We offer encouragement, affirmation, and respect when and where it is needed. There's no longer any reason for us to withhold what we're able to provide. As a result, our lives are more connected and far more joyful.

ASK YOURSELF

» How are you making sure your own needs are met these days?

» What are some of the ways you are providing for others?

ASK GOD

Lord Jesus, you modeled a life of giving to others. I thank you that you're teaching me to care for myself so that I can also care for others. Show me how to bless those around me today.

Acting, Not Reacting

Then the way you live will always honor and please the Lord, and
your lives will produce every kind of good fruit. All the while, you
will grow as you learn to know God better and better.

COLOSSIANS 1:10

Have you ever driven with someone who is prone to road rage? (Maybe you've been that person.) He might yell or make obscene gestures, slam on his brakes, or swerve around another car in a dangerous game that's happening in his mind. Sometimes he'll assign nefarious motives to someone who drives too fast or too slow or in the "wrong" lane. Mile by crazy mile, he is reacting rather than acting—and imperiling everyone who shares the road with him.

When Paul was in prison, he wrote a letter to the church in Colosse, urging them to live in ways that please the Lord. And the life he describes is one of acting in response to God rather than reacting to circumstances. It's a life of growing fruitfully rather than being bounced around like a ball in a pinball machine. The more we grow in our relationship with God, the better equipped we'll be to live this way.

ASK YOURSELF

» In what kinds of situations are you most prone to lose control and react erratically or irrationally to people or circumstances? Why do you think these situations trigger you to react in this way? How can you avoid them?

» How can you learn to act more and react less?

ASK GOD

God, thank you that you are growing me into someone who acts in response to you rather than simply reacts to circumstances. Feed me with your Word and strengthen me to live a fruitful, productive life.

Plans for Good

"For I know the plans I have for you," says the LORD. "They are plans
for good and not for disaster, to give you a future and a hope."

JEREMIAH 29:11

When we face struggle—when a job slips away, when a spouse leaves, when a child suffers or a home is lost—we may wonder if God is really watching out for us. And when these themes of loss cycle back into our lives season after season, it's easy to lose hope, to fear that God no longer cares. We may even believe that God cares for *others* but no longer cares for us.

After God's people had been carted away to exile in Babylon, the prophet Jeremiah wrote the captives a letter addressing these very human assumptions. Jeremiah assured them that, despite their circumstances, God had not forgotten them. He acknowledged their difficulties but promised that God still had a good plan for them—to bring them home and restore their fortunes. All God asked of them in return was to seek him (see Jeremiah 29:13-14).

Whatever you're facing today, be assured that God is with you. No matter what it looks like, he can be trusted with your present and your future.

ASK YOURSELF

> » What is your "Babylon"? Have you faced—or are you facing—a situation that drains your hope and makes you wonder if God cares?

> » What could help you trust God today for the future you can't yet see?

ASK GOD

God of Israel, thank you for the witness of the Scriptures that testifies to your faithfulness in the lives of your people. Though I can't always see the good you have planned for me, I know you are reliable. Today I choose to put my trust in you.

Sin Keeps Us Stuck

If I had not confessed the sin in my heart, the Lord would not have listened.
But God did listen! He paid attention to my prayer. Praise God, who did
not ignore my prayer or withdraw his unfailing love from me.

PSALM 66:18-20

Often it's easier for us to notice the sins that keep *others* stuck than to acknowledge the ones that keep *us* stuck. We can see so clearly the ways that sin is keeping someone else in bondage to lies, addiction, unforgiveness, or other death-dealing patterns. When it's our own sin, though, we often find it easier to remain blind.

But even when we are oblivious to our sin, our gracious God is faithful to reveal it when we ask for help. His Spirit will gently point out the areas of our lives where we are still in bondage and need to be set free. And as we face these sins and confess them, God hears us. God cares. God pays attention. He forgives our sins and promises never to withdraw his steadfast love from us.

ASK YOURSELF

» Why is it so easy to see others' sin and so hard to recognize your own? Have you seen this dynamic at work in your life?

» In what ways has the Spirit acted to reveal sin in your life? Have there been any big surprises?

» Are you aware of any current pockets of sin you need to address? What could you do to find clarity about this?

ASK GOD

God of all grace, I confess that it's easier for me to notice others' sin than to see my own. Forgive me. By your Spirit, expose the dark places in my heart that I might confess my sin to you and be set free. Lord, I trust in your unfailing love.

The Face You Need to See

May the Lord bless you and protect you. May the Lord smile on you and be gracious to you. May the Lord show you his favor and give you his peace.

NUMBERS 6:24-26

Some of us have lived our lives seeking approval, acceptance, and love from the faces of those around us: a parent, a teacher, a boss, a spouse. We developed the habit of turning to these human faces to get our needs meet. But because they were human, because they were by nature sinful, these people weren't able to meet the deepest needs of our hearts. Even the most beloved face wasn't enough for us—because there is just one face that can promise us life and keep that promise.

In the sixth chapter of Numbers, God commanded the priests of Israel to bless God's people with a special blessing. The original Hebrew explodes with imagery of God's face shining upon the people he loves. Can you imagine God turning his face toward you and smiling?

The blessing given to the Israelites is extended to you today as well. As you turn toward the light of God's smiling face, you can be set free from the disappointments and the death-dealing patterns that have kept you bound.

ASK YOURSELF

» Which human faces did you naturally turn to for approval when you were younger?

» Close your eyes and quiet your heart. Imagine God's gracious face smiling upon you.

ASK GOD

Father, thank you that you have blessed me with your presence. Open my eyes this day to see your face.

God Is Mine Forever

My health may fail, and my spirit may grow weak, but God
remains the strength of my heart; he is mine forever.

PSALM 73:26

When we're young and healthy, it's hard to imagine that our bodies will ever fail. But if we live long enough, there's a 100 percent chance that they will. Eyesight fades. Hearing dims. Muscles ache. Bones creak. Memory fades. I'll avoid some of the more unmentionable experiences, but they're difficult too.

The sobering truth is, every one of us occupies a body that is subject to the power of sin and death. And each of us will reach a point where that body fails us.

Many of us spend our lives depending on our strength, our wit, our beauty, our intelligence, and even our own faithfulness. But when our bodies are no longer dependable, God remains faithful. God's strength and faithfulness do not fail.

ASK YOURSELF

» Has your body or mind or spirit begun to fail in any way? What experiences remind you that you are mortal?

» Today, join your voice with the voice of the psalmist in announcing, "He is mine forever." Speak these words aloud and allow them to penetrate the depths of your heart.

ASK GOD

God who is the strength of my heart, I put my trust in you. I recognize the temptation to trust in my own abilities, but I also know those abilities will fail me. So from my birth until my death, I choose to rely on your strength, your power, and your faithfulness. Thank you that you are mine forever.

Reflecting the Face of God

Be happy with those who are happy, and weep with those who weep.

ROMANS 12:15

Have you ever noticed the eyes, face, voice, and posture of a gifted counselor or a truly faithful friend? Without a word, this attentive listener receives what you are sharing and reflects—with her body—what God's face might display when he listens to you. If you're sad, she might shed a tear. If you've been harmed, her face might twist into anger. If you're soaring with joy, a smile will stretch across her face. The good listener lets you know that you've been seen and heard—and loved.

The apostle Paul charges all of us to have this posture toward others, both those who are buoyant with happiness and those who are crushed with sorrow. With our faces, voices, and bodies, we can make God's care for others real and accessible. We can let them know that they are not alone. As we embody the truth that others are worth seeing and hearing and loving, we do the holy work with which we've been charged.

ASK YOURSELF

» Take a moment to consider the people you've encountered today. Have any been especially joyful or especially sorrowful?

» How can you more effectively show God's care through the way you listen and respond to this person?

ASK GOD

God of all compassion, thank you that you care about my life, my joys, and my sorrows. Lord, help me be an instrument of your compassion by reflecting your interest in and concern for others. Make me a faithful witness of your love.

I Am with You

Don't be afraid, for I am with you. Don't be discouraged, for I am your God. I will strengthen you and help you. I will hold you up with my victorious right hand.

ISAIAH 41:10

Suffering is isolating. It makes us feel alone. Afraid. Abandoned.

If we're facing a medical crisis, we might be alone in the MRI machine. If we're underemployed or unemployed, we know financial stress our friends can't fathom. If our families crumble, we each experience that rupture in a unique way. Our suspicions that others really don't "get" what we're going through are often true—and these thoughts only isolate us further.

When the people of Israel were suffering, God sent the prophet Isaiah with a message: "I am with you." God promised to strengthen them and help them. He reminded them that they were not alone.

We can count on that promise as well. When it feels as though others can't understand our suffering (which might be true), God is near. He promises to uphold us through our loneliest, most terrifying days.

ASK YOURSELF

» When in your life have you felt most alone? Did you know God then? What was your experience of him during those times?

» Is there a circumstance in your life today that you think others can't or won't understand fully? What can you do to remind yourself of God's presence?

ASK GOD

God who delivered your people from their suffering, I put my trust in you. Open my eyes to your nearness. Open my ears to hear your voice. I reject the lie that I am alone, because I know you are with me. Strengthen me and hold me up with your "victorious right hand."

A Living Sacrifice

Imitate God, therefore, in everything you do, because you are his dear children. Live a life filled with love, following the example of Christ. He loved us and offered himself as a sacrifice for us, a pleasing aroma to God.

EPHESIANS 5:1-2

What does it look like to imitate Someone who gave his life for us? Most of us will not be called to actually be nailed to a cross or even to die for our faith—though it does still happen. But in his letter to the church in Ephesus, Paul advises believers to imitate God in *everything* they do. He's not just talking about crucifixion and death. He's talking about how we *live*.

As you purpose to walk in the way of Jesus, God calls you to offer your life as a sacrifice of love for others. Sometimes you'll make sacrifices in the ways you love your family. Other times God may call you to give yourself to those in your church or in your neighborhood. And other times you'll be invited to sacrifice for folks you may not even know, for the sake of God's Kingdom. Today, live a life filled with love.

ASK YOURSELF

» Is there a small sacrifice God's quiet whisper is calling you to make today? Are you willing to give up time, money, energy, or privilege to imitate Christ?

» What is the difference between accommodating others' demands and choosing to give to them sacrificially? How can you care for yourself appropriately and still love others sacrificially?

ASK GOD

Jesus, Lamb of God, you gave your life for the world, and you gave your life for me. Thank you. Teach me how to imitate you in all of my living.

For the Sake of Little Ones

Anyone who welcomes a little child like this on my behalf is welcoming
me. But if you cause one of these little ones who trusts in me to fall
into sin, it would be better for you to have a large millstone tied
around your neck and be drowned in the depths of the sea.

MATTHEW 18:5-6

Jesus was passionate about the value of the simplest and most vulnerable among us—those he called "the least of these my brothers and sisters" (Matthew 25:40). By teaching and example, he urged his followers to care for, defend, and even identify with those that society might deem unimportant.

As someone on the road to recovery, you probably know some things about being vulnerable and needing protection. You've been learning to correct the deficiencies of your upbringing, to protect yourself, and to believe you are worth being cared for. Now, as you move toward health and maturity, you may be called to protect others—to guide and affirm them, to stand up for them and affirm their worth. As you put your newfound strength and confidence to work on behalf of the "little ones" Jesus loved, you can know him as well.

ASK YOURSELF

» As you learn to walk in healthy ways, who is God calling you to protect?

» Do you still have moments when you feel like a victim? How can you move past those moments and stand up for others who are experiencing what you once did?

ASK GOD

Jesus, I thank you that you valued the vulnerable and advocated for them. As I follow you, I want to do this too. Equip me to serve you by protecting and guiding these "little ones" you love.

Real Value

Riches won't help on the day of judgment, but right living can save you from death.

PROVERBS 11:4

We will never be good enough to earn our way into heaven. We will never have enough money to pay for entrance there, and nothing we can offer will ever be enough to gain us access to the heavenly realm. So we can keep our "riches"—God doesn't need them. When Jesus died on the cross for our sins, he paid the full price. Because of his sacrifice, we have been granted access to the throne of God.

Because money and possessions are so greatly valued in this world, it's easy to fall into believing that they can secure anything we need in life. This is a monumental error in human thinking and can create a false security that keeps us from God.

The truth is, material possessions are neither good nor bad. The place we give them in our lives determines their value and influence. Whether we have been blessed with little or with much, living a godly life is what really matters.

ASK YOURSELF

» What does it mean to you that Jesus has paid the full price for your admission into heaven?

» On what do you tend to spend your money? What does that tell you about your values?

ASK GOD

Dear Jesus, thank you for sending Jesus to die in my place on the cross. I want my values to reflect that awesome reality. Teach me how to fully appreciate the value of his sacrifice and honor it through the way I live.

Satisfied

Let the peace that comes from Christ rule in your hearts. For as members
of one body you are called to live in peace. And always be thankful.

COLOSSIANS 3:15

One of the popular prescriptions for satisfaction these days is to keep a gratitude journal. Research has proven that those who are daily able to name what
they're thankful for tend to be more satisfied than those who don't keep such a
record. And while the popular cultural trend doesn't specify to whom our gratitude should be directed, the Scriptures make clear who is to receive our thanks.

The church in Colosse that Paul addressed in today's verse had strayed
from what they'd been taught. Paul was writing to them about holy living. He
reminded them that they were called to peace but would only manage it when
they stayed close to Jesus. And then he suggested a way to access that peace:
"Always be thankful."

That's something to keep in mind. If you're lacking peace in your heart
today, or if you're feeling grumpy and dissatisfied, try Paul's remedy. Say thank
you to God for all he's given you. Then . . . say it again.

ASK YOURSELF

> » Have you ever tried keeping a gratitude journal? If so, what was your
> experience? If not, would you consider keeping one?

> » What can you sincerely thank God for today? Make a little list and then
> pray it.

ASK GOD

God, you are the giver of all good gifts. Forgive me for living as though I deserve
what I've received. Thank you for all that you've given to sustain my life and
my faith in you. You are a generous God. Continue to sow a spirit of gratitude
in my heart.

You Do Matter

What is the price of two sparrows—one copper coin? But not a
single sparrow can fall to the ground without your Father knowing
it. And the very hairs on your head are all numbered.

MATTHEW 10:29-30

Our world is perfectly balanced to sustain life: plants, animals, natural resources, and people. God created them all, and he keeps track of them all. From the insects that crawl upon the ground to the birds that fly far above it, the Lord knows everything that happens to each of them. The Bible says that "not a single sparrow can fall to the ground without your Father knowing it. And the very hairs on your head are all numbered." Wow!

If ever you feel that you do not count in the grand scheme of things, if ever you feel that your life has no real value, touch your head. Yes, touch your head. Every hair that you can feel there, God has counted and made note of.

You matter that much to him. You are that important. You are here for a reason.

ASK YOURSELF

» Do it! Place your hand on your head and take a minute to realize just how intimately God knows you.

» When you feel unimportant and undervalued, what can you do to remind yourself how much you mean to your heavenly Father?

ASK GOD

Dear Jesus, help me to realize just how much you care about me. Remind me daily that every movement I make is known to you. Thank you for loving me enough to know every facet and fiber of my being. Help me to recognize my own value in this life and use the talents that you have given me for your glory.

Eternal Investment

What do you benefit if you gain the whole world but lose your
own soul? Is anything worth more than your soul?

MATTHEW 16:26

When you make a financial investment, if you are wise, you'll make sure to choose what gives the best return. No one in their right mind would invest their earnings in something that was guaranteed to fade away or lose money.

The same is true of your time and energy. If you do not invest them wisely, you run the risk of ending up in spiritual or emotional bankruptcy.

Every morning when you awaken, you have a choice of how you will invest your time and energy that day. You can allocate them either to the things of this world or to your spiritual growth and the furthering of God's Kingdom. The distinctions are often subtle, but they are distinctions just the same. Be careful that you do not expend so many resources on the world's demands that you have no time to invest in what is eternal.

ASK YOURSELF

» Does the amount of time that you spend on your spiritual growth reflect its value?

» What does it mean in practical terms to invest in eternal things? What kinds of decisions and activities represent such an investment?

ASK GOD

Dear Lord Jesus, often the responsibilities of everyday life consume me, and I have no time or energy left for anything else. Forgive me. Teach me how to allocate time each day to spend in your Word, to pray, and to meditate on who you are and what you would have me do with my life. Instead of simply reacting to what the world throws at me each day, may I draw on the deep reserve of your love and wisdom.

You Can—But Do You Want To?

You say, "I am allowed to do anything"—but not everything is good for you. And
even though "I am allowed to do anything," I must not become a slave to anything.

1 CORINTHIANS 6:12

There are reasons that children are not allowed to make decisions concerning
the direction of their lives. Their brains are not fully developed, and they have
not yet acquired the knowledge and experience they need for making wise
choices. So children are likely to do anything that looks fun without regard for
the potential outcome.

Sadly, this tendency can continue into adulthood—and adults don't have
the excuse that children do.

The freedom to make choices can be a blessing or a curse, depending upon
the level of wisdom we use in making choices. This freedom makes us solely
responsible for the outcome of our lives, and that is no small responsibility. In
a sense, the choices we make each day determine the people we are and the
direction our lives will take.

Are you making wise decisions, decisions that are geared toward making
you a better person and bringing you into a more intimate relationship with
Jesus?

ASK YOURSELF

» Do you think we really have freedom in every choice we make? Why or
   why not?

» What are some areas of your life (if any) where your poor decision-
   making is evident? What can you do to reverse this trend?

ASK GOD

Dear Father, give me the wisdom to live in a way that will bring me closer to
you. Help me to make careful, mature, and intelligent decisions in every aspect
of my life. Do not allow me to become a slave to anything.

He Knows—and Loves

*Nothing in all creation is hidden from God. Everything is naked and
exposed before his eyes, and he is the one to whom we are accountable.*

HEBREWS 4:13

After Adam and Eve sinned in the Garden of Eden, they hid from God. What
were they thinking? They had walked and talked with him. They knew him
intimately, and yet they were attempting to hide from him. Why would they
think that was even possible? More important, why would they think it was
necessary?

The devil wants us to believe that if God really knew what we were like, he
wouldn't love us. But God knows all and sees all—and loves us no matter what
we do. There is nowhere to hide from his eyes and no reason to try.

When you think about how much God loves you, why would you ever want
to hide from him? He knows everything there is to know about you, and he
loves you anyway. That is the definition of true love.

The next time you have done something that you wish you could hide from
the Lord, remember that "nothing in all creation is hidden from God." Don't
waste your time. Simply ask God's forgiveness and move forward.

ASK YOURSELF

» What kinds of experiences make you want to hide?

» What can you do to become more open and honest before the Lord?

ASK GOD

Dear heavenly Father, I make so many mistakes in my life, and yet you love
me. Thank you. Help me to be transparent in my relationship with you. You
know everything that takes place in my life anyway. Please help me to own up
to my mistakes so that I can ask for your forgiveness and grow closer to you
in the process.

Don't Worry

Don't worry about anything; instead, pray about everything. Tell
God what you need, and thank him for all he has done. Then you will
experience God's peace, which exceeds anything we can understand. His
peace will guard your hearts and minds as you live in Christ Jesus.

PHILIPPIANS 4:6-7

In 1988, when a catchy song by Bobby McFerrin caught the ear of America, young and old began whistling and singing, "Don't worry. Be happy." While the melody was contagious, the simplistic prescription for dealing with life's troubles hardly seemed useful to those crushed under the weight of real concerns. Just telling someone to stop worrying doesn't help them do it.

So when we read the same words, "Don't worry," from the pen of the apostle Paul to the early church in Philippi, we're apt to be a little skeptical. But Paul goes on to pair his "don't worry" prescription with something that actually does lift our burdens: *"Pray about everything."* He promises that when we let God know what we need and give thanks for what he's done, we will experience a peace that's beyond human comprehension. Today you can offer your burdens to God and let them go. And then you really can begin to let go of your worry.

ASK YOURSELF

» What is the biggest worry you hold in your heart today?

» How might you begin letting that worry go?

ASK GOD

God of grace, you have made yourself known as one who sets your people free. You freed the Israelites from slavery in Egypt, and you free from sin all who trust in Jesus. God, today I offer you my worries, releasing them into your care.

Resisting Temptation

*The temptations in your life are no different from what others experience. And
God is faithful. He will not allow the temptation to be more than you can stand.
When you are tempted, he will show you a way out so that you can endure.*

1 CORINTHIANS 10:13

Each one of us faces temptations that pull us away from the life God has for us.
One person may be tempted by what's in the refrigerator. Another is tempted
by what's in a bottle. Someone else might be lured by what's on the Internet or
in a closet or under the covers or on sale at the mall. We're tempted daily by
that which distracts us from God's good design for our lives.

God knows what our lives are like. As Hebrews 4:15 reminds us, Jesus
was tempted in the same ways we are. But the promise we discover in the
Scriptures is that temptation is not our master. In fact, the one who mastered
temptation—but did not sin—gives us everything we need to resist. Like a
secret door in a maze of deception and confusion, Jesus offers us a safe exit
from any situation.

ASK YOURSELF

» Is a particular area of temptation especially difficult for you to avoid?
  Why do you think it calls so strongly to you?

» Do you remember a time when Jesus gave you a way out of temptation?
  What happened? Were you able to take advantage of that opportunity,
  or did you give in?

ASK GOD

Jesus, I thank you that you know what my life is like. You understand in your
bones the temptations I face. I trust that you will give me all I need to resist
temptation in your name.

Fix Your Focus

We don't look at the troubles we can see now; rather, we fix our gaze on things that cannot be seen. For the things we see now will soon be gone, but the things we cannot see will last forever.

2 CORINTHIANS 4:18

Perspective is a funny thing. Two people can look at the same situation and see it entirely differently. This has everything to do with their individual vantage points. When you stand very close to something, it is all you can see. If you back up and get a broader perspective, the entire focus changes.

Every day we make choices about how we will respond to what comes up in our lives. We choose what we will give attention to and what we will allow to consume our time and energy. The apostle Paul, in his second letter to the Christians at Corinth, has some relevant advice for making these choices. He suggests that we shouldn't invest too much of ourselves in today's troubles because they will pass. Instead, we should change our perspective and invest ourselves in what will last forever.

ASK YOURSELF

» Do you tend to be overly concerned with the "little troubles" that each day brings? What can you do to shift your focus and spend more time on the things of God?

» What can you do here on earth that has eternal consequences?

ASK GOD

Dear Jesus, I know I allow myself to become too concerned with the issues each day brings. I fret about things that may never become an issue, wasting precious time in the process. Help me, Lord, to learn how to shift my focus from the temporal to the eternal and how to invest my time wisely.

Your Actions Matter

Keep a close watch on how you live and on your teaching. Stay true to what is right
for the sake of your own salvation and the salvation of those who hear you.

1 TIMOTHY 4:16

When a woman is pregnant, everything she does affects not only her but also her baby. She has a huge responsibility for a life in addition to her own. If she doesn't take this responsibility seriously, both she and the baby can suffer.

Christians have a similar responsibility for the unsaved around them. They are accountable for not only the actions in their own lives but also how those actions may affect the faith of others.

When you woke up this morning, you probably had a lot of responsibilities on your mind—everything from making sure the family is clothed and fed to getting yourself to work on time to making sure the bills have been paid. But of the many responsibilities you may have in this world, the one that outranks all others is that you "stay true to what is right for the sake of your own salvation and the salvation of those who hear you."

ASK YOURSELF

» What do you feel most responsible for in life?

» How do you respond to the idea that when you choose to stray from what you know to be right, your actions could have a negative effect on the faith of others? Can you think of a specific instance when that might be true?

ASK GOD

Dear Lord, open my eyes to the fact that my choices in life don't just impact me. Please teach me to lean upon you for the wisdom and guidance that I need every day.

Strength in Weakness

Three different times I begged the Lord to take it away. Each time he said, "My grace is all you need. My power works best in weakness." So now I am glad to boast about my weaknesses, so that the power of Christ can work through me.... For when I am weak, then I am strong.

2 CORINTHIANS 12:8-10

The apostle Paul struggled with a painful and debilitating condition he called his "thorn in the flesh." We don't know exactly what this condition was, but it could be likened to those things in our lives that Satan uses to frustrate us and make us feel hopeless. Paul begged the Lord again and again to heal him of this condition, and each time God's answer was no. But with each no came a promise: In Paul's weakness, God's power would shine.

As we look at the mistakes, hurts, failures, and wounds in our lives, we would do well to remember God's promise to Paul. God's power works best in those places where we are powerless.

ASK YOURSELF

» What do you think would happen if you quit trying so hard to fix all your mistakes, hurts, and wounds and instead trusted God to be enough? What stops you from doing that?

» Do you understand what Paul meant when he said, "When I am weak, then I am strong"? Have you ever experienced that dynamic in your life?

ASK GOD

Dear Lord, I've tried so hard to "get fixed"—to correct all those mistakes, heal all my hurts—and in many ways I'm still struggling. Help me to trust what you're doing in my life. Help me even to rejoice in my weaknesses because there I will encounter your strength.

A Guide for God's People

Such things were written in the Scriptures long ago to teach us. And the Scriptures give us hope and encouragement as we wait patiently for God's promises to be fulfilled.

ROMANS 15:4

The early church included everyone who had put their faith in Jesus, the Son of God. But this diverse group was not without controversy. Some believers were Jewish, like Jesus, and others weren't. So these very different Christian brothers and sisters had to figure out how to live and worship together. Would they still practice Jewish dietary laws, or would those laws be erased? This was just one of the questions they were asking. There wasn't a manual for the new thing God was doing.

Paul taught the young church that although they didn't have step-by-step instructions for meshing as a community, God's Scriptures could still guide them in their life together. This is true for us, too, in our very complicated age. As we face issues that first-century folk couldn't have dreamed of (Internet porn? pregnancy surrogates? gay marriage?), the Scriptures can provide us the wisdom and guidance we need to live faithfully.

ASK YOURSELF

> » Are you facing a difficult issue or wondering about something not
> specifically addressed in the Scriptures? What is it?

> » Where can you find principles to guide you as you seek to be faithful
> to God regarding issues not specifically mentioned in Scripture?

ASK GOD

God of all wisdom, I thank you that you have breathed life into your holy Word. Send your Spirit to open my eyes and ears as I study and meditate on Scripture and seek wisdom in my faith community. Speak, Lord, for your servants are listening.

The Joy of God's Healing

The Sun of Righteousness will rise with healing in his wings. And you
will go free, leaping with joy like calves let out to pasture.

MALACHI 4:2

The process of taking your life back involves work—emotional work. And a big part of that work is facing the past pain that led you to develop false selves to present to the world. These false selves may have helped you cope, but they also promoted emotional habits of hiding and shame that kept you from growing and healing. But you don't have to stay that way. The prophet Malachi assures us that we really can be healed, that we can find freedom and, best of all, that we can experience joy.

The joy comes when we realize we never really had to bury our real selves—the ones God created. He knows all our weaknesses and failures and loves us anyway. The furthest thing from God's mind is that we have be perfect to be real. Think how exciting it will be to relate to a loving God just as we are, without hiding or pretending. We may even find ourselves leaping for joy.

ASK YOURSELF

» What "false self" characteristics have you adopted in the past? How did they help you cope? How did they hurt you?

» When have you experienced joy? Describe what it felt like.

ASK GOD

Dear Lord, give me patience on this journey of taking my life back. Help me to get to know my real self and to better understand the events that led me to replace it with my false self. Help me understand how much you love the real me.

How Long, Lord?

*The Lord isn't really being slow about his promise, as some people
think. No, he is being patient for your sake. He does not want
anyone to be destroyed, but wants everyone to repent.*

2 PETER 3:9

"Why does it take so long, Lord?" we sometimes cry out in frustration as we
walk the long road of taking our lives back. We want healing *now*! But then
we remember how long it took us to develop a reactive, dysfunctional way
of living. Most of us started building our reactive selves when we were very
young, and at the time it seemed like our only option. We thought our real self
was unacceptable, so we set out to create what we thought was the solution—
becoming someone we were not. It worked for a while, but it ended up creating
more problems than it solved.

Of course, we would love for God to just reach in and zap us into wholeness,
but that's not how God typically works. Instead, he is slow and patient because
he wants us to learn important lessons as we go through the healing process.
There's an advantage for us in God's slowness.

ASK YOURSELF

» What are some of the frustrations you have encountered on your road
to healing? What has made you impatient?

» What are some of the things you have learned about yourself and about
God on the same journey?

ASK GOD

Dear Lord, I'm sorry I get so impatient with you at times. Help me to see what
you want me to see and learn what you want me to learn. And help me to
understand better why healing takes so long.

SCRIPTURE INDEX

Genesis 1:27 . . . . Day 330	Psalm 27:9-10 . . . . Day 127
Genesis 16:13 . . . . Day 265	Psalm 27:14 . . . . Day 276
Exodus 2:24-25 . . . . Day 70	Psalm 28:7 . . . . Day 69
Exodus 3:2 . . . . Day 29	Psalm 29:11 . . . . Day 47
Leviticus 19:18 . . . . Day 123	Psalm 32:2 . . . . Day 327
Leviticus 20:6 . . . . Day 188	Psalm 32:7 . . . . Day 263
Leviticus 25:17 . . . . Day 214	Psalm 34:4-5 . . . . Day 78
Numbers 6:24-26 . . . . Day 346	Psalm 34:14 . . . . Day 252
Numbers 23:19 . . . . Day 40	Psalm 34:18 . . . . Day 331
Deuteronomy 31:8 . . . . . . Day 76	Psalm 37:23-24 . . . . Day 13
Joshua 1:5 . . . . Day 247	Psalm 37:37 . . . . Day 308
Joshua 1:9 . . . . Day 4	Psalm 40:1-2 . . . . Day 192
Judges 18:6 . . . . Day 1	Psalm 40:8 . . . . Day 210
1 Samuel 15:22 . . . . Day 248	Psalm 46:1-3 . . . . Day 322
1 Samuel 16:7 . . . . Day 52	Psalm 52:8 . . . . Day 153
2 Samuel 22:28 . . . . Day 81	Psalm 54:1 . . . . Day 256
1 Chronicles 16:11 . . . . . . Day 281	Psalm 55:22 . . . . Day 5
1 Chronicles 28:9 . . . . Day 175	Psalm 56:11 . . . . Day 296
2 Chronicles 32:5-7 . . . . . . Day 74	Psalm 57:7 . . . . Day 212
Nehemiah 9:2 . . . . Day 107	Psalm 61:1-2 . . . . Day 131
Nehemiah 9:37 . . . . Day 105	Psalm 66:18-20 . . . . Day 345
Job 5:11 . . . . Day 280	Psalm 69:32 . . . . Day 235
Job 5:17 . . . . Day 249	Psalm 71:23 . . . . Day 129
Psalm 4:4 . . . . Day 150	Psalm 72:12 . . . . Day 206
Psalm 8:4-5 . . . . Day 17	Psalm 73:26 . . . . Day 347
Psalm 16:8 . . . . Day 262	Psalm 85:8 . . . . Day 299
Psalm 19:8 . . . . Day 67	Psalm 86:15 . . . . Day 229
Psalm 21:7 . . . . Day 104	Psalm 90:12 . . . . Day 161
Psalm 23:4 . . . . Day 173	Psalm 92:4 . . . . Day 208
Psalm 25:7 . . . . Day 100	Psalm 92:12 . . . . Day 124
Psalm 27:1 . . . . Day 91	Psalm 94:18 . . . . Day 97

Psalm 94:19 . . . . Day 255
Psalm 103:8 . . . . Day 95
Psalm 103:11 . . . . Day 56
Psalm 106:1 . . . . Day 138
Psalm 109:4 . . . . Day 94
Psalm 112:1, 7 . . . . Day 272
Psalm 112:1, 8 . . . . Day 82
Psalm 116:1 . . . . Day 287
Psalm 116:1-2 . . . . Day 186
Psalm 118:24 . . . . Day 36
Psalm 119:36 . . . . Day 92
Psalm 119:49-50 . . . . Day 223
Psalm 119:61 . . . . Day 64
Psalm 119:143 . . . . Day 203
Psalm 119:165 . . . . Day 303
Psalm 121:5 . . . . Day 14
Psalm 126:5 . . . . Day 126
Psalm 139:7-8 . . . . Day 93
Psalm 139:8-10 . . . . Day 155
Psalm 146:3-5 . . . . Day 108
Psalm 147:2-3 . . . . Day 218
Proverbs 1:7 . . . . Day 57
Proverbs 1:17, 19 . . . . Day 16
Proverbs 1:33 . . . . Day 46
Proverbs 2:7 . . . . Day 139
Proverbs 3:5 . . . . Day 250
Proverbs 3:5-6 . . . . Day 320
Proverbs 3:6 . . . . Day 197
Proverbs 3:9-10 . . . . Day 326
Proverbs 3:11-12 . . . . Day 311
Proverbs 4:6 . . . . Day 89
Proverbs 4:23 . . . . Day 120
Proverbs 5:22 . . . . Day 307
Proverbs 9:6 . . . . Day 169
Proverbs 9:8 . . . . Day 88
Proverbs 9:12 . . . . Day 142
Proverbs 10:4 . . . . Day 237
Proverbs 10:9 . . . . Day 314
Proverbs 10:10 . . . . Day 253
Proverbs 10:12 . . . . Day 160
Proverbs 10:24 . . . . Day 316
Proverbs 11:4 . . . . Day 352
Proverbs 11:24 . . . . Day 318
Proverbs 11:25 . . . . Day 342
Proverbs 12:14 . . . . Day 163
Proverbs 12:15 . . . . Day 319
Proverbs 12:16 . . . . Day 187
Proverbs 12:20 . . . . Day 254
Proverbs 12:23 . . . . Day 266
Proverbs 12:25 . . . . Day 136

Proverbs 14:3 . . . . Day 41
Proverbs 14:9 . . . . Day 147
Proverbs 14:10 . . . . Day 204
Proverbs 15:15 . . . . Day 23
Proverbs 15:17 . . . . Day 103
Proverbs 15:21 . . . . Day 202
Proverbs 15:32 . . . . Day 111
Proverbs 16:2 . . . . Day 246
Proverbs 16:6-7 . . . . Day 283
Proverbs 16:32 . . . . Day 245
Proverbs 16:33 . . . . Day 134
Proverbs 17:1 . . . . Day 302
Proverbs 17:9 . . . . Day 61
Proverbs 17:17 . . . . Day 286
Proverbs 18:13 . . . . Day 240
Proverbs 18:15 . . . . Day 42
Proverbs 18:21 . . . . Day 101
Proverbs 19:8 . . . . Day 37
Proverbs 20:22 . . . . Day 332
Proverbs 20:24 . . . . Day 241
Proverbs 21:4 . . . . Day 216
Proverbs 21:5 . . . . Day 58
Proverbs 24:16 . . . . Day 59
Proverbs 27:12 . . . . Day 205
Proverbs 28:13 . . . . Day 55
Proverbs 29:26 . . . . Day 271
Proverbs 30:8-9 . . . . Day 225
Ecclesiastes 6:9 . . . . Day 65
Ecclesiastes 7:14 . . . . Day 43
Isaiah 26:3 . . . . Day 189
Isaiah 30:18 . . . . Day 87
Isaiah 32:16-17 . . . . Day 336
Isaiah 40:7-8 . . . . Day 339
Isaiah 40:29 . . . . Day 8
Isaiah 40:31 . . . . Day 152
Isaiah 41:10 . . . . Day 349
Isaiah 43:1 . . . . Day 54
Isaiah 43:2-3 . . . . Day 53
Isaiah 49:4 . . . . Day 200
Isaiah 49:15 . . . . Day 279
Isaiah 57:10 . . . . Day 151
Isaiah 59:1-2 . . . . Day 341
Jeremiah 6:14 . . . . Day 180
Jeremiah 17:7-8 . . . . Day 199
Jeremiah 29:11 . . . . Day 344
Jeremiah 31:13 . . . . Day 145, Day 297
Jeremiah 31:25 . . . . Day 195
Lamentations 3:18-21 . . . Day 11
Lamentations 3:22-23 . . . Day 99, Day 324
Lamentations 3:31-32 . . . Day 68

Ezekiel 36:26 . . . . Day 172

Hosea 13:6 . . . . Day 185

Micah 6:8 . . . . Day 60

Micah 7:7-8 . . . . Day 33

Nahum 1:7 . . . . Day 190

Zephaniah 3:17 . . . . Day 21

Zechariah 10:2 . . . . Day 260

Malachi 4:2 . . . . Day 364

Matthew 5:14-15 . . . . Day 273

Matthew 5:16 . . . . Day 264

Matthew 5:37 . . . . Day 224

Matthew 5:43-44 . . . . Day 239

Matthew 6:6 . . . . Day 288

Matthew 6:12 . . . . Day 96

Matthew 6:20-21 . . . . Day 236

Matthew 6:28-29 . . . . Day 110

Matthew 6:31-32 . . . . Day 170

Matthew 6:33 . . . . Day 90

Matthew 6:33-34 . . . . Day 333

Matthew 7:3-4 . . . . Day 84

Matthew 7:4 . . . . Day 278

Matthew 7:7 . . . . Day 270

Matthew 9:12-13 . . . . Day 66

Matthew 9:20-22 . . . . Day 215

Matthew 10:29-30 . . . . . . Day 354

Matthew 10:29-31 . . . . . . Day 179

Matthew 11:4-5 . . . . Day 300

Matthew 11:28 . . . . Day 243

Matthew 11:28-30 . . . . . . Day 72

Matthew 11:29 . . . . Day 282

Matthew 16:25 . . . . Day 12

Matthew 16:26 . . . . Day 355

Matthew 18:4 . . . . Day 135

Matthew 18:5-6 . . . . Day 351

Matthew 23:11-12 . . . . . . Day 130

Matthew 26:37-38 . . . . . . Day 34

Mark 2:3-4 . . . . Day 15

Mark 8:23-24 . . . . Day 335

Mark 9:24 . . . . Day 166

Mark 13:11 . . . . Day 148

Mark 14:44 . . . . Day 257

Mark 16:15 . . . . Day 198

Luke 1:11-12 . . . . Day 31

Luke 2:52 . . . . Day 244

Luke 4:18 . . . . Day 112

Luke 6:21 . . . . Day 118

Luke 6:30 . . . . Day 274

Luke 7:16 . . . . Day 38

Luke 9:23 . . . . Day 114

Luke 9:24 . . . . Day 309

Luke 11:39 . . . . Day 22

Luke 12:25-26 . . . . Day 268

John 3:18 . . . . Day 9

John 4:23 . . . . Day 313

John 4:23-24 . . . . Day 174

John 5:5-6 . . . . Day 3

John 8:31-34 . . . . Day 329

John 8:44 . . . . Day 115

John 9:11 . . . . Day 219

John 10:10 . . . . Day 26

John 11:33-35 . . . . Day 119

John 12:25 . . . . Day 83

John 12:46 . . . . Day 20

John 13:34 . . . . Day 226

John 14:27 . . . . Day 45, Day 258

John 15:19 . . . . Day 79

John 16:13 . . . . Day 290

John 16:24 . . . . Day 196

John 16:33 . . . . Day 209, Day 306

John 17:17-19 . . . . Day 217

Acts 2:44-45 . . . . Day 137

Acts 9:33-34 . . . . Day 328

Romans 2:15 . . . . Day 275

Romans 2:23 . . . . Day 267

Romans 3:20 . . . . Day 176

Romans 3:22 . . . . Day 149

Romans 4:8 . . . . Day 30

Romans 5:3 . . . . Day 165

Romans 5:4 . . . . Day 259

Romans 5:6, 10 . . . . Day 315

Romans 6:4 . . . . Day 221

Romans 6:6 . . . . Day 181

Romans 7:15, 19 . . . . Day 125

Romans 8:6 . . . . Day 117, Day 285

Romans 8:28 . . . . Day 62

Romans 8:31 . . . . Day 334

Romans 8:39 . . . . Day 128

Romans 10:16-17 . . . . Day 233

Romans 11:33 . . . . Day 167

Romans 12:1 . . . . Day 158

Romans 12:2 . . . . Day 32

Romans 12:3 . . . . Day 277

Romans 12:11-12 . . . . Day 35

Romans 12:12 . . . . Day 109

Romans 12:15 . . . . Day 348

Romans 12:16 . . . . Day 269

Romans 14:19 . . . . Day 154

Romans 15:4 . . . . Day 363

Romans 15:13 . . . . Day 177, Day 295

Romans 16:20 . . . . Day 178

1 Corinthians 1:20 ...... Day 207
1 Corinthians 2:9 .... Day 234
1 Corinthians 5:6 .... Day 140
1 Corinthians 6:12 ...... Day 356
1 Corinthians 10:13 ..... Day 359
1 Corinthians 12:12 ..... Day 121
1 Corinthians 13:4 ...... Day 310
1 Corinthians 13:11 ..... Day 6
1 Corinthians 14:33 ..... Day 182
1 Corinthians 16:2 ...... Day 106
2 Corinthians 1:3 .... Day 159
2 Corinthians 1:4 .... Day 116
2 Corinthians 4:7 .... Day 28
2 Corinthians 4:18 ...... Day 360
2 Corinthians 5:17 ...... Day 7
2 Corinthians 5:20 ...... Day 317
2 Corinthians 10:4-5..... Day 143
2 Corinthians 12:8-10.... Day 362
Galatians 1:10 .... Day 39
Galatians 3:3 .... Day 141
Galatians 3:22 .... Day 25
Galatians 5:13 .... Day 146
Galatians 5:22-23 .... Day 113, Day 183
Galatians 5:24 .... Day 261
Galatians 6:2 .... Day 301
Galatians 6:2, 4-5 .... Day 44
Galatians 6:3 .... Day 338
Ephesians 1:18......... Day 228
Ephesians 2:9.......... Day 98
Ephesians 2:20-21...... Day 325
Ephesians 3:17......... Day 50
Ephesians 3:19......... Day 77
Ephesians 4:2.......... Day 10
Ephesians 4:14-15...... Day 220
Ephesians 4:31-32...... Day 222
Ephesians 5:1-2........ Day 350
Ephesians 6:7.......... Day 323
Ephesians 6:11......... Day 49
Philippians 2:5-6........ Day 162
Philippians 2:6-7........ Day 321
Philippians 4:6-7........ Day 358
Philippians 4:7......... Day 144
Philippians 4:8......... Day 312
Colossians 1:10 .... Day 343
Colossians 1:11-12 ...... Day 293
Colossians 1:19-20 ...... Day 157
Colossians 2:7 .... Day 102
Colossians 3:2-3 .... Day 242

Colossians 3:12-13 ...... Day 304
Colossians 3:15 .... Day 86,
    Day 353
Colossians 3:23-24 ...... Day 63
1 Thessalonians 4:11 .... Day 194
1 Thessalonians 5:11 .... Day 284
1 Thessalonians 5:14 .... Day 133
1 Thessalonians 5:15 .... Day 193
1 Timothy 4:8 .... Day 337
1 Timothy 4:12 .... Day 298
1 Timothy 4:16 .... Day 361
1 Timothy 6:10 .... Day 71
2 Timothy 1:7 .... Day 122
2 Timothy 2:15 .... Day 305
2 Timothy 2:22 .... Day 184
Titus 2:12............. Day 294
Hebrews 3:6........... Day 211
Hebrews 3:14.......... Day 340
Hebrews 4:13.......... Day 357
Hebrews 4:15-16....... Day 18
Hebrews 10:25......... Day 292
Hebrews 11:6.......... Day 213
Hebrews 12:1-2........ Day 85
Hebrews 12:14......... Day 227
Hebrews 13:5.......... Day 75
Hebrews 13:6-7........ Day 2
James 1:2, 5 .... Day 19
James 1:3-4 .... Day 132
James 1:12 .... Day 73
James 1:17 .... Day 231
James 5:16 .... Day 80
1 Peter 1:6, 12 .... Day 164
1 Peter 2:2 .... Day 24
1 Peter 2:11 .... Day 171
1 Peter 3:11 .... Day 230
1 Peter 5:5-7.......... Day 238
1 Peter 5:10 .... Day 191
2 Peter 1:2 .... Day 48
2 Peter 3:9 .... Day 365
2 Peter 3:18 .... Day 291
1 John 2:5............. Day 51
1 John 3:20-21......... Day 27
1 John 4:4............. Day 289
1 John 4:10............ Day 168
1 John 5:4............. Day 201
1 John 5:5............. Day 156
1 John 5:14............ Day 251
2 John 1:6............. Day 232

TOPICAL INDEX

Abandonment............ Days 28, 68, 75, 76,
    127, 128, 175, 247, 349

Abuse/Neglect............ Days 14, 70, 256,
    284

Acceptance by God .... Days 7, 9, 68, 78, 99

Accepting Ourselves (see "Self-Worth")

Accepting Responsibility... Day 331

Accomplishment ....Days 15, 16, 81, 266

Acting Out, Acting In...... Day 2

Addiction............... Days 284, 119, 279,
    284

Anger .... Days 57, 61, 89, 95,
    123, 134, 143, 150, 193, 222, 301, 331

Anxiety.................. Days 5, 32, 91, 122,
    170, 203, 205

Approval/Affirmation ..... Days 6, 22, 39, 81,
    130, 169, 176, 264, 305, 330, 343, 346

Arguments (see "Contention")

Assumptions .... Days 14, 82, 344

Attacking Others.......... Day 86

Attacking Yourself .... Day 82

Attacks, Spiritual.......... Days 144, 183, 260

Authority .... Days 100, 117, 249

Belonging............... Days 47, 70, 125,
    179, 261, 289, 340

Belonging, Not/Not
    Fitting In .... Days 79, 245, 289

Bitterness................ Days 204, 222, 341

Blessing .... Days 16, 40, 48,
    101, 137, 225, 258, 346

Blindness............... Days 89, 130, 205,
    219, 234, 300, 345

Boundaries .... Days 1, 49, 74, 227,
    282

Brokenness .... Days 191, 218

Burdens .... Days 5, 9, 44, 72,
    155, 181, 195, 238, 243, 283, 301, 358

Caregivers .... Day 280

Caring for Others .... Days 7, 44, 51, 130,
    133, 226, 321, 338, 342, 348, 351

Change of Thinking/
    Perspective .... Days 11, 32, 82,
    143, 169, 200, 212, 312, 323, 360

Changing Other People .... Day 94

Character, God's .... Days 40, 330

Character (Morality) ...... Days 36, 95, 245,
    259, 314

Childhood Pain/Losses/
    Wounds .... Days 6, 26, 115,
    127, 199, 279, 331

Childishness/Immaturity .. Days 6, 216, 220,
    249

Childlikeness/Innocence... Days 135, 233, 258,
    270, 351

Choices/Choosing......... Days 23, 32, 103,
    117, 132, 142, 207, 210, 250, 285, 294, 312,
    320, 355, 356, 360

Clarity.................. Days 20, 304, 345

Comfort (Needing/Seeking/
    Finding).............. Days 113, 116, 155,
    159, 195, 203, 206, 223, 287, 297, 306

Common Sense.......... Day 139

Communication (with God)
    .... Days 46, 104, 144,
    188, 196, 228, 251, 341

Communication (with Other People)
.... Days 154, 240, 341

Comparison (to Others) ... Day 78

Compassion............... Days 38, 68, 95, 338

Condemnation .... Days 9, 125

Confession (to God)....... Days 5, 27, 55, 107, 196, 227, 341, 345

Confession (to Another Person) .... Days 27, 80, 222

Confidence .... Days 4, 69, 82, 97, 108, 109, 173, 206, 211, 212, 235, 272, 276, 295, 316, 336

Conflict .... Days 45, 132, 224, 227, 253, 304

Conscience............... Days 147, 275

Contention............... Days 86, 88, 160, 249

Contentment............. Days 43, 65, 75, 225

Control, Appropriate ...... Days 106, 312

Control, Inability to Maintain .... Days 16, 22, 97, 131, 134, 150

Control, Relinquishing to God/ Holy Spirit............ Days 5, 73, 83, 110, 111, 113, 117, 134, 158, 241, 283, 285, 296, 320

Controlling Behavior ...... Days 83, 110, 111

Craving.................. Days 24, 71, 189, 208

Criticism/Critical Spirit.... Days 84, 86, 154, 278

Danger .... Days 64, 82, 91, 151, 190, 205, 260, 316, 322

Darkness .... Days 20, 33, 91, 165, 173, 228

Death, Physical .... Days 315, 347

Death, Spiritual .... Day 285

Decision Making (see "Choices/Choosing")

Denial.....................Days 18, 26, 57, 166

Desire/Desires............ Days 65, 71, 75, 92, 120, 151, 171, 188, 293, 302

Despair.................. Days 28, 136, 192

Disappointment .... Days 10, 168, 200, 229, 257, 346

Discipline (Correction) .... Days 88, 111, 249, 275, 311

Discipline/Self-Discipline .. Days 57, 187

Discomfort............... Day 191

Dishonesty.............. Day 139

Dissatisfaction/Discontentment
.... Days 65, 75, 353

Distraction.............. Days 44, 46, 170

Doubt/Unbelief.......... Days 29, 76, 126, 143, 166, 170, 234, 255, 300

Emptiness .... Day 265

Encouragement.......... Days 4, 74, 76, 101, 116, 133, 154, 255, 292, 342

Endurance .... Days 36, 132, 259, 293

Enthusiasm/Excitement ... Days 35, 38, 208, 258, 270, 323

Equality .... Days 149, 216

Evil .... Days 71, 156, 165, 178, 216, 230, 254, 283, 294

Expectations .... Days 10, 61, 94, 198, 229, 271, 287

Failure .... Days 27, 30, 59, 80, 100, 127, 176, 200, 243, 248, 278, 365

Faith/Belief .... Days 2, 5, 11, 25, 29, 102, 104, 110, 149, 156, 166, 213, 215, 233, 247, 262, 328, 332, 334, 335

Faithfulness, God's .... Days 11, 40, 70, 99, 104, 138, 155, 173, 229, 315, 320, 331, 333, 336, 345, 347

Fear..................... Days 9, 21, 31, 82, 89, 91, 114, 119, 122, 173, 226, 248, 260, 264, 265, 272, 290, 294, 315, 316, 349

Feelings .... Days 26, 34, 57, 89, 119, 128, 150, 155

Flaws/Shortcomings....... Days 10, 59, 60, 61, 84, 100, 127, 160, 168, 298, 304, 310, 331

Flesh, the .... Days 239, 261, 276

Focus .... Days 11, 23, 39, 46, 52, 59, 65, 85, 98, 142, 170, 189, 235, 271, 309, 323, 333, 360

Foolishness .... Days 41, 42, 142, 163, 187, 250, 266, 278, 299

Forgiveness .... Days 55, 60, 66, 96, 101, 127, 147, 158, 196, 217, 222, 304, 331, 341, 345, 357

Freedom................. Days 1, 2, 25, 75, 78, 129, 135, 146, 212, 222, 313, 329, 331, 364

Fruit of the Spirit .... Days 63, 113, 183

Fruitfulness/Bearing Fruit . Days 283, 343

Fulfillment............... Days 81, 137, 168, 210, 271, 302

Generational Patterns/Sins.. Day 107

Gifts from God . . . . Days 23, 31, 36, 45, 57, 137, 138, 162, 172, 231, 258, 303, 324, 353

Giving to Other People . . . . Days 133, 224, 274, 282, 318, 321

God, Image of . . . . Day 330

God's Love . . . . Days 13, 21, 68, 98, 99, 100, 127, 128, 138, 168, 175, 179, 226, 232, 243, 279, 310, 311, 315, 346, 354, 357

God's Presence . . . . Days 38, 53, 70

God's View of Us . . . . Days 21, 52, 100, 129, 265

God's Will . . . . Days 197, 210, 267, 305, 336

Good Intentions . . . . Day 51

Goodness . . . . Days 57, 60, 62, 113, 165, 170, 183, 194, 308

Good Works . . . . Days 22, 130, 193, 230, 252

Grace . . . . Days 18, 48, 221, 222, 229, 291, 298, 335

Gratitude . . . . Days 60, 62, 65, 98, 138, 162, 165, 194, 249, 258, 327, 353

Greed . . . . Day 65

Grounding, Spiritual . . . . . . Days 14, 50, 339

Guidance . . . . Days 13, 33, 46, 67, 73, 104, 122, 155, 197, 200, 203, 211, 250, 275, 281, 299, 303, 320, 363

Guilt . . . . Days 27, 55, 57, 80, 147, 181, 290

Happiness . . . . Days 23, 43, 75, 249, 348

Healing . . . . Days 3, 15, 33, 66, 96, 180, 186, 191, 215, 217, 218, 219, 231, 264, 301, 329, 331, 334, 335, 340, 362, 364

Heart, the . . . . Days 23, 96, 120, 144, 228

Help, Asking for . . . . Days 33, 38, 231

Help from God . . . . Days 2, 33, 108

Helping Appropriately . . . . . Days 3, 7, 15, 44, 338, 342, 350

Hiding from God . . . . Days 55, 93, 175, 357

Hiding from Self . . . . Days 265, 364

Hiding from Truth/ Reality . . . . Days 172, 277

Holiness . . . . Days 30, 47, 56, 196, 214, 227, 294, 304

Holy Spirit/Comforter . . . . . Days 91, 112, 113, 117, 122, 148, 173, 180, 183, 210, 228, 276, 285, 289, 290

Honesty . . . . Days 80, 139, 174, 180, 277, 308, 327, 357

Hope/Hopefulness . . . . Days 11, 36, 109, 177, 215, 223, 228, 255, 259, 316, 344, 363

Hopelessness . . . . Days 11, 59, 186, 215, 328, 344

Humility . . . . Days 41, 60, 81, 130, 135, 162, 235, 238, 266, 282, 321, 338

Identity . . . . Days 77, 289

Influences, Harmful/Negative . . . . Days 120, 230, 260

Initiative . . . . Day 284

Insecurity . . . . Days 77, 114

Insight . . . . Day 67

Instruction, God's . . . . Days 4, 46, 64, 67, 193, 210, 239, 248, 303, 363

Integrated Lives . . . . Day 244

Integrity . . . . Days 139, 314

Intimacy with God . . . . Days 54, 179, 354, 357

Inventory, "Fearless Moral"/Heart . . . . Days 27, 204, 277

Investment . . . . Days 58, 83, 337, 355

Isolating/Isolation . . . . Days 53, 78, 226, 289, 349

Journey/Journey of Healing . . . . Days 1, 2, 197, 202, 215, 241, 282, 284, 286, 299, 335

Joy/Rejoicing . . . . Days 21, 36, 126, 164, 254, 293, 297, 327, 348

Judgment, God's . . . . Days 9, 352

Judgment, Good . . . . Days 139, 169, 250, 320

Judgmental Attitudes /Judging Others . . . . Days 2, 10, 269

Justice/Injustice . . . . Days 118, 271, 332, 336

Kindness . . . . Days 99, 191, 214, 222, 304, 310

Knowledge . . . . Days 42, 48, 167, 259, 266, 291, 356

Leadership . . . . Days 4, 117, 130, 260, 298

Letting Go . . . . Days 61, 114, 147, 181, 204, 274, 358

Lies/Deception/Deceit . . . . . Days 115, 254, 290

Listening to God/Hearing God . . . . Days 46, 111, 112, 115, 210 , 211, 214, 233, 249, 275, 276, 299

Listening to One Another .. Days 269, 301, 319, 340

Loneliness/Feeling Alone .. Days 155, 159, 173, 204, 226, 247, 331, 349

Love .... Days 21, 31, 51, 61, 68, 71, 78, 168, 310

Love, God's (see "God's love")

Love for God .... Days 51, 62

Love for Other People ..... Days 51, 94, 123, 154, 160, 226, 232, 235, 239, 274, 350

Manipulation............. Days 224, 256

Maturity/Adulthood ...... Days 6, 42, 220

Meaning................. Days 65, 90

Mercy/Mercies, God's...... Days 11, 55, 99

Micromanagement........ Days 110, 241

Misery .... Days 105, 297

Money/Finances.......... Days 16, 43, 65, 71, 106, 170, 194, 225, 326

Motives/Motivation ...... Days 22, 92, 130, 246, 305, 323

Needs .... Days 71, 75, 90, 137, 170, 177, 225, 305, 333

No, Saying .... Days 74, 85, 224, 294

Obedience .... Days 51, 60, 67, 112, 148, 210, 248, 267

Pain.................... Days 26, 28, 126, 204, 218, 287, 297, 306

Parents/Parenting........ Days 68, 100, 107, 127, 331

Past, the .... Days 100, 107, 217, 331

Patience .... Days 10, 35, 63, 73, 95, 133, 245, 276, 335

Peace................... Days 46, 106, 160, 227, 254, 283, 302, 303, 306, 308

Peace from God .... Days 45, 47, 48, 86, 112, 144, 177, 182, 189, 209, 258, 285, 336, 358

Peacemaking............ Days 230, 252, 253, 304

People Pleasing.......... Days 39, 85

Perfectionism .... Days 59, 61

Perseverance............ Days 59, 335

Perspective.............. Days 16, 212, 242, 268, 360

Placating .... Days 18, 227

Plans/Planning.......... Days 40, 58, 106, 202, 203, 205

Plans, God's .... Days 165, 211, 344

Pleasing God.............Days 39, 60, 63, 350

Power, God's .... Days 8, 28, 74, 152

Power, Human........... Days 8, 25

Prayer and Quiet Time .... Days 35, 87, 94, 108, 109, 144, 223, 251, 281, 288, 313, 337, 358

Preparation .... Days 148, 203, 205

Pride................... Days 41, 81, 98, 140, 266, 338

Priorities .... Days 58, 302, 337

Progress .... Days 59, 264, 298

Promises, God's.......... Days 4, 70, 75, 165, 223, 234, 296, 344, 362

Prosperity .... Days 43, 58

Protection, God's........ Days 14, 49, 69, 91, 144, 173, 190, 206, 263, 311, 322

Purpose .... Days 26, 62, 200

Reactive Living/Lifestyle/ Behavior/Patterns ..... Days 1, 2, 12, 32, 37, 74, 80, 85, 86, 101, 114, 118, 142, 169, 187, 257, 343, 362

Rebellion .... Days 13, 143, 220

Reconciliation........... Days 147, 157, 222, 227, 304

Recovery .... Days 2, 4, 35, 38, 42, 59, 80, 127, 137, 169, 186, 221, 304, 305, 333, 351

Recovery Groups/Twelve-Step Programs............. Days 27, 277, 292, 340

Recovery Resources .... Days 26, 99, 196, 231, 324, 355

Relapse.................. Day 59

Relationship with God..... Days 19, 48, 56, 79, 87, 158, 185, 199, 200, 208, 313, 341

Relationships with People.. Days 3, 10, 37, 51, 61, 79, 101, 103, 117, 160, 226, 229, 257, 265, 286, 304, 340

Resilience............... Day 28

Responsibility .... Days 118, 134, 198, 317, 356, 361

Responsive Lifestyle/ Behavior/Patterns ..... Days 37, 114, 172, 320

Rest/Renewal/Refreshment..Days 72, 107, 152, 172, 195, 203, 209, 255, 325

Restitution............... Day 147

Restoration .... Days 107, 191, 222, 223, 315

Reverence/Awe . . . . Days 38, 56, 164, 214

Role Models. . . . . Day 254

Sacrifice . . . . Days 30, 100, 149, 293, 321, 327, 350

Safety . . . . Days 1, 49, 91, 131, 192, 226, 305

Salvation . . . . Days 30, 98, 198, 259, 317, 361

Satan/Devil . . . . Days 49, 115, 178, 183, 184, 228, 254, 290, 307, 365

Satisfaction . . . . Days 26, 48, 71, 75

Security . . . . Days 43, 49, 91, 144, 190, 322, 352

Self, False and Real/True . . . Days 1, 32, 244, 265, 364

Self-Acceptance . . . . Day 295

Self-Care . . . . Days 7, 9, 37, 44, 338

Self-Centeredness/
Selfishness. . . . . Days 37, 114, 229

Self-Condemnation . . . . Day 9

Self-Confidence . . . . Day 323

Self-Control. . . . . Days 113, 150, 183, 187

Self-Entrapment . . . . Day 307

Self-Pity . . . . Day 195

Self-Promotion . . . . Day 81

Self-Worth. . . . . Days 6, 14, 17, 21, 43, 77, 81, 129, 168, 179, 301, 330, 352, 354

Service . . . . Days 35, 39, 63, 130, 146, 175, 235

Shame. . . . . Days 27, 55, 78, 89, 93, 181, 290

Sidetracked, Getting. . . . . . . Days 132, 156, 165, 202, 299

Simplicity. . . . . Days 133, 351

Sin. . . . . Days 5, 18, 30, 55, 66, 84, 107, 117, 140, 150, 181, 196, 216, 261, 277, 307, 315, 329, 341, 345, 357

Sin, Acknowledging . . . . Days 66, 80, 180

Sin, Unconfessed. . . . . Day 341

Solitude . . . . Day 204

Stability . . . . Days 102, 314, 325

Standards, God's/Biblical. . . Days 176, 200, 245, 308

Status . . . . Days 111, 149, 196, 269

Stress . . . . Days 36, 61

Suffering . . . . Days 70, 191, 215, 218, 259, 280, 284, 334, 349

Surrender/Giving Over
to God . . . . Days 5, 25, 28, 83, 96, 158, 283

Temptation . . . . Days 18, 73, 142, 184, 224, 261, 277, 359

Thankfulness (see "Gratitude")

Trust in God . . . . Days 2, 50, 76, 132, 144, 152, 153, 167, 190, 200, 204, 212, 259, 296, 318, 320, 328, 333, 334

Trust in Other People. . . . . . Days 27, 53, 118, 229, 296, 301

Understanding . . . . Days 8, 14, 18, 19, 34

Values. . . . . Days 10, 171, 232, 236, 352

Victory in Christ. . . . . Days 157, 201, 289, 306

Vision/Sight. . . . . Days 20, 29, 33, 40, 219, 228, 330

Weakness. . . . . Days 18, 364, 365

Weariness/Exhaustion. . . . . Days 8, 72, 152, 195, 215, 288, 324

Wisdom . . . . Days 19, 42, 101, 134, 142, 161, 167, 187, 207, 250, 266, 294, 333, 356, 363

Work. . . . . Days 58, 74, 92, 194, 200, 237, 252, 323

Worry/Worries . . . . Days 62, 72, 91, 97, 109, 110, 136, 170, 238, 241, 268, 333, 358

Worship . . . . Days 96, 313

Wounds/Woundedness . . . . Days 2, 6, 53, 180, 191, 218, 264, 364

Yes, Saying. . . . . Days 85, 224, 294

ABOUT THE AUTHORS

Stephen Arterburn, M.Ed., is the founder and chairman of New Life Ministries—the nation's largest faith-based broadcast, counseling, and treatment ministry. He is also the host of the nationally syndicated *New Life Live!* daily radio program, which airs on more than 180 radio stations nationwide, on Sirius XM radio, and on television. Steve is the founder of the Women of Faith conferences, attended by more than five million women. A nationally known public speaker, Steve has been featured in national media venues such as *Oprah*, *ABC World News Tonight*, *Good Morning America*, *CNN Live*, the *New York Times*, *USA Today*, *US News & World Report*, and *Rolling Stone*. In August 2000, Steve was inducted into the National Speakers Association's Hall of Fame. A bestselling author, Steve has more than ten million books in print, including the popular Every Man's Battle series. He is a multiple Gold Medallion–winning author and has been nominated for numerous other writing awards. He is also an award-winning study Bible editor of ten projects, including the *Life Recovery Bible*.

Steve has degrees from Baylor University and the University of North Texas, as well as two honorary doctorates. He resides with his family in Indiana.

David Stoop, Ph.D, is a licensed clinical psychologist in California. He received a master's in theology from Fuller Theological Seminary and a doctorate from the University of Southern California. He is frequently heard as a cohost on the nationally syndicated *New Life Live!* radio and TV program. David is the founder and director of the Center for Family Therapy in Newport Beach, California. He is also an adjunct professor at Fuller Seminary and serves on the executive board of the American Association of Christian Counselors. David is a Gold Medallion–winning author who has written more than thirty books, including *Forgiving What You'll Never Forget* and *Rethink How You Think*. He resides with his wife, Jan, in Newport Beach, California, and they have three sons and six grandchildren.

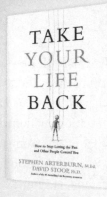

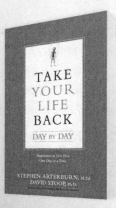

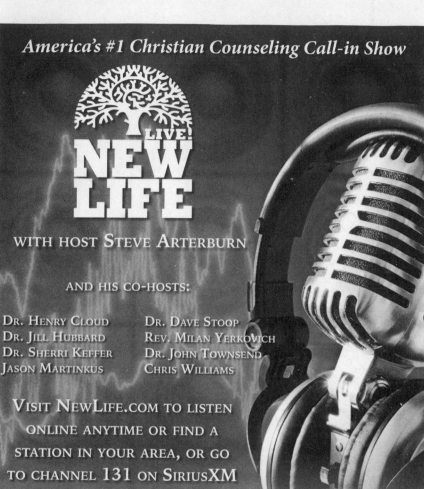